Tell The Truth And Shame The devil!

"The Untold Story of a Pastor's Wife"

By Theresa Ann Clark

Copyright © 2015 by Theresa Ann Clark
All rights reserved
Printed in the United States of America

No part of this book may be used or reproduced in any manner whatsoever without written permission from the Publisher.

Trinity & Talbot Publishing, LLC
P.O. Box 38503
Charlotte, NC 28278

Author is available for motivational speaking engagements and book signing events. Bulk sales are also available.

For more information contact:
Trinity & Talbot Marketing Dept. at 980-267-0436
Email: trinityandtalbotpub@gmail.com
Related link: www.theuntoldstoryofapastorswife.com

ISBN 978-0-9970786-0-2 (hardcover)
ISBN 978-0-9970786-1-9 (paperback)
ISBN 978-0-9970786-2-6 (e-book)

All names and identifying details have been changed and are fictitious to protect the privacy of individuals.

This book is dedicated to those that are looking for hope, searching for peace, and yearning for love, while in the midst of living through a hopeless situation. May the words and strength contained within this book bring deliverance and freedom to everyone who reads it.

Also dedicated to my precious Butterscotch, the most handsome Red Tabby ever created.

May 6, 1994 – August 6, 2012

THERESA ANN CLARK

Acknowledgements

I thank God my heavenly Father for Jesus and for giving me life and life more abundantly. I thank Him for health, knowledge, strength, and enabling me to write this book, for without God I am nothing. I would like to express my love, appreciation and thanks to those family members and friends that stood by me through all of my differences. I love you all for listening to me during my low points. To my father and mother, thank you for bringing me up to be who I am today, I love you both endlessly. To my sister Brenda, thank you for believing in me and for all of the encouragement you bestowed upon me. To my God-daughters, beautiful times are ahead for us, God-mommy loves you more than you know. Those of you that found it not robbery to listen to parts of my book as I was in the process of writing, and helping to critique it, I am eternally grateful, thank you! To Gwynn, my best friend, you are an UNUSUAL ANGEL sent directly from above, I am eternally grateful to you always, I Love You!! To my ex-husband, thank you for the knowledge of the Word, and for the financial support that you have bestowed upon me throughout the years. **Some of the words and context may be graphic for anyone under eighteen and not meant to offend anyone by any means, but with hope of deliverance for those that find themselves living a lie!**

Preface

If you or someone you know find yourselves inflicted by any form of turmoil and are entertaining the thought of marriage, whether it be to an ordinary person; a political figure; a community leader; a person of power; or a pastor, someone presumably on the straight and narrow; reading this book before making a decision may save you from a lifetime of heartache. It may also be used for a reference guide exemplifying how to get out of a grueling situation with your dignity intact, and succeed in life.

My hope is that this book will serve as a source of strength; if you are already experiencing signs of verbal or any other kind of abuse, please know that you're not alone and there's always a road to freedom, but you must be willing to take it. It's unfathomable that so many people for so many years have been going through this, yet they have remained quiet, and for the most part, remained with their spouses.

As you will soon find out, the wrong, or should I say the right person married a pastor, and maybe God is using me to free others, and to send out the message that none of His children should be abused, even if it's at the cost of an ordained person's reputation. It took me sixteen years to realize the necessity of speaking out on the issue because I was trying to figure it all out, not quite understanding what was happening to me.

I praise the Lord, study the Word and tithe, but yet I was a miserable Christian. Because of my beliefs, and the way my parents brought me up, I'm not afraid of anything or anyone, and decided to expose the evil that lurked in the home of one pastor in particular, and perhaps many of other people.

A pastor's wife is so busy helping others in need by encouraging them, and giving spiritual advice because we are devoted to fulfilling our obligations as leaders in our churches. Being overpowered by the burden of others, we don't realize that we are the very ones in need of freedom from whatever it is we might be going through, which can sometimes be a form of abuse. Unfortunately, some of us are not what you would call a sounding board for the pastor, but a punching bag.

There is a crisis organization and/or help hotline for almost every situation in the world; child abuse, battered women, women shelters, the homeless, alcoholics anonymous, etc., but it doesn't end with those that are commonly known. There is an untouched sect of people that have gone unobserved for centuries, and it is unfortunately the very person symbolizing strength Sunday after Sunday; your beautifully dressed, bible toting, praising, specially seated pastor's wife, that needs a helpline. Do not be fooled by the pomp and circumstance on Sundays.

As pastor's wives, we have monthly meetings to focus on our goals and such church business, but we all sit there amongst one another and don't even touch on the true situation as to fool each other. For those of us that are experiencing this, a real support system is needed where we can tell the truth and shame the devil while lifting each other up. We need to shy away from embarrassment and it shouldn't be an issue, we haven't committed this crime but are victims to it. We're too afraid and ashamed to admit how we are really living because we shudder to think that another Christian can out-Christian us, or that our rebuker doesn't work, or that we don't know how to use the power bestowed upon us by God to defeat the enemy.

Although some of us may be living through hell on earth, in our subconscious mind there is still that underlying thought that pastors are walking the walk as we see on Sundays which makes us believe and think to ourselves that this can only possibly be happening to me. We too are fooled by other pastor's wives' outer appearance, but if we were to dare follow some of them home; I'm sure we'd be surprised. Since pastor's wives are used to keeping everything hush-hush, we should induct that same law into a private support system and maybe, just maybe because we are taking a stand, pastors and other authoritative figures will change for the sake of risking being exposed. I'm not starting a war against pastors as my respect will always remain intact toward them; however, I do endeavor to encourage those that are shackled by abuse to be freed.

If you are reading this and are a Christian, I advise that you stay devoted to your church and your pastor because no matter who is preaching or teaching, if that person is telling the truth, then God's Word will always be God's Word which is Truth. No one's evilness or goodness can change His Word, remember that. Do your own studying and research asking God for revelation and understanding of what you've been taught to be sure that at least your pastor is spreading the correct good news. Use the Word for your edification and don't worry about the pastor applying it to his/her own life, because there is no way for you to know what goes on behind closed doors. All we can do is pray that our leaders *are* living right. Many may strongly disagree with me on this, but this is my opinion and how I feel. There have been wonderful teachers of the gospel out there that we've learned from, to later find out that they were some sort of a freak. Benefit from the Word that the pastor preaches to strengthen yourself; let it give you hope and courage to be able to leave an abusive marriage or situation, at least that's what I did, and its working. A husband is supposed to treat and love his wife like Christ does the church, so if that's not happening in your life, recognize it fast and do away with discontent. Ephesians 5:21-33 from the Message version of the bible states: "Out of respect for Christ, be courteously reverent to one another. Wives, understand and support your husbands in ways that show your support for Christ. The husband provides leadership to his wife the way Christ does to His church, not by domineering but by cherishing. So just as the church submits to Christ as He exercises such leadership, wives should likewise submit to their husbands. Husbands, go all out in your love for your wives, exactly as Christ did for the church, a love marked by giving, not getting. Christ's love makes the church whole. His words evoke her beauty. Everything He does and says is designed to bring the best out of her, dressing her in dazzling white silk, radiant with holiness. And that is how husbands ought to love their wives. They're really doing themselves a favor, since they're already 'one' in marriage. No-one abuses his own body, does he? No, he feeds and pampers it. That's how Christ treats us, the church, since we are part of His body. And this is why a man leaves father and mother and cherishes his wife. No longer two, they become 'one flesh.' This is a huge mystery, and I don't pretend to understand it all. What is clearest to me is the way Christ treats the church. And this provides a good picture of how each husband is to treat his wife, loving himself in loving her, and how each wife is to honor her husband."

    It's terrible that the very person I expected to understand that scripture doesn't. If the tragedies that are revealed in this book can happen to a pastor's wife, it can happen to anyone.

Chapter One

It was winter, and the garage like most, had no heat, and there were piles of junk everywhere. From tables to ladders, unused clothes to old broken down vacuum cleaners, and many of those large industrial garbage bags filled with empty bottles of booze, to name a few, was a part of the dusty scenery.

Thanks to my dad for his God given talent to build, that the two car garage was converted and compartmentalized into three areas. The interior door that opened from the downstairs den into the garage was made of steel and had a keyless heavy duty sliding bolt lock. The first area entered into when coming through that door was the larger space for one car, except a car couldn't fit in there at that particular time in question due to the junk. On the other side of the unpainted drywall which was installed, was a decent size office for Hank, and a much smaller room for the laundry machines. An exterior door coupled with a screen door lead to the outside from Hank's office. The typical car garage door that rolls up overhead was left intact for the larger side of the garage, allowing two different ways to exit to the outside.

The concrete ground was stony cold, the roar of the furnace was like an unending hum, and it had to be dismal for him to have been locked in there alone for roughly thirty minutes, as long as it took me to get to the precinct and back.

That fiasco was so devastating and humiliating to me. The red lights were flashing and lighting up the entire corner where our primary residence was, or the so-called parsonage. I used the term "So-called" purposely, because the church didn't own that beautiful corner home, we did.

However, being one of the worst of many tormenting episodes, I needed backup, so I drove to the police precinct and had them follow me back home. I had no choice but to get the po-damn-leese as my grandma would say instead of "Police." I needed to leave that night for the sake of my mental state, but Hank was blocking me, and he wanted to physically fight to keep me there. As bad as it was and the hatred I felt toward him at that point, I was protecting Hank and wouldn't fight him because I would have killed him, hence the scrimmage just to get him off of me. I couldn't leave him locked in a cold garage all night, so I needed the cops to let him out with the assurance of my leaving safely.

It was around one o'clock in the morning, two cars trailed me and my heart was not only broken but pounding; thank God they didn't use the sirens on the way or the majority of the neighborhood would have been awakened.

As I exited the car to go back into the house, I noticed a car with tinted windows parked a few houses down with the headlights off not to be conspicuous, and it was him, watching in fear unable to help me. It was shocking as well as refreshing to see that someone biologically unrelated to me cared enough to be there for me although helpless. I befriended Samuel some years prior while riding the railroad with the everyday crowd. Although to me, Sam seemed to have a touch of sugar in his tank, he was very caring, attentive, understanding and respectful, which made me feel very comfortable confiding in him regarding my personal issues. When I texted him that I was heading to the precinct, I never expected to actually see him watching in the background.

My parents were sitting directly in front of my house because I called them on my way to the precinct. Rev. Defenbar never ever got over the fact that my parents, as he would say, had the nerve to be there. After that incident he would always say, "Your parents had no right to be running over here getting in our business just because you called them." He harped on that for years, and he honestly thought he was right. Is it a possibility that Hank grew up with unconcerned parents that would ignore him and deny him if he asked for their help? My parents love me unconditionally like any normal parent would love a child. What father among people would give his son a serpent if he asks for a fish? I was the modern day damsel in distress, and I reached out to my parents for help and support of me personally. They weren't called to get involved verbally, and their opinion wasn't needed or solicited, I just needed a ride to their house because I didn't want to drive Hank's car. Not once did they get out of their car. I handled my business with the police, and afterwards I left Hank there that night alone.

As the police approached the front door, I was telling them, "He's locked in the garage, naked with no clothes on," so I thought, but Hank had found an old trench coat to wrap around his feeble body frame. Hank's frail looks were self inflicted, and happened rapidly as his depression took more of a toll on him once he realized that our marriage had been over for a few years. We were already nine years into the marriage and sleeping in separate bedrooms on different levels of the house. I slept upstairs and he slept downstairs.

When I first met him, his looks were very easy on the eyes. He stood around five feet eight and had a great posture. His skin was light brown with red undertones. He had keen features; his nose was semi-sharp and perfectly shaped, his face was oval with high cheekbones, and his neatly trimmed mustache rested upon his medium sized lips. His eyes were dark brown and his ears didn't stick out, but were perfectly positioned close enough to his head. The soft salt and pepper hair and his nice hairline gave him a distinguished look especially when he was dressed in his size forty-four suits that were accessorized to the nines. He had broad shoulders and looked robust. However, sometimes his smile reminded me of a photo I've seen of Cab Calloway.

Those looks changed dramatically as he became smaller; his face and eyes were sunken in, and his cheekbones were protruding. It looked as if his height dropped two or three inches also, and his suits had to be altered because they hung on him as if on a coat rack. Due to lack of exercise, the extra skin just sagged. His shoulder blades had become like razors, his head shrunk, and you could practically see his skeleton. He was too thin and it didn't become him at all. He looked hungry and not well; there was no meat on his bones. He wore two pairs of jogging pants, using the first pair as meat to help hold up the second pair. I believe a strong wind would have blown him right down the street; he'd need to anchor himself with a brick. This all happened because he allowed his inner troubles to stop him from eating and caring about his wellbeing.

The police went inside, two of them, and they let Hank out of the garage. They spoke to him and then waited for me to leave as per my request. That was the night of all nights. Hank had been drinking, as was customary. When I arrived home that evening the house was dark, which was a hint, and he started calling me whores, talking about my mother and telling me that I was nothing, etc. Enough was enough and I didn't want the stress that night, and refused to tolerate such behavior. I wanted to leave, get out of the house, but he was determined to hold me prisoner and block me from exiting. When he saw me grab my purse and start for the door, he jumped in front of me so I couldn't get down the stairs. I pushed my way pass him and ran down the stairs as did he, and he blocked the front door. Hank was wearing a t-shirt only. I remembered that I could get out through the garage, so I bolted down the next flight of stairs to the steel door, sliding the bolt lock as fast as I could, but by the time I reached the exterior garage door, Hank was right behind me and we began tussling. As we tumbled to the cold concrete floor in this physical bout, my head nearly hit a pipe in the garage. I was finally able to break loose as the adrenaline flowed, and I ran like the dickens before he could get off the ground. I slammed the garage door closed and put the bolt lock on, I was too angry, stirred up and shaken from the scrimmage to care that he was naked and cold. I grabbed my keys and ran out of the house as I could literally hear my heart beating in my ears. I put the key into the ignition and backed out of the driveway in a flash, and headed to the police precinct.

There was always an abundance of arguments but that was the only time I needed to get the law involved. I often wondered whether or not I was the only first lady going through such harsh turmoil. My second thought was that I need to inspire or help others to overcome abusive situations, and in order to do that I would need to tell my story reluctantly, as I didn't lead a transparent life.

Due to the fact that Rev. Defenbar was both my husband and pastor, unfortunately not my friend, I interchangeably used his titles. His complete title is Rev. Dr. Hank J. Defenbar. However, when we were home I referred to him as "Hank," with the exception of calling him to the phone for anyone associated with the church circuit, and then it was "Rev. Defenbar, telephone!" When speaking of him to others, including those that were only in the secular world, it was "Reverend Defenbar." At church, be it on Sunday or during the week, it was always either "Pastor Defenbar" mainly, or "Reverend Defenbar."

No matter the amount of respect I've shown him, he has tried to kill me softly from the inside out. I have never been as emotionally and mentally unhappy in my life as I was during our marriage. He always said extremely stressful and ignorant things to me like, "I know you're waiting for me to die!" He would say that out of the ether, unattached to an argument.

Although I saw the bad road as early as our first year of marriage, after that episode I was looking for a way out more vigorously than ever, yet graciously. Undoubtedly, my Heavenly Father is El-Elyon and His works never cease to amaze me. I had to endure many things for sixteen years which seemed endless, but God in His infinite wisdom finally opened a door for me to leave and I exited stage left. All that I went through, the abuse inflicted upon me, the way I handled it to get to my freedom by the faith I had to exercise, the patience I had to retain, and how God kept me, will send most people on a whirlwind. Some of the episodes are unfathomable, but they happened and will shock you, leaving you in disbelief, not only because of the brutality, but also because somehow I didn't end up in the psyche ward.

Chapter Two

It took nothing to egg Hank on. All he needed was someone to remotely agree with what he was saying or what he was thinking, and anything that I personally said around him would be used against me constantly. I always had to warn friends and family, without explanation, *not* to say anything about me; good, bad, or indifferent when around Reverend. Unbeknownst to them, he would turn any good or bad situation around and use it as a weapon in the hopes of harming me, and he'd stay on that kick until someone gave him something else to feed off of. When in the presence of others, I was always listening and watching so I could buck my eyes at them if I heard them going in the wrong direction. It was always smart to keep the conversation off of me, and I know that's weird, but Reverend Hank J. Defenbar was weird.

One day, Essie, the eldest of my siblings, was visiting along with Gertrude, a cousin of ours, who was later revealed as a turncoat, and we all sat chatting with Hank. When our family gathers, any funny subject is liable to come up. In our conversation, I was being sarcastic to the fact that my siblings and I were sheltered growing up, which Hank already knew, so I said, "Yeah, we were ho's right Essie, we were all ho's." Essie knew I was being silly, and really didn't pay me any attention. I called one of my sisters that lives out of State, the one next to me in age, and said, "Hey Lele, aren't we ho's?" She fell out laughing because at that time she had already been married for twenty-eight years to her first and only boyfriend. I then told her what we were talking about, and hung up. I thought nothing of it.

At that point I hadn't yet caught on, and I had no idea that Hank was going to run *that* in the ground literally for the remainder of our marriage. Even though he had already been calling me a whore for years, that comment gave him backup material as far as he was concerned, and something to solidify what he'd been saying.

I had been accused of the butcher, the baker, and the candlestick maker, right after I said "I do," and it didn't stop. It was obvious that a man like that had to be insecure in *himself*.

Unfortunately I was a glutton for punishment and chose to remain in denial or oblivion regarding Hank's evil tactics hoping he'd change, but I should have known better. The stress of being perpetually tormented by Hank had become so burdensome on my psyche in the years *prior* to my making the "ho" comment that it only intensified. Mary Ellen, my best friend at that time, was trying to help me figure out a way, if there was a way, to possibly live with this. As long as I was staying there trying to co-exist with the pastor, who was being guided by demons, something needed to be done. With that tidbit added on, life was about to become horrid, and looking back, I'm glad that I had already begun to do what Mary Ellen divulged she thought I should do in the beginning.

Throughout the years of our marriage, Mary Ellen was my voice of reason. As if she had some sort of epiphany or something, she said to me in her soft spoken voice, "Lydia, when Hank starts, just ignore him, don't say anything back, just let him talk to himself, and he'll eventually shut-up because no-one can argue alone."
"Ok, I'll try that," I said.
Hank wasn't wrapped too tight, it's like his two hundred man army didn't have any men, and he proved Mary Ellen's theory to be wrong.

I have never in my life felt so demoralized by anyone, friend or foe. When I decided to take Mary Ellen's advice of trying to ignore Hank, I was tormented by a monologue, who would have thought? I feel better using a word that doesn't exist, by saying, who would've *thunk* it.

I sat at the kitchen table eating my dinner, and Hank must have been drinking because the vulgarity that spewed from his mouth was enough for me to shoot him if I had a gun. I'm so glad no guns were in *our* house.

To be able to talk to a woman, or any human being like that, is in and of itself agonizing, malicious, unethical, cruel, and unacceptable. It took all I had to hush and not respond. Tears wanted to come, but I held them back. I couldn't help but think, "Punch this dude in his face Lydia!" I shuddered, and my insides were doing acrobatics as I clenched my teeth listening to him, feeling less than human. I've always been afraid of monsters from childhood, and I didn't even know what a monster looked like, but now I do.

In normal circumstances, one would have to say something in order for another to get started on any conversation, no matter what the subject may be. Oft times, I'd be sharing my secret drama with Mary Ellen, and she would stop me and say, "Wait, wait." I knew what was coming, so I'd just look up at her with wide eyes, as wide as they'd stretch, with a serious expressionless face, just waiting for her question. Immediately from my look she would burst into a laugh, but still continue with her question.

She'd ask, "What did I miss, what part did I miss, did I miss something?" "Nothing," I'd yell. "That was the beginning of the argument, he just came upstairs and started like you're starting a car, it came out of nowhere, and I didn't say anything to prompt it."

For the world, Mary Ellen couldn't digest the fact that Hank could argue alone and out of the ether. Although she's heard many stories starting like that since the beginning of my marriage to Hank, she would still ask, "What did I miss?" Hank's behavior was so incomprehensible that up until the end she was still having a hard time believing it.

Mary Ellen said something very valuable to me, and that was, "No-one will believe what you're saying, especially against a community leader of Pastor Defenbar's caliber. It's little you against big him, you'll never win, you better start recording him." As I thought about it, she was correct. No-one would ever believe me, because in the pulpit, Pastor Defenbar was ecclesiastic. On the contrary, the tapes would corroborate my side of the story. That was the best idea I've ever heard and also the most brilliant, so I immediately went out and purchased a tiny voice activated recorder which could fit in a pocket. That took place six years prior to any day spa business being imagined, or my being aware of any construction worker's existence, which was another person that I was accused of down the line, go figure! Hank didn't know, but every time he got raunchy and I grew weary of the argument, on my way out of the front door I'd say, "That's ok, I got you bitch," because he was being recorded.

Church was still carrying on in the eyes of the parishioners, as I played the part, having sometimes been cursed out on the way *to* church on Sunday morning, but that never stopped my praise, it made me praise all the more harder. My praise is real, and I felt it in my gut as I do now. I would shout because although I was going through hell on earth, I had faith, and knew that God was working on my situation, even though I couldn't see it or feel it. Also, I was so thankful to God for giving me strength to continue in my walk, not skipping a beat; working, praising Him, and completing school, without interruption. When I think of His agape love, my soul cries out Hallelujah! I would begin to get full, and tears of joy would flow like a river. There was a song we sang in church that always touched me deeply because it's so apropos to my life, and it's called, "I Never Lost My Praise." The lyrics testify to the fact that I never lost my hope, joy, faith, or praise, and that my praise is still here. A couple of times, I just took off and ran around the church during service, I just had to run for the Lord.

Anyway, I couldn't finish my meal in peace because the monologue man had just walked into the kitchen. I really should've hit myself in the head and said, "I should have had a V8," because isn't a sermon like a monologue? That was a walk in the park for him. Well, I was on a new thing that day for trial purposes and that was, *not to respond.*

As the one man band started, it really sounded as if I had a previous conversation with him. His voice was crude, evil, and harsh, like a demon, as he spoke with disdain and disgust. There was a roar to his pitch, and he screamed the entire monologue.

He started by saying, "You haven't contributed nothing, to not one thing that I have put in....that I have invested in my life. This house, our second home, nothing in it, you're a thief, and I wish you would leave. You need to go back to your damn mama, who spoiled you to death, and made you less than a woman, you ain't nothing, you're not even a woman. Look at all this crap here in the middle of the damn floor in the walkway that nobody can even get through to get to a closet to fix up with clothes that *I* bought you. And I sit next to you at night, and you ignore me like I'm some robot sitting up there, that you ain't gotta be messing with. I ain't taking that crap no more, somebody gotta go, and I ain't going. You can go back to your nigga, go back to the construction worker. Yes, I believe everything that woman said about you, and I know you did it, because you said from the very beginning, you were a whore. You cheated on every man that you known, so what would make me any different? You got on the phone and called your sisters, and said that ya'll are whores, in disrespect for me, to let me know that that's what you were, because you told me that from the first time I met you. Every man you ever known, you cheated on. You think I will continue to support you? Your mama needs to take you back, you said she didn't want to give you up, I will tell her, take-your-butt-back, cause you ain't no good to me. You don't pay one bill, not one bill have you paid in this house since you lived here, not one bill. Cause I've taken care of you, and you think that you can treat me any way you want to, and go out and fuck somebody else, with your crazy ass self. Yeah go out and fuck somebody else. (He goes downstairs briefly then returns) Come back down here and turn these lights off down here. Get outta my life, cause I'm about to go crazy on you, and I'm gonna let everybody else know, I'm not going to jail over you. You're trying to provoke me to get me outta here so you can take whatever, so you and your family can take over whatever I left here, and I'm gonna let everybody know, you got a husband you haven't slept with in six months. You been out parading your butt to somebody else, I been paying your bills, bills in this house, paid bills at the other house, bills over that business and all that stuff, and you treat me the way you treat me and I'm tired of it, and I'm about to lose my mind on it, and you betta leave me alone, you betta get out of my sight. And it's probably all your plan, because you done it before. Everybody who is close to me, I told about you, ain't nothing to you, you ain't never been nothing. Damn cat running up and down the damn hallways, and up and down the stairs and so forth because you don't come home and take care of him, you expect me to take care of him? I wouldn't put my life in your hands at all. -- A long silent pause -- You came back to me because your ex wouldn't accept your ass, you came back to me because the construction worker fooled your ass, I told you from the time I saw you down at that business, you shouldn't have been down there by yourself, but you persisted in doing it, and you covered his ass all along, you ain't cover mine. You covered his ass, you covered his fucking ass, and I have supported you and given you thousands of dollars, thousands of dollars damn freaking ass son-of-a-bitch you. And I have supported you all during that damn time, and you still refuse to be with me, and let me be your husband. And you think that you can stay in this house and turn me down, and not have sex with me? You crazy, you are absolutely out of your freaking mind. Go back to the damn niggas that you been fucking, and that's what you are, you got on the phone, and tried to make your sisters believe that all of you were whores. Right in this house, with Essie sitting up here, got on the phone saying, "Yeah, you know we're all whores," and you the only one that confess to the fact that you were. That's all you have ever been in your life, you screwed everybody in your home town. That's why that woman said she didn't want you nowhere around her husband. I ain't going no place, I'll stand here, and you go to your business and sleep, and I will take my car back, cause I do have keys. I will take my car back before I leave from here. I'm tired of you freaking over me. The other night, I took you out for dinner, and spent eighty something dollars. Then you come back up here talking bout, "I'm watching lifetime," and put on all your clothes so I couldn't touch you, you stupid, no I'm stupid, yup. Go down to your business, that's where I want you to go. Go down there, burn up the heat there, don't burn up this heat here, the church has to pay for this. You don't deserve to stay in this place. I gave you a brand new house totally furnished, look at this place now, look at it, you ain't nothing."

I had to walk out, and as I was leaving, I was so vex I could have spit, and I screamed, "Oh please, go to hell, go to hell, you-go-to-HELL, your mother is there," and I left the house. I had been inundated over the years constantly, with verbal and mental abuse.

I wanted to answer him back blow for blow, but I had to prove a point to Mary Ellen, which was that there was nothing anyone could have told me to do that would have worked, because that man behaved in a sick manner.

How dare he fix his lips to say I didn't pay any bills around that house; he didn't either, those were perks that came with his job. Was I supposed to reimburse the church for paying him his due? I'm being facetious, but that's the reality of it. He had great big balls to say the house was a mess, and he couldn't walk down the hallway. Of course the house was a mess, he didn't know how to clean, and wouldn't if he did, and he didn't let me clean. Every time I attempted to clean the house, he would come behind me fighting for no reason, which was habitual. He would tell me where to start, he would tell me not to touch his room or his office, he would then start snowballing one subject after another, and the name calling would begin. I would be so darn disgusted, that I couldn't even clean in peace, so I'd drop whatever I was doing, get in my car, and leave for hours, and there went another day the house didn't get cleaned. Without exaggeration, that literally happened every single time, the same old thing. He never picked up after himself, nor dumped his plate, nor did he wipe up his spilled liquids, and that angered me like you wouldn't believe. He would sit his plate with bones on it outside his room door as if he were at a hotel. I would call Mary Ellen complaining, and she would always say, "Even though you don't like the fact that he doesn't pick up after himself, you should pick it up, because ultimately you're the one that will always end up doing it anyway. Lydia you're just creating more work for yourself." She was right, but I still would get so mad and leave his mess right where it was, and then days or weeks down the line I eventually cleaned it up because it was indubitable that he was never going to do it.

  Reverend Defenbar is a smart man, and he knew that his ruthless speech and behavior would chase me out of the house anytime I would try to clean. Nevertheless, he would complain to people that I didn't clean, and how dirty the house was, and I just wanted to choke the life out of him for saying that, just squeeze his neck until he couldn't breathe. The anger burned inside, how dare he talk about me like that when he knew he wouldn't let me clean. Why didn't he tell those he spoke to that he cursed me out every time I attempted to clean? Why didn't he tell the truth and shame the devil?

  Mary Ellen would say to me, "Just clean your house and ignore him." Unfortunately, it's very hard for someone to understand when they aren't in the situation. Hank had been extremely nasty for the entirety of our marriage, and I was so beat down with his nasty tone of voice, and his filthy words, that my ears couldn't take it, I had to run. His voice and words, would burn inside my gut, so it wasn't a matter of ignoring him, I mentally and physically couldn't take hearing him. My fist would ball up, I couldn't stand the ground he walked on, and he deserved to live just the way he was living. He was pure evil.

  Hank didn't just lie, but he spoke them with conviction. What woman, or person, would tell their spouse or significant other that they've cheated on their previous mate, be it true or not? How could Hank have argued with such anger that I've cheated on everyone I've been with? Who ever told him that, and where did it come from? I've never been accused of cheating by anyone I've dated, except Hank; so how can he accuse me on their behalf?

When Hank would go away to visit his family, attend a meeting, or go to our second home, I would take advantage of that time and clean the entire house to a pristine shine, walls included. He would come back to a beautiful house, and it started all over again. I began to tell him, "Why don't you go away so I can clean, I can't clean with you here." Every time I'd say that, he would say in his nasty cutting voice, "You're using that as an excuse because you don't clean, and you just want to get rid of me." Talking to him was so impossible and I hated having to. He said that I came back to him because my ex wouldn't accept me and the construction worker fooled me, but I'm still confused about where he thought I went, I never knew that I left.

The very next morning after that grueling monologue, I was standing in the kitchen at the sink, he came up the stairs and stood behind me with his body slightly against mine so that I could feel his piece, and tapped me on my hip like I was something he was attracted to. He did not mention the night before, nor did he give an apology, he was just going along like everything was fine. I believe that was when I unequivocally knew that he was bipolar. He couldn't see my face, but the entire *second* that I stood there before swiftly moving toward the fridge as if I needed something, I squinted my eyes and balled up my lips in disbelief. I wanted to take my left hand and cap my fist on my right hand with it for more power, and take it on a downward swing with my elbow coming up in the back, and elbow that brother as hard as I could. However, I don't like confusion, so I covered those feelings up in my movement, not my facial expression, which he couldn't see anyway. I swiftly, yet gently moved away, I didn't snatch away. Did he really believe he could touch me and that I would want him to touch me, ever?

Although these horrendous things were going on in my life, I had to suffer through them alone, silently, other than Mary Ellen and my first cousin Lamont at times. When I had to run out in the middle of the night, I had no-one, but that was when Jesus was carrying me, and I only saw one set of footprints.

Chapter Three

Whether I was right or wrong, to Hank I was always wrong, and it was always his family against my family in his head, although his family had no idea and neither did mine. Well, I had had about enough when he brought his son Scooter to live with us early on in the marriage. I might have taken crap off of Hank, but I'll be darned if I was going to take it off of a kid that's living in *my* house. Initially, Scooter would come only for visits over a weekend to see his dad at times, and ironically every time he would leave to go back home, a piece of Hank's jewelry would go missing.

Hank and I had gold jewelry coming out of the ears, as we both had a passion for jewelry which is probably the only thing we ever agreed on, although with that too, I had to play my hand right to get a new piece of it just on G.P.

Back then, we would always purchase expensive pieces for each other, especially for birthdays, anniversaries, and Christmas. Every vacation we took, we would always bring back more gold, and the guys on Forty-Seventh Street in New York City were our friends and loved to see us coming. Nothing was ever too expensive for either of us. However, we kept our jewelry in five different jewelry boxes, and would notice anything missing in an instant because we always utilized our jewelry for every occasion, including our daily pieces. Scooter wasn't aware of that, and I was like a mother hawk over our jewelry.

    I purchased a fourteen karat gold jaguar ring for Hank that was a casual piece he could wear every day, and he did. After a Scooter weekend, one evening we were having dinner, and I looked at Hank's hand and said, "Where is the jaguar ring?"
I'm sure he had already known Scooter's M.O., but was too embarrassed to tell me, so he said, "I must have misplaced it, I can't find it."
My thieftennas went up because we didn't lose anything, but I remained quiet without saying a word, it was part of the set up. I said to myself, "Uh-huh, we'll see about this." The next day, I started the hunt in looking for the ring, not to recover anything.
I began to hound Hank about it and he said, "I'll buy another one and replace it, I don't know how I lost it."
Indeed, Hank purchased another one just like it.

    Scooter came up for another visit, and when he left that time, a genuine Gucci watch of Hank's left too. This time I boldly told Hank, "Scooter is stealing your jewelry." Why did I say that?
Hank got to hollering and said, "Don't you say my son is a thief, my family don't steal, your family steals, all of ya'll are fucking thieves."
"Well then what happened to your jewelry Hank?" I put emphasis on the "k" in "Hank."
"I don't know what happened to it, but my son didn't steal it!"

Hank screamed out of sheer frustration of not having an answer and his son being exposed, when his family is supposed to be so much greater than mine.

"So what are you telling me Hank, that the ring and the watch grew some damn legs, and decided to get up and walk the hell out of here?"

"Oh, go to hell Lydia."

"No, you and that thief son of yours can go to hell!"

That argument went on and on. He was fighting a losing battle with me on that one, but he stood his ground in defending his son for months until I confronted his son, threatening him with the martial art Wushu.

Every time Hank started an argument with me for nothing as usual, and said my mother didn't raise me right, I'd tell him that he raised a thief, and the battle was on again as he continued to defend Scooter.

A year or so had passed, and I being the compassionate, forgiving person that I am, was asked by Hank if I'd be ok with Scooter coming to live with us. I said "Ok," thinking I could keep an eye on Scooter because after all it *was* his son.

I'm a woman, yet a handy-man for lack of a better term, because growing up I was the one always by my dad's side watching him fix everything, and I'm a quick study.

Prior to Scooter's move-in date, my actions spoke volumes to Hank, however, I didn't say a word and neither did he, but by watching me he understood my motive. Unfortunately, I had to go into Fort Knox mode. I simply went to Home Depot for the purchase of two keyed-entry door knobs to replace the closet entry door knobs that were on our bedroom doors. Our bedroom had a door leading into the hallway, and another door leading into the connecting bathroom.

The entire hallway on the upper level was mirrored on both sides, including the double bi-fold accordion linen closet doors, literally from the floor to the ceiling as was our bedroom. The master's suite wasn't the size of a master's suite so we used mirrors to give the appearance of a larger space. Once our bedroom door was closed, from the inside perspective it seemed like a maze or funny house and it was hard to tell where the door was. The doors, closet, and walls were all mirrored; you needed to look for the handle to identify the door if you weren't familiar with its location.

Once we were locked down Scooter moved in and I kept an eye on him, but had to bite my tongue in letting him know that I knew what he stole and that he was a thief. Therefore, I couldn't even warn him not to steal anything which was bursting at my seams. I had to pretend like nothing ever happened, but I was going to find a way to get him if it took me forever and a day.

I told Hank, "When Scooter moves in here do not argue in front of him so he can report back to his mother how we don't get along. If you want to argue, let's take it in the bedroom but not in front of Scooter." Hank somewhat agreed by nodding. The first opportunity Hank got, he cursed me out in front of Scooter which made me angry, so I gave Scooter something he probably never seen before, and something to write home about. Since that first day very bad arguments took place in front of Scooter. I was embarrassed to be acting like such a fool as an adult but I'm no punk and wasn't going out like one. I had to fight back although it was ridiculous and I hated it. How could Hank disrespect me, his wife, in front of his son, I felt terribly degraded. I later found out from Scooter that Hank did the same thing to *his* mother, the only difference was that she wasn't a warrior like me. Like they say, don't come like lettuce, all head and no behind, you got to bring some to get some.

Months had passed, and I thought nothing of leaving a checkbook on the dining room table because I was only interested in the jewels growing legs and walking. One day I opened the bank statement; lo and behold there it was, a stolen check with Hank's signature forged by Scooter. I was waiting, tapping my feet, just itching to see Hank justify *this one*. Scooter was too young and ignorant to know that the bank mailed out a monthly statement with all cashed checks; talk about America's Dumbest Criminals! By the time Hank arrived home I was livid knowing that I had to lock up *everything* that wasn't nailed down. It angered me that I had to live in a prison in my own home and something had to give.

Hank arrived home, walked in the house, and I immediately showed him the statement and his face looked perplexed. He didn't speak a word to me, but he yelled for Scooter to come upstairs because Hank will curse him out too. Hank was maaad and embarrassed.
Hank said, "Scooter, did you do this?"
Not that Hank didn't believe it, but in a here's your chance to redeem yourself manner. Scooter was scared to pieces, not knowing that I was the one he needed to be afraid of because standing close enough to me I'm sure you could see steam coming off of my head.
In a low key voice Scooter said, "Yes, I'm sorry."
"You're stealing from *me*? I'm the one that takes care of your stupid behind, and don't you ever steal from me again." Hank went on and on. Scooter was turning red with his light skinned self. He solemnly went back downstairs feeling totally embarrassed, but *I* wasn't done, it was my turn.

I was hot under the collar so I marched in my room, put on some jogging pants, a tee-shirt, and some sneakers, and Hank was looking at me but he knew *not this time*, and he left me alone. The kitchen was directly above the downstairs living room. Hank stood in the kitchen quietly, listening without interrupting me because he knew that as the woman of the house I had every right. He also knew I would have lost my mind had he tried to stop me.
I went downstairs screaming, "Scooter come out here!"

Here was my big opportunity to bring up the stolen goods too. With my Wushu skills I jumped into a horse stance with my right fist drawn back at my hip facing upward and my left arm extended with that fist facing downward ready to do the male punch. I glared at him, and he was scared as he could be. He had no idea that I really knew how to fight, and I was fit and muscular.
"I'm gonna ask you one time, and if you say 'No,' or lie to me, I'm gonna punch you in your fucking face. Now, did you steal your fathers Gucci watch and jaguar ring? Let me see you lie, just one time, lie!" I screamed like a crazy woman.
Immediately he admitted to it.
He then said, "I pawned the ring, but I broke the watch, I'll go get it and bring it back."
That's all I needed and I went upstairs, looked at Hank, rolled my eyes and said, "I told you he took it, that shit ain't got no legs."

We got over that, and he did bring the broken watch back from his mother's house. I was still in hawk mode, watching, watching, and watching. I wondered if he had changed after being busted, so after a substantial amount of time had passed, I set him up, well, actually he set himself up, when he stole my keys. Although I was still in church and at the church doing my thing throughout the week when needed and on Sundays, I was living through chaos and nobody knew. Screaming and arguing with Hank, and watching Scooter was the bulk of my life.

Now I don't know what possessed Scooter to think that he was wiser than I was, but he tried me. We made him go to work, so he got a job at the local twenty-four hour convenient store. One day I was preparing to take him to work and I went to the key rack in the kitchen where all keys were left, and my large key chain was missing. I love key chains and everything was on mine, it was quite large. For one, I never lose my keys which Scooter obviously wasn't aware of; and two, that key chain was too large for me to lose. I asked had anyone seen my keys and they both said no, then Scooter chimed in, "You must have lost them." Hmmm I thought, and my thieftenna started to go up a little. Then he questioned us twice about how long we'd be at the church service that night because we had a revival going on, and my thieftenna went up a little more. What difference would that have made if he's at work until midnight, I thought. Things that make you go hmmm.

I immediately moved into detective mode, one of my many traits, and I started thinking to myself, *"Ok, Scooter waits until there is Revival at our church, and he knew he needed to pick a time that Hank and I would be out of the house, and that happens to be the day I lose my keys? So, he's planning to double back when I drop him off at work, to rob us."* I began my setup. I had to play that one out because if I had let Hank know what I was thinking, he'd tell Scooter. I went along with everyone, took my bath, got dressed, put on my make-up, and did my hair.

"Ok Scooter, let's go, I have to come back and get your father for church." I took the spare keys, and off we went.

As we were driving down the street, Scooter made an enormous mistake, and not just by bringing up my keys again, but he said, "Lydia, you always lose your keys." I thought "BINGO," this rascal stole my keys, and is coming back for the kill just as sure as the world. His intention was to secure the fact that I thought I lost them so that he doesn't become a suspect. I've never lost my keys, besides, that was the first incident that he's ever witnessed, so for him to make that claim was inappropriate. Then he reiterated the time his dad and I were to return, and I thought, "GOTCHA!"

When I returned home after dropping Scooter off, I told the good reverend, "I don't feel so well, I'm not going to church tonight." I still didn't tell him anything so not to blow it. I tricked both of them. I looked from the bay window to watch Hank pulling out of the driveway, and then I started to set the scene.

    I changed quickly into all black ninja clothes and white sneakers because I didn't know how soon Scooter was coming back, and then I locked our bedroom door. I turned off all the lights in the house except the porch light to make everything look the way it did when we were gone. My heart was pounding as to what I might do, so I grabbed the butcher knife from the kitchen drawer just in case this dude thought out of fear to fight me with something. I hid in the room across the hall from our bedroom with the door slightly ajar so I could see my bedroom door. I sat at the window in the pitch black. Boom boom, boom boom, boom boom, was the sound of my heart as I peered out of the window waiting for a taxi to pull up. After an hour had passed, a taxi surely pulled up, and my heart was about to beat out of my chest, and I was saying, "Oh God." Scooter jumped out of the cab and sped to the door, taking the stairs two at a time, and he was happy. At that time I jumped to the door, peeping out into the black hallway, and I heard him downstairs jingling that huge key ring of mine. On his way running up the stairs in a hurry, he fricking yelled at my cat, my baby, and said loudly while rushing, "Get out the way you stupid cat!" I should have cut his ass then. I waited, and then he came walking down the hall; I didn't want to leave any room for excuse, so I decided to wait until he was at least four steps into my bedroom. My eyes were glaring at him through the crack as I silenced my breathing, darn near holding my breath because he was so close, I could have just reached out and cut'em. He unlocked the door with *my* keys and walked in. I jumped out with the knife in my hand, pointing it at him and roared, "Ah ha, got your ass, now you get the fuck outta here now before I kill you, and give me my damn keys you liar!" He left the house immediately and walked back to work. Holding his head down he didn't say a word, and was as red as a tomato. He probably crapped on himself because I have a boisterous voice to begin with, the house was dark and silent, one of the cars was gone, and he thought he was alone. When I roared "*Ah Ha,*" he must have thought he had just been shot or that a spaceship landed. I bet he wanted nothing more than to get beamed up at *that* moment. I was seriously shaking and I jumped in the car and sped off to the church. I pulled into the back parking lot and then ran in and got an usher to get Reverend Defenbar. He came out and I told him about the whole set up, and boy was he furious. He went back into the sanctuary, sort of like Bush did when he heard about the twin towers, and calmly took his seat as if nothing happened. Rev. Defenbar remained and continued until the service was over, and I went back home.

When Hank got home, I told him simply without arguing, "Your son is welcome to stay here and you don't have to make him leave, but I'm leaving. I can't live in prison, looking around all the time, not feeling comfortable, and locking everything up."
Surprisingly the pastor said, "I understand."

At midnight we both picked Scooter up from work and Reverend lit into him, but I chose to say nothing. Scooter was scurred. Scooter was made to apologize to me, and he did, but he had to leave and go back to his mother, which was Reverend's choice.

Everything was back to normal, as far as not having to put my home on lockdown, but the verbal abuse worsened. Perhaps and most likely, Hank was secretly holding me accountable for his son having to leave.

Ten years later Scooter and I became closer, and he has grown out of that phase, thank God, and he is a nice young man today.

Chapter Four

In our sixth year of marital hell, I found myself sitting alone in the upper part of the split ranch while Hank was on the lower level in the bedroom that *he* chose to sleep in, but to hear him tell it, I kicked him out of our bedroom. In the living room upstairs were many plants; some were floor plants and some just sat *on* the floor, others were in the bay window as well as spread about on end tables. I had Chinese Evergreen, Croton, Dieffenbachia, Dracaena, Snake Plant, Golden Pothos, and the Corn Plant. There were times when Hank would complain about the plants and say, "It looks like a jungle around here." He would argue about any and everything.

The aqua greenish carpet matched a color in the upholstery of the couch and the room was cozy, designed for conversation only with the absence of a television. Although I was alone upstairs, the tension in the house was so thick you could have cut it with a knife, as was the case on a daily basis without exaggeration.

It was around seven o'clock in the evening in my quiet neighborhood during the month of November so it was dark out and I was trying to mentally escape Pastor Defenbar. I was his third wife, which should have been an enormous flashing red light signal to me, but it wasn't. I was blinded by love, but that will never happen again. For the most part, I'm an intelligent person so I often wondered why my becoming Defenbar's third wife didn't give me a clue that he wasn't the one. I should have heard a little voice saying, "Bad move, bad move."

I was considering returning to school to pursue a doctorate degree in order to busy myself and have something to do so that I spend less time in that wanna-be holy house. Pastor Defenbar told me that if I returned to school he would divorce me, so I'm not sure what kept me from Grad School. His words alone should have been incentive enough for me to go back.

Sometimes I think to myself, "How on God's green earth did I, of all people, end up married to a pastor anyway?" God sure has a way of testing folks. Not that being married to a pastor is a bad thing, because all of those other no-goods with highfalutin academic degrees are either on the down low, cheaters, let me get you all wet with sexy talk and don't call you for another two weeks type of mo-fo's, or devilish s.o.b's that don't know the Lord.

For the simple fact that I always had access to intelligent answers concerning biblical questions, and was able to grow much in the Word, for that reason only I count it a blessing having been married to the pastor of our great church. Ours was a church filled with the woman that cooks for every occasion; and Sister so and so that's in everybody's business but her own, at every funeral, will travel to a church meeting even if it's ten States away and stay in the best of hotels but puts her weekly dollar in the plate, sitting in the back of the church so that she can see everything, and don't anyone sit in her seat, you'd think she paid for it. Let's not forget about the lady that takes pride in the fact that she visits all of the sick, "I'm a Missionary!" she'd say, and I guess she would love to add, "So put that in your pipe and smoke it." Big dootyswat, and did she want a fricking cookie to go with that missionary pin? Back then I wished I could have told them that I only inherited them by default; I mean, do they really think that I prayed for God to send them to me?

Anywho, there I sat listening to jazz, and that's when I decided to write about it. I realized that what I was experiencing was the opposite of what the world believed happened behind the doors of a pastor's home. I needed to let other silent sufferers know that they weren't alone by my revealing and uncovering the dark secrets of our marriage.

Chapter Five

It all began back in 1964 when I was the last born of six children, five girls and one boy. Back then my parents were climbing the entrepreneurial ladder to success. My father was a successful general contractor and my mother also owned her own business making her mark in the world of gemstones, always travelling with me in tote doing gem and mineral shows across the country. Being people not born with a silver spoon in our mouths, we needed to be smart, wise, crafty, and talented.

Our house was large and we lived comfortably. There was a large eat-in-kitchen, five spacious bedrooms, a sizable living and dining room, and unfortunately one bathroom. However, we managed very well and it was never an issue, not as far as my memory goes. For some reason lately, I can't remember whether the chicken comes before the egg, or the egg before the chicken.

The suburbs of Long Island, New York, was where we were reared in a beautiful black and white corner house with a yard that seemed to me to have been massive in size back then. We lived in the nicest house on the block, God had blessed us. Our parents were staunch church folks back then, not that they don't go to church now every other Sunday, but back then they didn't miss a Sunday. Consequently, I ended up back in the church. The Word says in Proverbs 22:6, "Train up a child in the way he should go: and when he is old, he will not depart from it." Having a firm foundation, it baffled me how I ended up being abused by my husband.

Well, as fate would have it, I, me, moi, the dancer, the party girl, the spur of the moment ready when you are just let me get my shoes on girl, was the one that ended up married to a pastor, and I don't know if that was some sort of a bad joke or what. I mean let's add this thing up, what did I ever do to deserve to get a sermon on Sunday, cursed at on Monday, Fellowship night on Tuesday, cursed at on Wednesday, bible study on Thursday, cursed at on Friday, not speaking on Saturday, and back to church on Sunday? Gee whiz, I felt like Solomon Grundy, who was born on Monday, christened on Tuesday, married on Wednesday, took ill on Thursday, worse on Friday, died on Saturday, buried on Sunday, and that was the end of Solomon Grundy. I thought, "Well damn this!! Somehow this must come to an end, even though I attracted it into my life through prayer."

My mother is also an excellent seamstress and we were the best dressed children around. I was always a confident child and still am for that matter, unbelievably after all I've gone through. We were always taught that we can do anything that we want to do as far as setting goals and reaching them, to always be the best in whatever it is that we do, and not to blame anyone for what may befall us. Dad and mom told us that we were more than conquerors. My father has a saying when telling us to be the best at whatever we do, and that is, "If you're going to steal, rob a bank, always shoot for the top." Mama's saying is, "If it can be done, you can do it." Those were words that stuck with me all of my life, like oatmeal sticking to your ribs.

My mother made sure that I always wore ribbons and shoes to match my clothes, I just love that girly thing and everything must still be just so. I used to prance around in mama's shoes that were like boats on me, would walk around putting scotch tape on my fingernails so they'd be long, and had the nerve to paint them too. Although I had decent length hair, I'd put a white t-shirt over my head as if to have longer hair like Rapunzel. Would you believe that what we go through in childhood really stays with us throughout our lives, we just do it on a much larger scale. I am that same little person just seasoned. You can't catch me without my nails done, or a little extra hair on every now and then. Let's get real weave divas, let all women of all nationalities stand up too, my goodness more people wear weaves and extensions than I can shake a stick at. I had to pull the rug on that one being that Pastor Defenbar has a thing for women with long hair.

To not have ancestors born in America in those days made it difficult for people to get ahead easily. I must say we were privileged. The main key to my success is that we were taught that we weren't better than anyone, and absolutely no one was better than us. Therefore, we were told to dream big and accomplish them. Part of my dream was always to have a peaceful and respectful relationship. From what I know now, a healthy relationship is a part of prosperity. Rev. Defenbar with his ill ways was doomed by the law of attraction.

I've always been able to speak without intimidation and with authority to anyone, no matter what their status was or is in society or the business world. Once cut, everyone bleeds red. Furthermore, I've never seen a brinks truck behind a hearse, so basically we're all the same. Money is good to have, but it doesn't make the person, and everyone should be able to tell the next person, "You're no better than I am, and you can't take it with you."

I didn't start out as a child knowing what I wanted to be when I grew up like some people that pop out of their mama's behind saying, "Since I can remember, I always wanted to be XYZ;" it took me well over two decades before I really knew what it was I wanted to do. Although I can truly say it's always been inside of me, it just had to surface, and no it's not being a writer *or* a pastor's wife while we're on the subject of don't wanna be's. Try being married to Pastor Jeckyl and Reverend Hyde. Let's move on, as they would say in England "Carry-awn," oh how I love that accent.

As I sat there in the living room of one of my two homes, I was listening to an instrumental version of a song called "Hearts of Fire," which speaks about planting a flower and producing a pearl. I do believe that my parents planted this flower and grew a pearl. I don't say that out of conceit which is something I never even entertained, nor do I say it to pat myself on the back of my accomplishments in life. Without God, without Love, without Charity, let's get all the definitions in, without Jesus, don't get me preaching, I AM NOTHING, but it's a poor frog that don't waddle in his own pond.

Having that song playing in the background as I wrote made me realize the truth in it, and I would have been remiss had I not mentioned it. Un huh, yup, that word became a habit from church, "REMISS." There was this sister that would use that word during announcements, always saying, "I would be remiss if I didn't say…." blah blah blah.

I didn't know back then what I was destined to do but hey, if you seek ye first the Kingdom, come on Saints you know the rest, but then again let me not take that for granted. For those that don't know but should know; those of a different faith and different walks of life; and those that sit and listen to a sermon and leave the sanctuary doing the exact opposite of what the pastor just preached his heart out about folks; the scripture says in Matthew 6:33, "But seek ye first the kingdom of God, and His righteousness; and all these things shall be added unto you." Get it, got it, good!

My brother and I were naturals at dancing and we loved it, it was an art to us, it was in our bones unlike our other siblings who had rhythm only because we were a dancing family. I have no idea how we ended up with rhythm anyway, we seemed to have had a monopoly on dancing.

My parents always took pride in me because I am the last born, not the favorite, but the last born. I was always enrolled in activities that had the potential of making millions because my parent's goal was to expose me to things that could benefit me later in life. I've had private tennis lessons, which were fun but didn't hold my interest. Only had I known that these sisters were emerging, I would have stuck with it and given them a run for their money, having been as athletic as I was growing up. I've taken dance, acting, and private singing lessons at some of the top schools with some well known instructors, and I also appeared in Off-Broadway plays in New York City. Unfortunately, Hank didn't realize that my upbringing instilled great self esteem within me. He lacked in understanding that I am strong willed and strong minded, and that there was nothing derogatory he could ever say to cause me to think differently of myself.

After getting a black-eye in the eighth grade by a sucker punch thrown in my direction by a classmate, my mom sent me for Wushu lessons, which is a form of martial arts. I guess my mom said to herself, naw naw naw NOT MINE Sistah, and that never happened again. My hands were registered in New York City through my martial arts school, and the next fight I had, my opponent ended up in the emergency room, literally.

Thanks to my parents, I'm a well rounded individual. I've traveled oversees a few times on flights that have taken thirteen hours in one direction. I was brought up being exposed to an extensive amount of classical music in my mother's office, which was her music of choice and no-one dared come in her office and change the station. From high school age I was able to work through the summer with my mom, I've had interactions with owners of businesses, I have an education, I was reared in the church, and I've travelled across the world to name a few things that contribute to my well roundedness. All of these things plus some gives me my wholeness. Having this background, it's unnerving to know that folks in the church had the audacity to gossip and say my husband's name made me. They don't know from whence I've come, and neither did Hank.

Chapter Six

I'm a person that loves to laugh and I've always been that way. "Live, Love, Laugh" is a motto I've adopted, and I especially like it when I'm laughing so hard until I cry, better yet until I can't breathe.

Lamont, who now lives hundreds of miles away from me is extremely funny, and when I need a real good laugh I just call him, and we start cracking up for no apparent reason as soon as we hear the others' voice. I guess the memories flood our minds. I surely miss him being right next to me, he is one funny human being and a tongue speaking, bible studying, prayer warrior to boot. Lamont and I laughed so hard one time we thought we'd die because we couldn't stop laughing to catch our breath. I knew that any man I marry would have to make me laugh.

The pastor is funny believe it or not, and when he's funny he's really funny, but when he's mean he's hateful, which was ninety eight percent of the time.

My sense of humor is great although some sensitive church members didn't think so. They were always looking to turn something a person said into a negative thing, or try to make it seem as though harm was meant. I was speaking with someone at church and I mentioned a very kind woman that was humble and I really liked her. She happened to walk up on my conversation and I said "speaking of which," and she went to the pastor crying and saying that I called her a "witch." Years later she left the church. Individuals fitting those criteria need to pray a little harder!

I remember going out after I reached the age to do so, to clubs that had comedians for part of the night and I would always sit in the front to intentionally get picked on, but they'd never say a word about me, never one wise crack. This concerned me after one particular night when a comedian picked on everyone in the front row one after another. It was a narrow row and consisted of only five seats, but when he reached me he stopped. I approached him at the bar after the show to question him, and I couldn't believe the answer he gave me. It was for the simple reason that he couldn't look at me because I'd make *him* laugh. That goes to show how hard I laugh, and naturally I'm a happy person. I've been told many times that I've missed my calling, and that I should have been a comedienne, but I beg to differ, I don't think I'm all that funny. How is it that with all the joy that's naturally inside of me, it wasn't enough to obliterate the hell I was living through in that marriage?

I've prayed about it for years literally, waiting on the Lord and being of good cheer, waiting on Him to change the pastor. I understand that God works in His own time and not ours, neither do I get angry with God, but sometimes I felt as if I was in a position to say the words that Jesus said, "Father, why hast Thou forsaken me?" That feeling has occurred more than once during that time in my life.

Now for the sake of lay people, Hank was after all my husband, man first, pastor second; so before others start judging about someone's calling, they need to understand the circumstances of being a man first.

The pastor and I being the head of the church unfortunately couldn't tell anyone our personal issues, hey, we're not supposed to have those kinds of problems. Only if you're a pew member you can have those problems, well wake up America!!! We are people too wackadoo wackadoo wackadoo.

Maybe I am a bit funny because I make myself laugh at times and no-one has to be around, but it's not so serious that I think I can make a living off of being a comedienne. I just tell the truth, and the truth is always much funnier than just making up some fictitious statement to get a laugh. When a comedian makes a joke about real life scenarios, things that has happened to him/her, or things that they've seen happen, it's more real and much funnier.

Although I was going through some of the worst situations, and knowing that I had to escape one day and would, I still had a joy deep within my soul. I was able to genuinely smile and laugh at the people and things that gave me that feeling.

Chapter Seven

Growing up I never fully trusted anyone except God as my father always taught me, and I don't know whether it's right or not, or whether it's just one man's opinion, but it's instilled in me. My dad always told me a story which is seemingly his version of a worldly parable and it goes a little something like this: *There was a little boy that climbed on top of a house and couldn't get down. When his father saw him, he told his son to jump assuring him that he'll catch him; so when the little boy jumped, the dad just turned and walked away and said to his son, "Never trust anybody."* Well needless to say, as awful as that sounds and although I could never understand why a dad would do that to his child, I never trusted anyone one hundred percent.

When I first met Mary Ellen I was in my mid twenties, and over the course of twenty years I've learned to trust her to a degree that I consider greater than average. I know her innermost secrets, and likewise she knows mine. I thank God for her being in my life at that time because as a first lady there is no one that we can talk to or trust without the risk of exposing the personal business of the first family. There are always a few church goers that have a way of twisting things, especially the evil ones, just to start a rumor, gossip, or to try and get rid of you if they don't like you.

In the church there are some naïve people that think pastors and first ladies are the untouchables, impervious, and should be able to walk on water like Peter. Well, let me be the one to burst their bubble and bring them into reality. A pastor is like anyone else in the area of being born in sin and shaped in iniquity, which is the reason for Jesus. However, most pastors possess biblical exegesis with a more in depth study of the Word than the average person. I believe they're highly anointed, but they must stay on their knees more than we because the devil wants to stop them in their tracks from spreading the Good News. Given these factors, they still can't do a darn thing about being born of a woman, they *are* flesh, bone and blood.

There may be a few exceptions of pastors here and there that walk the straight and narrow; and I used the word "may" because I lived that life, and although I didn't go home with all of them, I wouldn't put anything past anyone. I'm sure it was a struggle with trials and tribulations for those on the straight and narrow reaching that point because hey, they darn sure weren't born that way. Saints don't overlook this because ALL pastors do not walk the straight and narrow, HELLO. I truly believe my husband was anointed by God which is the reason satan wanted him badly, but unfortunately Rev. Defenbar didn't have the faith to exercise his power given to him by God to overcome that demon, thereby abusing and desecrating his anointing.

Most people that claim to be practicing Christians that go home cursing up a storm after church, would just put their holy suits on and die if they heard that the pastor said a curse word. Get over it, they're human too, at least I've never heard of a farm that bears pastors. Disciples are made, not born.

As far as first ladies are concerned, heck we weren't called to be pastors so you can get over that all together. Don't get me wrong, all Christians should strive more and more to be Christ like but don't get your panties in a bunch if you see us accidentally acting out of character too.

Once God ordains someone they don't become un-ordained just because tests and trials come. If the naïve folks knew inside information on what really transpires behind some closed doors, they would be running around saying, "Oh my God, the pastor or first lady said so and so or did so and so, he ain't no real pastor." In reality, that type of person isn't really practicing Christianity. Remember, Jesus died for all of us!

Then there are those that are struck with jealousy that think they wish, and I said "Think they wish" because if they knew, they wouldn't wish it, that they had what the pastor's wife has, not knowing what it is some of us go through or went through to have what we have. As much pain and anguish as I've been through married to that rascal, every one of them would turn tail and say, "Feet don't fail me now." So as you can see, we can't say a word to people, and must endure this with Jesus alone.

Fortunately, I was blessed with Mary Ellen, who also is a Christian and always respected my then husband as a pastor no matter what. She lives in her church's basement, well, she may as well, because if she's not at church for little Ralph's drum lessons, she's there for Kayla and Karla's praise dance rehearsals, or the three of them having choir rehearsal, or some meeting.

Her marriage isn't like mine although it's still a marriage. She can't get her husband in a church if she paid him, but it's all good as they met that way so nothing has changed. I do believe however, had I met her after

I said "I do," I would not have become close to her either, but we've known each other for at least 8 years prior to my marriage. I do know people that I've known longer, but they fit into one of those "Oh no, not the pastor!" categories I mentioned earlier.

Needless to say, outside of my family she's one that I didn't mind opening up to. As a matter of fact, there are some people in my family that I can't talk to, and some that I don't want to talk to, not because they would have spilled the beans but because they too would have disregarded the pastor's calling. Most of them becoming too darn nosey would've started telling me what I should have and shouldn't have done.

Mary Ellen is as nosey as Pearl on the television sitcom "227," but she'll listen as a friend and only give her opinion when I ask for it, or when she senses that I'm looking for one.

I've learned that the cliché "It's lonely at the top" is true, but the part that goes unnoticed is that it also hurts. With having to keep mostly everything hidden inside protecting my abuser, made me feel inadequate as a human. Why was I so adamant about protecting him after what he'd done to me? What was it that made me still care? Who was I viewing Hank to be? When would I let out these behind the scene secrets? Where would I end up by telling these truths?

Chapter Eight

When I first found out that pastors had an ordinary side was long before my pastor-husband came along; it was when a pastor that was married tried to come on to me. He started offering to buy me things and wanting to take me out while undressing me with his eyes like I was candy. The person I was dating at the time, along with my mother, said not to accept anything and that this particular pastor wanted more than met the eye. Thank God I listened and took heed.

Sure enough, the person that he targeted next was fooled by his title, taken advantage of, and her husband ended up moving her out of State because of that situation. I was appalled to see a pastor behave in such a way because I used to be one of those naïve pew members too. I thought all pastors were on the up and up, but fortunately although shocked, I had enough common sense and wisdom to know that they're human beings first. I never exposed him, and continued to respect him as a pastor.

Hallelujah, God is good, because little did I know; I would be married to a pastor, being subject to the same scrutiny. Perhaps, had I exposed that pastor, someone would probably have made accusations about us as well. I believe and know for a fact that what goes around comes around. Good or bad, people get back what they give out and I only gave that pastor respect. Although Rev. Defenbar behaved in ways that were embarrassing to me in public, I never heard gossip about it. In respecting pastors, I don't discriminate based on whether I believe they're a bad person or a good person; I respect the title.

Chapter Nine

Although my siblings and I were brought up in church, we stopped going at some point when I was between the ages of ten and twelve. I'm not sure of the reason, but I believe it had something to do with our car. We attended a Baptist church that was roughly thirty five minutes from our home. Thank goodness none of us lost our values concerning God.

I started to go back to church when I was in my twenties, after I reached the point of no return with Harold, my first and ex-husband. He smoked marijuana like the plant was free. I married at a young age the first time and it lasted only two years as was predicted by an uncle of mine. Harold would pick me up after church and go right to the spot designated for purchasing weed which was some demonic act as far as I was concerned. I'm sure most Christians will agree with me on that one. I won't mention his nationality to prevent stereotyping, but after he lost his job he lied about looking for work. He decided on his own to just sit on his behind and collect unemployment until that ran out, then he had the nerve to get an extension. He smoked cigarettes and smelled like a dirty ashtray at all times. His toenails were dirty and it made me cringe to look at him or touch him, oh heck no he had to go. He became a totally different person than he was when we met.

When I met Harold he was well put together and his hygiene was excellent. He had a high position at his place of employment which was at a fortune five hundred company in Manhattan, and he did all of the hiring and firing. However, when his entire department was outsourced resulting in him being laid off, he crumbled under pressure and couldn't get back on track. I eventually kicked his behind out. Now that may sound harsh, but doggonnit he shouldn't have given up. When life gives you a lemon, make lemonade!

Harold knew that I used to be a hypochondriac before I fully understood God's Word on healing, and that nutt had the nerve to call me trying to get me back by saying, "I have a problem." He said that in the hopes of it coming across as if he had an epiphany and realized his contribution in the breakup and was then willing to make it better, but I was thinking differently. Right away I shouted, *"What you got! I'm putting on my shoes, and I'm on my way to the emergency room!"* He then said, "No, no, I'm addicted to marijuana," well what a relief that was. I felt at that moment like I hit the Mega Millions. Marijuana was something we always fought about because he would disagree with me that he had a problem.

During that time in the midst of those fights, I knew no-where else to turn, so I found a church to seek God's help. Nothing seemed to work, therefore, Harold and I divorced. Years later, I eventually changed churches, and that's where I met Pastor Defenbar who arrived five years after I joined.

I had no idea that my life was headed for a downward spiral, and that I would soon be living in a hell that I knew not of. I never saw it coming.

Chapter Ten

I was baptized as a child along with my siblings and I mean submerged under the water, not sprinkled as some denominations do. Being baptized once is all a person gets in the connectional church that Pastor Defenbar is associated with. Concerning the six children my parents bore, some of us were on the usher board, and others in the choir, but rest assured we were working for Christ.

Pastor Defenbar was a great pastor and teacher. During his tenure I learned abundantly and felt more of a closeness with Christ. I wanted to be baptized again while I could understand more clearly what was happening, but it doesn't work that way. I thank God that at least I remember everything that happened when I was being baptized as a child.

Oh how I thank God for my parents. I especially thank God for Jesus because He is the one that sustained me and prepared me to become a pastor's wife unbeknownst to me. He also prepared me for what I was about to encounter at the new church with those desperate women, or should I call them panty throwers or pastor chasers? However, I'm uncertain about His preparing me to have dealt with Pastor Defenbar's bullcrap although ultimately He did. I just don't understand, and I'm not sure whether or not I was ready for the hell that was to come, although I can handle myself very well. I'm no killer but don't push me.

When I joined the new church I didn't know anyone there, and I would go in on Sunday mornings and sit midways in the sanctuary. The church had eight-hundred or so members on the roll at that time; since then the roll has fluctuated with deaths, births, and those coming and going.

The sanctuary was large with two aisles on each side, and one long beautiful aisle down the center, which eventually became the aisle of doom by way of my walking down it to get married. There was plush crimson color carpeting throughout the church that reminded me of Jesus' blood, and the pulpit area stretched across the entire front with the choir loft located directly behind. In the pulpit were chairs that looked like they were built only for kings to sit on with cushions matching the carpet.

The pastor in all of his glory would sit there every Sunday morning in the largest chair like Papa Bear. He wore beautiful robes, some made out of material that had inlaid crosses, and all of them were adorned with doctoral bars which added to his already distinguished look. My mother being the excellent seamstress that she is, also made a few of his robes. He wore a fourteen carat gold chain approximately thirty-six to forty inches long with a custom made fourteen carat gold cross. The cross was proportioned, and both the horizontal and vertical bars stretched three and a half inches long with a large black onyx square cabochon in the center. The cross hung over his robe and what a majestic look that was. With a pipe organ to his right, and another expensive keyboard and piano to his left, he would look out over his flock and yes, he did seem untouchable, I just wish I hadn't touched him.

There were lighted candles and live plants gracing the altar along with the podium and other sacred tables that were draped in beautiful cloths corresponding with the liturgical calendar colors depending on whether it was the Advent season, or Epiphany, etc. Professionally made banners, also made by my mother, hung on either side of the sanctuary with a scripture uplifting our Lord and Savior Jesus Christ which reminds me of a sign that once graced our home.

A year or so after we were married, we put a spiritual sign inside our home over the front door which I took down because of the things that went on in there and the language being used, I felt we were defiling the Lord.

The many pews were in the form of long benches with comfortable crimson color cushions to match the rest of the décor in the sanctuary, you know, the ones with the book holder on the back for the bibles, hymn books, and fans. However, in our church the hymn books seemed to be far and few between, other than the ones in the choir loft. I guess some people didn't feel as bad clipping a hymn book as opposed to the holy bible which is probably why we couldn't find a hymn book in every pew out in the congregation. Then again, I honestly don't know the true story as to whether or not there were ever many hymn books to begin with, or what could have happened to them. The many chairs in the choir loft also had red cushioned seating. Speaking of the choir, there were a few of the members that were evil toward me some years back, prior to my joining the choir. I never said an unkind word to any of them, they just had bad spirits.

Chapter Eleven

My husband was a handsome man, however, that didn't mean a hill of beans to me and never has. Going back to my teenage years until now, I've actually never dated anyone for their looks which was evident by some of those Neanderthal looking jackrabbits I've dated. For the most part they were all nice people, which was what my decisions were based upon.

Unfortunately, there's the ignorant religious that can see a handsome pastor that's a bachelor and think he's the one for them because they like his style or his swagger. I truly believe it's because they're desperate for a man and frustrated. The married as well as the unmarried women were just plain ole jealous of me. Anyone in their right mind wouldn't or shouldn't judge a book by its cover, but then again, I guess we should never underestimate a dried up woman looking to be lubricated; she is apt to do or say anything, just like a woman pms-ing, six in one hand, half dozen in the other. If they could have imagined what they would have been living with, and what they would have had to endure, and if there was a legit reason by any stretch of the imagination why they didn't like me at first, they would've been happy that I was the one to have gotten stuck with him.

I, on the other hand, had someone in my life when Pastor Defenbar was sent to our church, but at that time the guy that I was with had one foot out the door and the other foot on a banana peel which was due to the cognizance of our own relationship issues. That very fact didn't have any bearing on why or how I ended up with the pastor.

It was my prayers that got me into that marriage; you are to be careful of what you ask for, and be very precise. No matter who I was dating, my prayers were always for a God fearing husband that would go to church with me every Sunday as I remember my parents doing. I prayed that he was to be well educated, handsome, and a responsible person. I received all of that, however, I failed to request NO Jeckyl and Hyde, and someone to respect me and love me for who I am. We must be precise when asking of the Lord. I guess God said, "Are you sure you want someone to go to church with you *every* Sunday? I'll go you one better!"

So there I sat midways in the sanctuary every Sunday morning at eleven o'clock, which is around the time most churches start.

I didn't know anyone in that church at all and no one knew me although I grew up in that town. There was a handful that knew *of* me because of school. My family wasn't the type of family that got involved with others in the community, nor did we mingle too much, so the town gossip never involved any of us. If anyone pretended as if they knew us when, trust me, they're lying. I was never at a party or at a bar when so and so went down, and neither were my siblings. I went to church, and wasn't allowed to go around the corner to the candy store until my eighteenth birthday, so if anyone said that I was seen somewhere, it was in their dreams.

Well, once I became involved with the pastor, all of a sudden most of the women in the church started to speculate and testalie, not testify, but testalie, including the married ones. Jealousy is a booga and will get you nowhere. They were so jealous that some of them left to join other churches, and the ones that stayed, tried to be a thorn in my flesh but soon found out that I am not the one, wrong chick, wrong day.

Prior to getting married, a fourteen year old girl whose mother and father are still married to this day, approached me and said, "I heard you're sleeping with the pastor," and I looked her dead in the eye with a smug look on my face and said, "Tell your mama she's just jealous."

There was one woman that really shocked me because she is a quiet person with a gentle spirit and would never cause a problem to anyone. I went to her house one evening to either drop off or pick up something and she greeted me at the door saying, "You didn't give anyone else a chance." Was I supposed to make an announcement in church asking if anyone wanted a shot at my man before he and I walked down the aisle or while I was making my wedding plans? Who does that?

Some of them imagined that they were in competition with me, but there wasn't any competition because little did they know, I was resting comfortably in a relationship with our pastor while they ran around like crazy throwing panties. One sister well past my age, walked in the church, lifted her dress to me and said, "My legs look better than yours, you're no competition." What a hoot that was. I smiled and said, "God bless you," and walked away from her.

Chapter Twelve

I was never ashamed to praise the Lord publicly which I did. I was always a faithful member, and because of my personality I met people with speed who seemed to have loved me until I got married.

I found out much later that when I would walk around to drop my offering in the plate, the pastor wasn't only attracted to my praise but my figure caught his attention too. Yes, pastors like it too, so do priests, and that shouldn't be hard to believe. There are only two men that I know of that truly abstained from sex, and that's Jesus, and the Apostle Paul. Look at those freaky priests that have been in the spotlight as pedophiles, they are flesh and blood my friend.

Unfortunately, *my* sex life with Pastor Defenbar had been a living hell almost from the beginning, especially when I realized that he was into something else for sexual pleasures which outraged me.

On the contrary, our pastor was a smooth man because he outwardly walked righteous and never let anyone know what he was thinking; therefore, I had no clue prior to his approach that he ever had any interest in me. We innocently went out to dinner a few times, at first with my girlfriend Vanesia in tow because I didn't want to be alone with him. Eventually I started to realize through Vanesia's persuasion his interest in me, and that he was an ordinary man after all, having a need of companionship too.

Vanesia and I had a friendship that stemmed from high school. We became close as young adults and worshipped together at church becoming junior trustees. Prior to actually meeting Rev. Defenbar, I remember teasing her and saying, "I'm going to marry the pastor." I knew I'd get a laugh because of the age difference between the pastor and me.

As our relationship further developed, Hank and I decided to get married so that we could openly be together and not become tempted, and we didn't want to live apart. Our wedding was the talk of the town and the entire congregation was invited including many others; friends, family, co-workers, clergy, etc. The wedding was beautiful with the white limos, a wedding cake made like a cathedral with spiral stairs on each side, and all the trimmings a bride could dream of. Although invited, the envious sat across the street in cars just to watch, they were lined up. Due to the amount of people and the expense a hall would have been, we chose to have a four-thousand square foot white tent with Astroturf erected on the church grounds for our reception which was close to five hundred people. I felt like a princess that day. Well that was it, once I became his wife and the first lady, I discovered who he *really* was.

Our first year of marriage was an eye opener. I really found out first-hand how some pastors are behind closed doors, more so than what I found out from my previous experience with a pastorman trying to come on to me. The first time I heard Reverend Defenbar curse, I was flabbergasted yet again like the people I spoke about previously, and I proceeded to curse him out as he did me, let the games begin! Yes, I uncontrollably stooped to his level, pardon moi, but my verbal reflexes sometimes get in the way of things.

Because he was a pastor, in the beginning of our relationship I never even thought about cursing at him or around him because I ignorantly thought that pastors were truly what you see on Sunday mornings. For the most part, I also believed that they literally lived it by practicing what they preached twenty-four, seven, three-sixty-five; every one of them. Well Lordie-mercy what an untruth!!

After our nuptials, things started to get ugly for some reason or another, more like *another* because he had no reason to think that I was stupid and dumb although he called me "Young and dumb" the entire time of our new marriage. He would say it with such a profound, nasty, and hateful disposition, until I received yet another academic degree. While I was working toward my degrees, during arguments Hank would always say, "I know you're going to leave as soon as you get your degree just like my other wives did." As a newlywed those words hurt because a thought like that would never have crossed my mind. I actually thought he would get better and that he was going through a phase. In retrospect I'm wondering if he premeditated being evil to me and knew he'd chase me away. However, I left eight years after acquiring a degree, which had nothing to do with why I left. How was it that he was so prophetic in what he said? Because you *will* have what *you* say!

As life would have it, Vanesia and I grew apart and lost contact due to that hellish marriage of mine. For me, the onset of our friendship going topsy-turvy was due to my alienating our bond in trying to please my new husband. She was my best friend at that time and I never invited her to my new home, not once. I was too embarrassed to tell her that Hank wouldn't allow it because she was engaged to my ex's best friend. Her wedding was one year after mine and Hank forbade me to be in her wedding, but thank God she persisted and would not allow me to back out. God knows I would have regretted it. Vanesia being an official in our church wanted her pastor to perform her ceremony but Hank gave an excuse as to why he couldn't be there. He childishly refused to even attend her wedding because my ex and I were in it, although not partners. I've never felt so bad in losing a friend, it hurt me deeply; she was my sister.

Having double standards, Hank thought he could have some topless dancing woman that he used to date and love, call my house as supposedly some friend without any repercussions, well damn that! Don't tell me it's raining, and you're peeing on me; I know about those so-called "Friends." Hank had already told me prior to our marriage that he and this woman caller had a teenage son together which is Scooter. He tried to use his son as an excuse to speak to the mother, but that was by no means going to work with me. My philosophy was that Scooter had reached his late teens and knew how to call his father if he needed him, and I put an end to that baby mama drama as far as I knew. What I didn't know didn't hurt.

I was fortunate enough to answer her phone call one night when Reverend Defenbar wasn't home. I took that opportunity to tell her plainly, that if she continued to call my house, it was going to be me, her, and the ground. What I meant by that was, I was going to hit her, and she was going to hit the ground.

I felt as though he always hated me for ending his bullcrap relationship with that old flame, but it made me no never mind.

It's no secret that a select few of pastors have babies out of wedlock, and then take their unworthy butts in the pulpit on Sunday mornings looking like the untouchables. Well-known ministers were found guilty of having children out of wedlock; they were obviously doing more than praying.

I am able to continue having the highest respect for pastors although I'm aware of the real deal. Some are truly called by God; they have to be in order to deal with all of those different personalities and demonic forces in the church. Due to my knowledge and understanding of the Word, and in spite of what I've suffered, through it all, I believe that while they're on duty in the church, most pastors are sincere about what they do. Maybe I'll just speak for Pastor Defenbar. *He* was sincere and took his assignment seriously while at church, and the Lord used him as an instrument to speak to His people. Jesus says that *He* is "The Truth," therefore, if the pastor speaks the truth, then its truth come from God. It's just that satan does his job well; which is to kill, steal, and destroy, ruining the lives of those that allow him to. Pastors are one of the devil's main targets because of what they do and what they stand for.

It's an unspoken and unwritten law that first ladies just don't speak to family members or anyone about certain situations when it comes to a personal issue between her and the pastor. We protect and respect our husbands, at least in front of people, as any other woman protects her husband in public. There are past first ladies of the United States that chose to stand by their President husbands as an outward sign of protection and support when he did wrong.

Just as laypeople struggle to live the best Christian life that they can, so do pastors, or they wouldn't have a testimony without a test and the gospel wouldn't mean much. Can I get a witness?

Making excuses and covering for our husbands doesn't make it right, but unfortunately it's what some women do.

Chapter Thirteen

In the early days as well as throughout our entire marriage relationship, we clashed in absolutely everything. I'm unable to say "Yeah, those were the good ole days!" The first few years were like being married to the devil himself, until I found out that I was actually married *to* the devil.

The pastor always had someone from the church that took on the job of housework to clean his home the entire time of his bachelorhood and he continued with that custom after we were married. Having someone cater to all of his needs his entire life, as his father and grandfather were pastors also, did more damage than good. Pastor Hank doesn't know how to clean anything. Although the proper cleaning products were in the closet at his disposal, he'd use dish detergent for shampoo, use shampoo to wash out socks, and use Lysol toilet bowl cleaner to clean the stove, etc. When I corrected him as nicely as I could saying, as I picked up the bottle, "Why is this here, what did you use it for?" He immediately would bark and go off the deep end for no reason with hatred and funkiness in his voice saying, "I used it to clean the stove!" Since he was already going crazy, I tried to be as passive as I could in hopes of turning his attitude around and would say, "Oh, well this is for the toilet bowl, see," as I pointed to the words "TOILET BOWL CLEANER." He would snap and proceed to curse me out saying, "I don't give a damn, you're always so critical, I'm sick of this fucking house, leave me the hell alone." At that point I was like whoa, and I would find somewhere to go and get out of there, even if it was just to a coffee shop.

After we married, I got rid of the house keeper because there was no way I could let a nosey jealous church woman go through my private things and know everything about me. Besides, I couldn't shake the thought that there was a possibility of my toothbrush being dipped into the toilet or spit getting in my juice while I was at work. Un un damn that, I don't trust people.

I hired someone from another country to clean my house that was trustworthy, came highly recommended, and doesn't know anything about any church folks. During the transition I did all of the cleaning and that's when I started to unravel the first hidden obsession that my husband had, which made me angry, disappointed, and disgusted with him, and it provoked many verbal fights.

I could never understand why any small trivial thing would set him off and make him so angry, and why he would take everything out of context all the time, but I soon found out.

When I cleaned in the closet and looked in the shelf, then on the floor way in the back, there it was in a bag, almost finished, sometimes finished, and sometimes new. I also found it under sofa pillows often or in old canvas tote bags. The words C-H-E-V-A-S--R-E-G-A-L jumped out at me like some 3-D movie and I thought I would pass out, as I stood there trembling with anger. I was living with and married to an alcoholic pastor, and I thought that was the extent of it but there was so much more.

Staying in the Word had to be the only thing that sustained him because it's mind-boggling how he went on with his calling extremely well, and carried himself no differently than any other distinguished gentleman. Yet, he drank either a fifth or a pint a day, and I'm not even sure whether or not they're one in the same which shows how much I know about drinking.

From then on, every time he said the word "If" and I had the opportunity, I would say, "If 'IF' was a 'FIFTH' we'd all be drunk." I would cry, pray, and ask God to stop him from drinking and to take the desire away from him, but it seemed as if God wasn't answering my prayer. You live and you learn, and I have come to the realization that God has given us our own free will, and if one doesn't want it, one won't get it, in spite of others' prayers.

Prior to his curbing the juice for a *moment*--because the curbing didn't last, he would need AA behind some heavy duty drinking crap like that--I was so afraid of the amount being consumed that I thought he would get cirrhosis of the liver, and I didn't want him to die on me.

For years I would constantly tell him, "You're killing yourself, I love you, please stop with the cigarettes and drinking." He smoked like a train, forcing me into second hand smoke. He had no respect or regard for me which was understandable because he didn't respect or have any regard for himself. There was a time when I started smoking his cigarettes with him until I came to my senses and knew I had to get out of there for several reasons. No-one in my immediate family smokes.

He had such a nasty temperament, but at one point it had gotten a little better, only turning out to be the calm before the storm. He grew horrifically worse than ever. It appeared that his behavior seemingly stemmed from his childhood or from being hurt by people he loved. He would say nasty things to me like "You're not perfect, why don't you fix *yourself*, and why don't you tell your ex-boyfriend to stop *his* habits, I bet you didn't tell him anything because that's who you love, you're a whore, your mama and your family is a whore, and I hate you."

Now what on God's green earth does the ex-boyfriend, who he doesn't even know and never met, nor had *I* seen or heard from in ten years at that point have to do with anything, and why was my family being persecuted? He always talked out of his head like a maniac. He brought up the name of my ex so much that I remember having to threaten him prior to our wedding. I told him that if he mentioned my ex-boyfriend one more time, that I was going to end our relationship, leave him, and call off our wedding, so he stopped for two weeks until *after* the wedding.

My ex's name never even came to my mind until that joker mentioned him. To hear him talk, one would think that we've had conversations about my ex, or that the pastor knew him or something but he didn't, now how weird is that?

When I would come home and find yet another bottle, I would start out by saying, "So you're drinking again," and that comment would set off the biggest argument ever. I would ask him to stop until I realized that was what he did and wanted to do, so I chose not to be nice any longer. One day I found a bottle and poured the clear liquid out, replaced it with water, and did a horrible job at pretending to be drunk. I wanted to make him see that it's not fun watching someone you love kill themselves, but that didn't work either. I was so upset, but it must have been comical to watch. I was talking with a slurred speech and walking crooked while stumbling in the same manner a comedian would when making fun of drunks. I didn't stop to realize that it wasn't Hank's reality but I gave it a shot anyway; a drunk person is a drunk person. He never mentioned the exchange I did of booze to water in his liquor bottle, he just ignored it.

He seemed to have thrived and made himself feel better by disparaging others whether he was drinking or not. He would belittle anyone that came to his mind, especially those he used to date and/or was married to. He always degraded and spoke poorly of his ex-wives and Scooter's mother, calling them bitches too. Because I knew him, I never believed anything he said, I only listened to appease him. This observation of mine was confirmed by one of the two of his loving sisters.

He would call me whores, bitches, and everything else that my parents didn't name me. He'd also talk about my mother, not that he had anything of cause to say about her but just to be evil and hit below the belt, but don't talk about my mother, those are fighting words. I would then retaliate, once again letting the verbal reflex get in the way; and I would stoop to his level by talking about his mother too, and God knows it was for no good reason whatsoever and all respect was lost.

I was not brought up to talk about anyone; that was some new kind of stuff to me. However, be it right or wrong, I was taught that if someone says something to hurt you or does something hurtful to you, then say it back or do it back to them, and I do. I'm a work in progress when it comes to someone talking about my mama, you can bet that! I'm praying on it though. I started to call him all kinds of things like; addicted drunk, bitch, jack ass, drunken or jackleg preacher, mutha f-er and anything else that I could think of because when someone talks about my mama, all is fair, I mean *all* is fair. As Lamont would say "Aaw hail naw." I would tell Hank that he's a wannabe preacher, and oh boy, why did I attack his ministry? I would attack his ministry every time he drank, thinking that since he took the insult so seriously maybe he would stop by realizing the comments being made were true. I was hoping he'd realize that it was a demonic force against him. Well nothing worked and our marriage worsened even more.

I would say in the midst of an argument "Let's pray," and his response was always "I don't want to pray." I never knew what I might say that would tick him off at any given moment. A first lady in Tennessee said the same thing, but she shot and killed her active pastor-husband in 2006. It could be something as simple as making a comment on what was viewed on television. I could be speaking to him about someone else's situation, which didn't have to be a negative comment, and he would literally get fighting mad. He would try to turn the situation on me as always and find a way to relate it to *my* life or *my* past in a negative way.

Being an entrepreneur, it had become intolerable to work from my home office. Prior to having to work from home, I rented a gutted building with only four exterior walls, single- handedly wrote a bonafide business plan which solely enabled me to acquire a quarter-of-a-million-dollar commercial loan, hired an architect, and opened a sheer luxury three thousand square foot day spa. The spa was something I had envisioned in college years before it actually manifested. I drew a sketch of how I wanted the spa to be laid out, and collected swatches made out of formica with the colors of the furniture, walls, and flooring. Everything was custom made, and I carried around the sketches of the manicure tables and the front desk unit which was drawn by the furniture company as I described it to them.

The spa was located in a middle to upper class neighborhood that had outdoor cafes, great restaurants, piano bars, dancing, and the like. My spa was the most beautiful business in that town, and some called it a museum. There were two entrances, one on the main highway, and the other at the back parking lot which ran alongside the railroad to New York City. The parking lot in the back transformed my back entrance into the main entrance. No expenses were spared in the construction of the spa, as the best of everything was used, including the name brand toilet bowls.

Upon entering, there was a coat closet to the right, and the main restroom to the left that was handicapped accessible which had a beautiful light green tile trimmed with a malachite color tile. There were three beautifully upholstered brown wood framed chairs in the waiting area, and a chocolate colored leather sofa. The custom made front desk matched the manicure tables, and was very large in the shape of a backwards letter 'J.' Sitting behind it was a lighted wall unit with nine glass shelves. Directly across from that was a retail section with jewelry. Immediately pass the front desk, waiting area, restroom, and retail, began our service area.

Custom made French doors with patterned frosted glass and fancy brass door handles shaped like a mustache leading into the spa area was to the right. The spa area consisted of a long hallway and nine rooms. The waiting room had light dimmers for ambiance, and two stone end tables with a matching coffee table. Candles and magazines sat on a stone sofa table that was against a wall, and a wonderful brown leather sofa matching the one in the nail area made it cozy. There were three spacious treatment rooms for massages and facials that had six-feet-long upper and lower wood cabinets with built in round stainless steel sinks; two changing rooms with robes, slippers, towels, spa headbands, and waist wraps; a restroom; a private beautician station for hair; and a seven-seater Jacuzzi room. An oversized door designated as the fire door as per building code was at the other end and led back into the nail salon area. In lieu of numbers, brass plates with engraved names representing the men that labored diligently in that project were above each treatment room for identification to the clients.

In the nail salon area were eight custom made manicure tables with wooden winged-corner Queen Anne legs. There were seven state-of-the-art pedicure stations that had fluted glass tubs with multi-colored lighting in the water, and nicely cushioned chairs that laid down on nearly a ninety degree angle with quiet gentle motors so it didn't look like someone getting the chair massage was having some sort of a fit. Above each pedicure station was an engraved brass plate that had the name of one of my sisters above it rather than numbers so that we could assign chairs to clients. The nail drying station was high tech with purple heating lamps on a timer for the hands and feet. All of our tools were sterilized in the autoclave machine that I purchased from the supplier that my dentist used, and packaged in dental packaging for each client. I also had a kitchen area to make coffee and drinks for clients. The kitchen wasn't enclosed, and was designed with wooden cabinets and glass doors, a sink, a microwave, a mini fridge, and a hot cabbie for towels. The entire spa was covered with hardwood flooring throughout, and tile flooring for the wet areas. Two flat screen televisions were mounted on the walls as well.

The colors in the salon were very serene and warm. Two different surround sound systems were incorporated so that only tranquil spa music played in the spa area, and light music played in the nail salon area, controlled only by me. Each treatment room had only a volume dial for the music, and a light dimmer. The Jacuzzi room was truly one of a kind. To get into the tub, there were two stairs with a third serving as a large platform, all tiled to match the floor. The walls were tiled from the floor to maybe six feet high in case of splashing, and the upper walls were painted in an ocean blue. An imitation floor plant sat on the platform along with beautifully folded towels. Tea lights were placed around the tub with only one burning essential oil for aroma.

Due to obvious reasons that the town's people couldn't grasp, my expenses started to exceed my revenue, so it behooved me to close after two years. Locking my doors on a project that I birthed was a bitter pill, but a valuable priceless lesson; however, it was acceptable because my vision statement doesn't include any one particular geographical area and it's not over. One woman asked me who owned the place, and that she knew they had to be millionaires, so I responded "You're looking at her." She then retracted her hands, looked me dead in my eyes and said twice, "You're shittin me," and she never returned.

Closing my business was right up Hank's alley because he felt his grip would be tighter being that I had no income and would need to depend on him, and he'd have the upper hand to make me suffer. From the inception of my building a spa, and all throughout its existence, Hank would always say, "I hope your business fails," and I don't know why or how he could be so evil to me because I always encouraged *him*. Many businesses and people were hit hard in 2007 by the bad economy that year, losing their homes and possessions. My SUV was repossessed, and the other Cadillac wasn't working properly at that time. I refused to ask Hank to use the Caddy he was driving so not to give him the satisfaction of telling me no. Hank thought he had me confined to the house, but I walked in the rain, rode my bike, took the train, etcetera. However, as I walked, I talked, thanking God out loud every step I took. I would say, "Thank you God for my new car," over and over. I had already received it by faith when I asked for it, so all that was left to do was to say, "Thank you God for my new car." I defeated the devil on every angle and never let him steal my joy, remembering he was defeated when he was kicked out of Heaven, he was defeated on the cross, and he's defeated by the words of my testimony.

Hank could have purchased a car for me, but he didn't until God sent one to me free of charge by way of Alex and Myra, and I didn't even ask for it. Alex and Myra were long time close friends from work. Two weeks after I was given a car, Hank went to the Cadillac dealer and purchased a new caddy. I guess he felt that he couldn't defeat me so he may as well join me. It was apparent that he didn't want it to go down that someone else cared for me, or did more for me than he did. We were back to having three cars, so when the used car given to me died, I was back to driving a Caddy.

After I tried working from home for a year, I had to rent office space in a luxury office building for another business of mine. In spite of having to fight Hank everyday and being subject to belittling and slurs, I never gave up. The office I rented came with secretaries, stocked pantries, and conference rooms. With twenty-four hour access, it ended up being my sanctuary away from home. Many nights I stayed there until one in the morning, sleeping on the chair. Even though there was discomfort in those chairs that became my makeshift bed, it was more comfortable than my house of horror where deep dark secrets and lies existed.

Chapter Fourteen

Depression mode was a constant with Hank, and it seemed as though he could never come out of it from Sunday afternoon through Saturday; nonetheless, he'd pull it together for Sunday morning services. I surfed the internet to find out the symptoms of depression and being bipolar in order to truly make that claim, and he fit all of the criteria.

His depression consumed the atmosphere of our home permanently, to the point that I dreaded going there. The closer I would get to my house when driving home from the office, or coming in from anywhere, I'd progressively get pains all throughout my body. The pain would start in my ears, then my head, then my neck and shoulders, and then my back. By the time I reached home, I was a ball of pain. The physical pain reminded me of when one has to urinate, the closer you get to the restroom, the worse the pressure gets.

I visited my sister in Raleigh, North Carolina for a week to babysit my nieces while she and her older daughter travelled to Puerto Rico. The peace of knowing that I didn't have to argue everyday brought such calmness to my mind and spirit. I thought to myself, "This is how I'm supposed to be living, and the way God intended it to be, peaceful like normal people."

After the week was over, I took an evening flight back home. Upon arrival at JFK in New York, I grabbed an airport taxi home because Hank was too mean to take a twenty minute ride to pick me up. During the ride to my house, although my mind wasn't consciously dreading an argument, my body reacted. As soon as my feet literally crossed the threshold of our front door, I broke out in terrible back spasms and couldn't move. Reverend Defenbar had to help me with my bags, and to the bed. It didn't dawn on me until later that subconsciously I hated that place and dreaded being there, so my body returned back to doing what it normally did upon going home.

No matter what was said to him, good, bad, or indifferent, when he was depressed his voice was piercing with anger, hatred, disgust, woe is me, and I lost my best friend kind of sound all balled up into one. This was a sure thing every day, however, the deeper he fell, the worst the symptoms.

He would drink and smoke all day without eating, causing tremendous weight loss, so much so that people thought he was sick, other than in the head. I would always be able to tell whether or not it was bad when I pulled into the driveway. The lights in the entire house would be out, and I don't know of anyone that likes pure darkness but the devil. Jesus is LIGHT! Nights like that I would hit the steering wheel, clinch my teeth and say, "Dammit," and take precaution as I entered the house. I watch "Snapped" and don't know what could be waiting around a dark corner. I would walk in like a ninja with my hands first, sliding them up against the wall in a backwards swimming motion flipping on every light as I got to it until the house was lit up like a Christmas tree.

Two antique cars were given to us, one to him, and one to me, from a friend that was moving to another State and had no way of transporting extra cars. We already had three cars that we were using, so I put those collectibles on Craigslist and made sure Hank was aware of that.

When he initiated conflict, I'm not sure whether or not it was premeditated, or he just wasn't aware of his own behavior. Can a human really *want* to argue everyday with someone they presumably love? I've never seen nothing like it. How can it be everyday for sixteen years? How I'm still standing is the real question.

As I sat at the desktop computer downstairs which was right next to his room, I was checking my email looking for a response to the ads for the cars.
He asked, "Is someone trying to buy both of them?"
"Here's a question about them, but they're not trying to buy them yet," I said.
As collectively as he could he replied, "I don't know what you were going to do with the money when you got it, you didn't mention that to me."
"I didn't mention it to anyone, I didn't mention it to me, I didn't mention nothing, because nothing happened."
"How are you going to negotiate with someone, and not say anything to me?" He said, getting all hyped up.
Oh boy, I knew it was coming, as soon as he turned a simple conversation into a controversial one, you best believe he's stirring up a fight.
"I didn't do anything yet," I said nonchalantly as I always did when I heard him becoming flustered, in hopes of calming him down, as to put out a fire before it got started.

I would say a breath prayer, "Lord let him realize this isn't a big deal, I can't take this anymore." Those breath prayers actually never worked.

He then said, "But you started negotiating with stuff, without mentioning anything to your husband."

Being obviously hopeful, he'd throw that "Husband" word around when he felt he needed it as a controlling tool but that didn't work with me. In essence, I prayed for a husband, but got a provider only. I give credit where its due, he was an excellent provider, however, it had become disturbing when he used the term "Husband."

I dreadfully continued in the conversation with, "Mention *what* to you, about putting the cars on Craigslist?"

"I didn't know they were on there," he said.

"Oh, so you didn't know they were on Craigslist?" I needed to make sure I heard that lie correctly.

"No, I did not know until I asked…."

I chimed in as to be in oblivion, "Until just now?" I said.

"Until I asked you about it the other day, and you told me what you'd done, because you were in there trying to find the keys out of my room."

"Right, I had just put them on Craigslist, so I told you the same day right?"

"Why would you go in my room trying to find keys to something that did not belong to you?"

Typical of Hank's snowballing arguments, since I put a pin in his fallacy of not telling him about Craigslist, the subject moves to why was I in his room looking for keys to a car that was given to *me*, although he was claiming it didn't belong to me.

"No, I knew where they were," I said, letting him know I wasn't looking for anything, I was simply getting them.

"Why would you go in my room and do that? I don't go in your room and do that kind of stuff."

"The car doesn't belong to me?" I asked him trying to jar his memory.

"No, it doesn't belong to you, not until he takes the plates off and transfers it into your name."

That was said in a funky manner as to enlighten me on such an elementary subject; he did anything to stress me out. That was sheer nitpicking, and I don't know why I entertained him.

"Ok then, it doesn't belong to you either," I said.

"You were trying to negotiate the one that was given to me," he retorted.

"Ok, you're just trying to pick a fight because you miss fighting or something?"

"I'm not trying to pick a fight."

I was so frustrated at that point, so I said, "Because right now what you're saying is just…..you're just…..for what?"

"No, you gonna do stuff, and not even tell me what you're doing."

"Well, I can't tell you no sooner than the same day. I couldn't call you while you were inside the prayer meeting, so I told you as soon as I saw you, when else was I gonna tell you? Should I have called you during the prayer meeting, and interrupted you?"

He got loud, "You didn't tell me anything about the car they gave me, you told me about the one given to you, which I don't care about."

That agonizing conversation became conflicted at that point, what was he talking about? OMGoodness!

"I couldn't tell you about anything; I didn't do anything until yesterday!" I said again with frustration.

"You cannot put mine on there."

He said that like I gave a darn. He actually said it as if it was going to hurt me. He had me confused with someone that cared.

"Alright, I'll take it off, you keep it and drive it or something." I immediately agreed with him thinking he'll be quiet.

"No, I'm going to trade it in." Again, he said that as if I cared.

That was the perfect time for me to have said "Really," but back then that term wasn't being used in that way.

I responded, "Ok, you do that, it's no big deal, it can't hurt. If someone responds about your car, I'll ignore them thats all."

"I don't care whether they respond or not, I can trade it in."

"That's fine, so…, that's fine." I let out a sigh, "Alright, let me go catch 'Army Wives.'"

Just when I thought it was over, he kept going, "You do stuff and you, you know with your family and so forth involved, and you don't include me."

I stretched my eyes in bewilderment, and thought to myself, "Did he just flip this argument again to a different subject?" I began to get tight because that was ridiculous.

"My family ain't got nothing to do with that car."

"Lydia you gonna….whatever you do, you gonna take care of your family, I know that, I know that from experience."

"If you know that, why are you talking about it?"

"You don't give a damn about me."

"Okay," I said in agreement, because he would always say that to get pity but I don't play that game.

"If you get some money, you gonna help them."

I thought to myself "Duh," and then I said, "Ok, if that's what you say that's fine, you can say what you want, I won't stop you."

"I know from experience," he repeated.

"Ok….do you have anything else to say, cause 'Army Wives' is coming on in two minutes."

"Like you got on the phone and called your mother to tell her I said I wasn't going to pay so and so, and so and so."

Hank was seriously using everything he had to start a big argument, as if he'd die without one.

I told him, "That's what you said."

Hank had said out of anger that he wasn't going to pay the mortgage any longer, which would ruin my mother's credit record.

"That was between you and me, not between her," he blurted out.

That statement in and of itself was evidence to the fact that he only wanted to talk trash behind closed doors, and never let anyone else know the things he was capable of saying and doing. One thing is for sure, he would always take care of finances, even when he didn't want to. That was the one good nature about him, but I got tired of hearing his crap, so I called his bluff. "Well her name is on the mortgage too, so I thought I'd tell her what you said."

"How did her name get on it?" He asked in mental blankness.

"Ask yourself," I told him.

"Don't ask me, I didn't put it on there."

We were really off to the races for something so nonsensical, how could this be? The arguments were so petty and draining, it was like hitting yourself in the head with a hammer over and over. That was literally how I lived life daily, with those boring, long drawn out, stressful, unconducive and trifling arguments. What was that for and why was he doing that?

"Alright, you said that before too, why do you keep saying it over and over? Gosh!" I said out of sheer frustration in the vein of shut up already, damn!

"Because you put me in a trick, that's why I don't know."

"Okayyy, alright, you miss your arguing, and you're starting up for nothing." I sarcastically chuckled and then said, "WOW!"

"You, Lydia, will take care of your mama, you gonna take care of your mama and daddy."

"Okay, alright, and…..yes I will, and now what?"

"Me….and me, you ain't give a shit about."

Here we go again, pity pity pity. He needed to feel sorry for himself, and I'm sure there's a medical term for that.

As we're still wasting breath I said, "Ok, that's what you say, ok, now what?"

"It's true."

"Ok, that's what you say!"

"It's proof about it."

"Alright, now what?"

"And then you ask me about going to the covenant, or something with you about something?" he asked.

I wasn't counting but what subject number was that? Totally unreal; we started with cars. It didn't make sense for me to engage in back and forth, but it was difficult to not respond when I had been buffeted for so long in that marriage. I had to protect myself, and my being quiet didn't stop Hank anyway.

I turned to him and said, "I didn't ask you about going into no covenant."

"You asked me about communion."

Why he even brought up communion with the devil so prevalent in him at that point exceeded my comprehension.

"Right, you said you were gonna commune, and I asked are you gonna wait and take it with me."

"That's a covenant," he said funkally.

"Ok, so if you decide not to do it that's on you, that's fine, I won't commune with you, but don't cry about it," I told him.

"You don't even consult me about stuff. I've asked you for *one* day."

TELL THE TRUTH AND SHAME THE DEVIL!

I thought to myself, "Hold on did this argument's subject just change again?" Keep in mind that was how all of my days were.

I was so tired of him heeing and hawing on this *one day* thing, and my reply was, "Oh, paleeeease!"

He enjoyed comparing our torn down relationship, which was based on his inabilities to cope with a wife, to other relationships that are normal, having a decent marriage that incorporates date nights. He yelled at me and argued every single day, especially when in a car and in public, and there were no exceptions. We could be in church, celebrating a birthday, anniversary, or be on vacation, etc., nothing was exempt from him giving me a break with peace. He was destined to ruin everything, as well as every occasion, including Christmas and Thanksgiving. I have felt so alone on those days for years. I tried to explain to him time and again, that I dreaded setting aside one day a week for us, so that he can fight me all day? No way Jose. I'm scratching my head wondering, what type of person is he to think anyone would enjoy being around him to suffer verbal abuse constantly, let alone set a day aside for it. However, he was so serious about that, and would say it with conviction, "*I ASKED YOU FOR ONE DAY*," as if it's supposed to help our marriage, or is an answer to his problems. I wanted to run seven days a week away from him, as fast as I possibly could, just run Forest run! So which of those seven days would I dare be willing to give him? The day that he called me a whore, or the day that he called my mama a whore? I would be in disbelief when he fixed his lips to mention us having "A day," and each time saying it in the midst of a heightened argument, I mean there's my incentive to want to have "A day." Obviously, he wasn't realizing the reason it would never happen was due to daily arguments like the one we were having at that moment! It made my fist want to ball up when he went there.

He continued saying, "For years."

"You sound like a broken record," I said as I rolled my eyes.
"That's right," he screamed.
"Aah, Pa-lease."
He kept on, "So how you gonna get into a covenant with somebody?"
"Alright, so fine, that's fine, now, now what, anything else?" I asked him.
"Nothing else."
"Ok" I said, and my inner spirit was saying, "Thank you Lord."
"Nothing else, as long as you know that I know….."
I said, "Un hun," as I listened.
He continued to talk after he said "Nothing else," and picked up right where he left off. "That you don't give a shit about what I do, you will fuck over me if you can."
"Okaaay," I said in disbelief of his carrying on. I wouldn't badger a dog the way he badgered me.
"Just like you have done with your business and everything else."
"Now what? Now what?" He just flipped the script again, now off to the business, this was inhuman.
"Because your mama….you and your mama."
I thought back to myself, "Wait a minute," then I asked, "Why are you cursing like that, did you take communion today in church?"
Still trying to get his point across he repeated, "Because your mother, you and your mother…."
"Did you take communion today in church?" I said, while cutting him off again.
"You and your mother…."
"Why you cursing like that?"
"What! I cussed?" He said acting stupid.
"You-didn't-just-say……"
He cuts me off, "NOOOO, I didn't cuss."

"You didn't use the word 'fuck'?"
"Is that a cuss word?"
"Is it, or is it not?" I asked.
Then Lucifer, who had control over his body and mouth reared his ugly head and he said, "Have you asked anybody to fuck you?"
"Absolutely not," I said with anger.
At that point I became more vexed over the fact that he was getting nasty for no reason, as that entire two hour argument was for no reason. Every day he went on and on like that, moving from one thing to the next until he managed to get the argument to a highly explosive one. A small disagreement never satisfied him and I hated that lifestyle with a passion.
"Bullshit," and he laughed like a demon, hea hea hea.
"Oh, you're a sick bastard," I said.
"What did you call me now? You called me a bastard? Then you're talking about my mother."
"That's exactly what I said, you're sick."
"You're talking about my mother," he said once again.
"Oh pa-leease," I shouted.
That astonished me that Reverend Hank can dish it, but he can't take it. Firstly, he knew as well as I did that I wasn't thinking about his mother, but he decided to get technical. He directly talked bad about my mother for naught, crossing the line, but if he remotely thought I was indirectly talking about his mother, it was an issue. I'm not cut out for that type of daily harassment, and I waited patiently to get out of that mess.
"You are talking about my mother," he continued.
"Ah, I didn't even mention your mother."
"Yes you did, you called me a bastard."
"That's right."
"Which means, I was born out of wedlock."

"Oh Hank go somewhere will ya?"

"No, you go somewhere."

"You just want to argue, you are sick!"

"You are sick! You're the one that's sick. You go out and stay six to seven hours a day."

I wondered who he knew that worked one or two hours a day.

"Sooo what," I screamed.

"And you tell me that *I'm* sick?"

"Being here with somebody like you, who would ever want to come home? Please."

Did Hank not yet realize that I didn't want to even be around him? I stayed out with a purpose. Revisiting these arguments word for word is haunting for me and causes my body to tense up even now. Unfortunately, it's necessary in order to portray the true effects of my past reality.

"Then why don't you move?"

"Why don't you be quiet? Eeeew," I said.

He sarcastically asked, "You think I'm stupid?"

"You are!"

"You go out and stay for seven hours, and I'm supposed to believe you?"

"I don't care if you don't. Why are you talking to me?"

"I know you don't."

"Why are you talking to me? You ain't nothing but the devil," I shouted.

"No, you are the devil."

So I told him, "You do that every communion Sunday, act like a fool."

"You are-a-devil, every day in the week."

"Why are you starting an argument?" I repeated twice.

"I'm not starting an argument."

I thought to myself, "Now I know I'm not having an outer body experience, and Hank isn't drunk this time either and didn't have a drink yet. We've been arguing over an hour, or was that a figment of my imagination? That creature just said he wasn't arguing. Perhaps it's normal to him, which explains why he does it every day."

I don't know what his idea of an argument is, but I said, "You're a liar, yes you did start an argument. I was on the computer, and here you come with that crap! cursing and everything."

"Because I understand what you were doing with the cars, and I knew where the money was going to go."

Originally, both antique cars were given to Hank, but he didn't accept both, and that's when the brother gave the other one to me. Hank was always so worried that I would share my money with my parents, so once he found out that I put it up for sale, he wanted it back.

"You don't understand nothing, you gave the car back! I understand *that*," I said.

"I didn't give the car back to nobody."

"Aw, you're just jealous."

"Of *you*?"

"Obviously, that's why now all of a sudden you want the car back."

"I'm jealous of you?"

"Why do you want the car back?"

"And you stuck me with two mortgages."

He just flipped the subject again like always, so I brought him back and repeated, "*Why* do you want the car back, because it was given to me?"

"I never gave it to you."

"It wasn't yours to give, you gave it back to the brother, ask him."

"He gave it to me, I didn't give him….."

I interrupted, "Okaayy, I don't want to talk to you, is that alright?"

That argument wasn't making any sense, it was very stressful, petty, and childish to say the least, and was a waste of breath, time, and energy; I'm confused just transposing it. Ninety-five percent of the arguments were as senseless as this one, and it angered me to see a marriage that could have been powerful, wasted over foolishness. During that period of time, I was believing heavily that "ALL things work together for GOOD, for those who love the Lord and who are called according to His purpose," because I didn't do anything that deserved living in hell on earth and Yahowah doesn't make any mistakes. I had to have gone through that bad marriage for a reason.

    Routinely, the very next morning some switch in his head had flipped, and he came upstairs as if nothing ever happened, not realizing that just the night before he added more "dis" to my "like" for him, which are permanent scars. I assumed that was his way of living, but I couldn't possibly go on like that, day in and day out, flipping and flopping.

    He asked me if I wanted to go out to the diner for breakfast because he wanted an omelet, and I said I didn't care. He then told me twice that he bought grape juice, and I didn't respond out of shock after he told me the night before during that chaotic argument that the Lord told him that we didn't need to commune together because we were *not* together. One thing was for sure, my heart was long gone and we definitely weren't together.

Chapter Fifteen

If I could have just learned to not talk to Hank at all, maybe I could have had some sense of peace. If I had my own opinion and disagreed with what he thought, then that was another fight. He tried me a couple of times at church in front of people and at times in front of his officers. I would get back at him in front of those same people at that very moment, and that broke him out of doing that for a while because it was embarrassing for a pastor to be disrespected by his wife in front of his members. My motto is, "You have to give respect to get respect." If someone disrespects me, best believe that I'm going to disrespect them back right then and there, so I'm quick to say "*chee-eck* yourself before you *wree-eck* yourself."

I recall one Sunday morning before service, he got nasty with me about something while people were in his office, so I tried to break the hinges off of his office door slamming it behind me, BA-BOOM! The walls shook, and I went right upstairs into the sanctuary to give God His. *The devil is a lie!*

He didn't care about the pastor thing being hush-hush, he seemingly was willing to put his harshness toward me in the streets. During our entire marriage I had to protect him from himself by cutting arguments down in public. I'd have to walk away, because telling him "Stop it, you're in public," didn't work. He was so embarrassing.

One Sunday morning I was at my wit's end after a tormented ride to church and I went directly into the secretary's office without giving any thought to what I was doing or exposing, I just needed someone. I closed her door behind me and fell to the floor sobbing simultaneously as I muttered "I can't take this anymore." Without explanation she just hugged me and prayed with me not knowing what else to do or say. She allowed me time to regain my composure prior to entering the sanctuary for service. I straightened up my face, held my head up, squared my shoulders, walked out of the office, shouted, danced, praised God, and no-one knew.

At times when I'd call Lamont complaining, he would tell me to "Kill-em," and I laughed at that joke but he said, "NO, kill-em." One day I called Lamont, it was always either him or Mary Ellen, and was hysterically crying about the continuance of abuse which had become gut wrenching at that point, and he said, "I TOLD YOU TO KILL-EM, YOU WOULDN'T BE GOING THROUGH THIS RIGHT NOW!" He always knew how to get me to laugh. Although I'm a very strong woman, every two to three months I would explode and just breakdown from living in constant torment. I would get in my car, peel off, and I'd call one of the two of them screaming and crying. If you keep chopping and chopping at a huge tree, it will eventually fall. After months of build-up, it would only take a minute into a situation to cause me to break down.

I don't think Hank and I ever had a legit argument, they were never over anything substantial, they were just out of the ether. If there was something legit to argue about I wouldn't feel as bad, but to get cursed and barked at and made to feel less than human over absolutely nothing is abominable. Literally, everyday these small badgerings would become explosive to the point of yelling to the top of our lungs, slamming doors, cursing up a storm, and my fleeing out of the house.

Thank God, after I would let it out I immediately picked myself right back up, and no one ever knew. I never cried in front of Reverend Defenbar over our arguments, but I had to let it out so I would leave the house. It was a cry of, "Lord, why am I still here, am I ever going to get out of this, when am I going to see the light at the end of the tunnel? I'm tired."

After he started sleeping in the lower part of the split ranch, every morning when the Lord woke me up I would lay motionless, listening to hear where he might be, because once he realized I was awake he'd immediately start an argument. When I would hear him walking towards my room, I closed my eyes and made that light snoring sound, and held my face expressionless thanks to acting school, then he would turn away. There were times that I'd lay awake for an hour or so before mother nature forced me up, then when he heard me in the bathroom all hell broke loose.

One morning as I awakened but haven't gotten up yet, I wasn't aware of his whereabouts in the house. He's very light on his feet, so without my hearing him he walked to the door and my eyes were open as I laid there. It seemed as if he was up walking to and fro to see who he could devour. His voice was distinguished, yet daunting; and he always spoke as if he had it all together. At any rate, he allowed evil ideas to enter into his head, and just rolled with whatever satan told him, which is the opposite of someone that has it all together. He wasn't even together enough to fight satan!

He started in on me before I could get out of bed and he said, "You know, you get angry with me Lydia because I ah...."

I cut him off in a low I'm just waking up voice, hadn't had coffee, and discombobulated to say the least, and I said, "I'm not angry with you."

"No, about certain things, like when it comes to money."

I immediately got defensive because he was already making things up. I replied, "No I don't," with emphasis on the "d" in don't.

"When it comes to money you tell me, 'oh don't worry about it.'"

"That's not angry with you, how do you call that angry because I said, 'don't worry about it?'"

"Because..."

"I don't get angry with you about nothing."

"You don't understand how I deal with money. I don't like pressure. In the areas that I don't like pressure in, I-manage-my-business there, not to get myself in pressure."

"What are you talking about now? You just....I mean..."

"We're talking about...."

"We weren't even talking, I was laying here sleep, now you come here talking about I get mad at you about money?"

"I have tried to talk with you about the finances and so forth, that we have gotten ourselves in, and to get you to sit down and we work on things together."

After years and years of constant bickering, the term "So forth" made me cringe when he said it. He puts a certain ring to it, and it sounds the same every time he funkally says it. The new word "Funkally," in the world according to Lydia, means saying something with a funky attitude. Why at that point in that marriage he thought I could remotely want to work together with him on anything, is beyond belief! There was no togetherness, he killed that so long ago.

So as I tried to stick to the subject, something he never does, I said, "I guess my only question is, where is this coming from?"

He seemed to evade that question, and he started to get riled up, and raised his voice.

"Because you never want to talk when I…, you got angry the other night…." He said that as if to say "Come to think of it."

The devil had just whispered that lie into his ear, because the accusation was only in *his* head, it actually didn't happen.

So I said, "I did not."

He continues his sentence right where I stopped him and says, "When I said something about money."

"No I didn't."

"When I was going to bed, you were around here slamming things around and so forth."

Oooh wee, there goes "So forth" again.

So I continued to challenge him saying, "Why are you lying like that, wait a minute, why are you lying, what did I slam?"

"The other night when you were cleaning and so forth."

"I wasn't slamming nothing."

"Well then that's just your way of being loud, and dealing with stuff."

For some reason he obviously thought that at that stage in the game, I still cared about that abandonedship, not relationship, and would waste my time doing things in order to be able to deal with it, when in fact, as far as I was concerned, there was nothing to deal with. The only thing I was slamming was my knees on the ground, praying to be delivered by Jehovah Jireh out of that demonic house.

So I continued, "But I didn't get mad at anything. I don't get mad the way you get mad at everything, why are you saying that?"

"You know what Lydia, you are not a rational person who tries to understand other people, I did not get myself in this mess."

I can't believe he fixed his lips to say that *I'm* not rational when he is the one who suffers from depression and won't do anything about it, harassed me daily, turned any easy conversation into a controversial one, and automatically barked instead of talk. Really!

"First of all, could you tell me what you're talking about?" I had to ask that question because who knows what satan told him to say that time!

"Got in *this* mess, this financial mess, because you tried to conduct a business and so forth, and would not include me in it."

"Hank, all I'm asking you is, what are you talking about, we just now weren't even talking?"

"I'm stuck with seven thousand dollars a month, of of of money that I gotta deal with to keep things going, and you say, 'oh don't worry about it.'"

Since he acted as if he didn't hear what I was saying, I put it another way as usual, and said, "Ok, I know the word I'm looking for, what *prompted* this conversation? Like we were just now not saying anything, and you walked upstairs out of nowhere, I don't get it. What prompted the conversation?"

"What prompted this conversation?" he asked, repeating my words.

"Yeah, you were just talking about….the last thing we talked about was food at the church for Family and Friends Day."

I had to bring to his remembrance the last conversation the night before, and that this wasn't even an extension of *that*!

He started, "Because again, you're telling…., we were talking about ah ah….you telling me something about food," he said in a frustrated and confused manner.

Having selective hearing, all he heard was the word "Food."

"No, I'm not telling you nothing *about* food, I said the last thing you and I spoke about was food at the church, and you just now came back and was totally somewhere else, what prompted you to say that?"

"Because people are always dealing with me, or thinking that I should do stuff, you should have taken care of that dinner thing, you should have cooked something."

He said that with such disdain, as if I didn't know how to do my job. He stepped up on his own and volunteered to cook black eyed peas for Family and Friends day in order to look good in front of his members because they enjoyed his cooking. Nonetheless, when we got home I was yelled at about his volunteering, go figure. I was still waiting for him to answer my question but he was on another topic.

"Ok, so what does that have to do with the money? Now how did you come back with the money issue? How did you flip?"

"Because that is the thing that is on my mind and bothers the hell out of me."

"Why do you let it bother the hell out of you?"

Technically speaking, anything that would have been capable of getting the hell out of him, should have been acceptable to me.

"Because I'm the one that's in charge of it and it falls on me!" he said.

"But you don't need to do that."

I always tried to explain to him that what he thinks about and stresses over, he's going to bring about in a fast way, but it goes right over his head every time.

His response was, "Because it don't fall on you, that's why it's easy for you to tell me don't worry about it."

"No, no, you really shouldn't."

"Well then give me some money!" he screamed.

"Yeah, I'm trying to do that."

"Don't tell me about trying, just give me some money."

"Well stop talking so negative about things." I yelled.

"If you had run business like business ought to be run, we wouldn't be in this predicament."

He was trying to reflect on my entrepreneurial skills.

"I did."

"You didn't know what you were doing."

"Yes I did."

"And you didn't consult me, the person that put the money out."

Aaaand we're off to this race for the hundredth time and he goes on in a snowball effect. His daily routine was precisely the same, going from why did you open a business in a prominent area, to getting ripped off by the electrician and plumber, to my father's business taking longer than it should have, and my not having enough slush fund to hold me over for a year. He never realized that those were the causes of me not having the cushion money that I factored in and anticipated, he would just say I didn't put enough money aside.

I had to tell him again, "If people rip you off, and take the money you had as cushion money to hold you over for a year, that has nothing to do with one's ability to run a business, so you got it confused."

"You had to spend money elsewhere, because you didn't have the money, you didn't have two hundred thousand dollars to run a business for a year or so, and that's how you got behind."

"No, that's not how I got behind, I got behind because of the construction which took money that wasn't estimated in the original contract, and it also took three months longer."

"Now who's the one that did all of the construction?" he asked.

"All I'm saying to you, is that between the electrician and the plumber, it took an extra thirty-five thousand dollars, and you've heard this story before."

"All of that has to be estimated."

"What, for someone to rip you off? You're supposed to estimate someone ripping you off?"

Granted, I could have sued them for breach of contract, but that would have delayed construction, cost attorney fees, and time that I didn't have. Therefore, I paid when they claimed that they ran across unforeseen expenses.

"Your father's business took longer than it should."

This very conversation had been rehearsed over three years and had become antiquated.

"Anyway, this is like three years old at this point, so what are you talking about? That's my thing about you being negative, stop dwelling on that, move on Hank!"

I always thought to myself "I wish he could understand that if he keeps looking back, he won't be able to see where he's going, and I don't know how to get that into his head."

He then said, "The thing is, how I've been treated in this situation and dealing with this situation."

"You know what, argue with yourself, you just want something to argue about."

"Bullshit," he screamed.

"You're looking for anything to argue about, you ain't talking about nothing that has to do with today. How are you arguing about something that's three years old?"

"I'm arguing about stuff that got me in the shit that I'm in now."

"Ok, so argue about something concerning today."

"With you and that construction worker, that thing freaked with me for about a year."

That he got incorrect, it was still freaking with him *three* years later. He harassed me without interruption on a daily basis about that man.

"And that's why you're stupid now," I said.

"No, you were stupid by treating me the way you did, because you should have confronted that fucking, that fucking situation."

I was thinking he was about to foam at the mouth as angry as he got when he talked about the construction worker that he and the devil put together in his head. Hank has blamed me about having another man, cursed me out, called me whores, bitches, and everything else, from day one of my marrying him. First I was being accused of my ex for the first three years, then my next ex for a few years, then someone at my job, then someone at the university, then one of the construction workers. It is abuse when you're constantly being accused of something you're not doing, and it's hurtful. Many times I thought to do something to make his claims legit, but I had no-one to do anything with.

"Hank, shut up, I'm not arguing with you about that, have that conversation by yourself."

He said, "Shut me up dammit."

"No, have that conversation by yourself."

"You get money out of me, then you gonna get smart, don't get smart with me!"

"I can get smart all I want, and it ain't nothing you gonna do about it, not one thing," and I said that hard.
"It is something I can do about it."
"Go ahead, let me see, come and shut me up, come and shut me up."
I should have told him, "You feeling froggy leap, you might walk over here, but you'll limp back!" As always, he found a way to wiggle my mama into his mouth during an argument, literally every argument, as if he had a vendetta against her for giving birth to me. Although numb to his arguments and hurling insults at that point, it was still like a dagger in my heart when he brought my mother into every single issue. She had no clue because I could never tell her that he did that. I guess I felt so terrible about it because she never talked about him, she loved him, and thought he was ok. It would hurt me to see her around him, knowing how he talked about her all the while smiling in her face, and I couldn't say anything.
"You can call your mama, or do anything you wanna do."
"I said come shut me up."
"You're not even worth shutting up Lydia."
"Alright then, ain't a damn thing you can do about me getting smart, cause I am smart."
"There's a damn thing I can do about money."
All he cares and worries about is money. He thinks love only consists of money. He can't tell anyone how he ever loved me, all he can and will say is what he spent on me. I will admit that he always bought me whatever I wanted, but I had to fight and argue to get it, and then suffer the repercussions of having it constantly thrown up in my face. It was like he kept a mental list. He wasn't even capable of giving out of love, he gave to use it against me. I eventually learned not to ask for what I wanted, I'd just say, "Wow, I love that, but it cost too much," or something of that nature

and I'd keep walking, and then he'd say, "Let's get it." In my mind, I'd do that knee up fist down thing in the motion of one blowing the horn of a Peterbilt eighteen wheeler truck, and think to myself, "Yesss!" Even so, that too was still thrown in my face, but at least I avoided the argument of acquiring whatever it was. He bought me a condo, a house, furs, diamonds, cars, etc., but could not speak to me for five minutes without barking and degrading me. I had to tell him that I'd much rather have nothing and be spoken to nicely and respectfully, but he never understood that, and I knew God had to get me away from him.

I worked a nine to five job the majority of our marriage, so the bulk of the time that I was tortured was when I had a job. During that long period, in the heat of an argument, I'd tell him to stick his money where the sun don't shine. I had a good job and didn't need his little money.

The argument continued, and I said to him, "I don't care, you said you can do something about me getting smart, no you can't, never!"
"That's why I-am-not gonna spend my last dime on your ass, because when you get out of trouble, you gonna go over to your mama, you'll help them before you help me, and you have proven that."
"Ok, show me how I proved it, you keep telling me I ain't got no money."
"You have helped...you will do stuff for them that you will not even do for me!"
"Like....like, what?"
"They can get on the phone and call you, and say we need so and so, and so and so, and you'll get up out of bed, and go down there and do it."
Did that demon think he was going to persuade me *not* to honor my father and mother? That devil right there ain't nothing but a liar!
So I said, "Oh, and if you told me you needed something, I wouldn't do it?"
"No."

"Give me one example where you told me what you needed, and I didn't do it."

"I asked you, I asked you about calling those people, about the bank situation, and you said, 'when I wake up I'll do it.'"

"And did I…," he tried to cut me off, but I didn't let him, and I went on to say, "Excuse me what bank situation, what bank situation?"

He coughs then starts to talk, "Uh, dummy….."

I cut him off and said, "Did I do it or not?"

"What…what close to six thousand dollars did I pay yesterday?" He asked.

"How did *you* pay it, you called them?" I sarcastically asked him.

"No, you called them when you…."

"Alright then, I thought you said you asked me to do something…" He cuts me off again.

"You called…..but I wanted it done…"

He was getting ready to tell me *when* he wanted it done, but I chimed in quickly.

"I don't jump cause you say jump, I was doing something else."

"Fuck you!" He retorted.

"No, you can do that to yourself, like you're doing."

"That's another problem."

"You can do that to yourself" I repeated.

"That's another problem."

"For who, for you? Not for me"

He continued, "That's a serious problem."

"Not for me, for you, that's your serious problem," I said.

Little did he know his days of ever touching me were over!

In a threatening voice he said, "You think I ain't gonna retaliate?"

"I don't care what you do."

"And I don't care what you do, I don't care whether you live here, or…or go someplace else, you ought to go and live with the niggas you want to be with."

I ignored him and left. That obtuse argument was so uncalled for and insignificant that it was one of those straws that broke the camel's back incidents, and I got in the car to call Lamont or Mary Ellen to cry, scream, and explode yet again. I was so tired of expending so much energy, and being totally aggravated over trivial things that the average person wouldn't even think to argue about.

Chapter Sixteen

Acting out in front of church folks had since gotten a little better with Hank; but every now and a blue moon he forgot who he was talking to. After eight years of being publicly humiliated I eventually ceased attending his bible studies, love feast and meetings. No matter what I would say or comment on, be it right or not exactly worded in *his* way, he tried his best to embarrass me, and it started to become evident with some of the members.

The older women would have the nerve, although they wanted to be helpful in fear of my getting attacked, to tell me "Shhh, don't say anything." That happened in bible study as well as in meetings, and it made me feel like a kid that didn't know the appropriate time to speak. It ultimately made me angry because how dare another woman or any person get between the conflicts of married people. That was *my* husband so I spoke anyway, and he attacked anyway, but that was my business.

After all, they weren't going home with us, so who was going to protect me there was my philosophy.

Pastor Defenbar was a teacher par excellence, and I was exposed to his study habits. I had a front row seat to biblical exegesis, therefore my understanding of the Word became clearer, as well as my thirst for the Word. Possessing this knowledge and being able to impart it upon others will be with me forever; and I pause, "Thank you Pastor Defenbar."

I was an evangelist in our denomination, approved by the head of our district; therefore, at times Pastor Defenbar would ask me to start devotions prior to a meeting or bible study. I led devotions many times with prayer, song, and scripture; sometimes singing a cappella if the musician was running late. There were times that it was like pulling teeth trying to get some to participate but I'd sing with gusto and enthusiasm and they'd eventually join in.

One of many meetings that's engraved in my mind was a Monday night church conference with roughly 50 people present, and more than one evangelist, myself included, was in attendance as always. The attendees consisted of presidents of organizations, ministers, active members, and nosey people. Pastor asked me to read a scripture, another to pray, and another to lead us in song, and being obedient I did so. I chose a scripture that I deemed relevant to the time we were in, so I opened my bible to it and gave a minute for others to find it. Although my bible was open, I didn't have to look at the scripture because it was on the table of my heart, as many scriptures are; therefore, I quoted it. Those that were reading along were obviously looking at the page and not at me. All of a sudden, Pastor Defenbar said in a sarcastic manner, "It's not necessary for you to show off because you know how to quote scripture."

Needless to say, I was dumbfounded, caught off guard, and didn't know what to say or do, so I just sat down and looked at Sis. Arletha who likes to think of herself as a big sister to me, and she shook her head in disarray. I couldn't have been more mortified and hurt that out of nowhere my husband could intentionally do that to me. I wanted to run out and go home, but I remained strong and stayed there although I didn't know what the look on my face was like. One thing I can't do is fix my face in order to hide my feelings. My insides were tight, I wanted to punch him, choke him, curse him out, and tell him "F U" because he was so darn evil and no-one knew it except me, and I had to pretend.

I felt anger toward myself for attempting to attend a meeting of his when in fact I knew better. I thought I'd be careful and remain quiet to perhaps get through the meeting without anything of that nature happening, but he threw me into the lion's den by asking me to read a scripture. I made sure that it was my very last meeting, bible study, love feast or anything, and I never went again. The only time we were in the church building together was on Sunday morning, a special event, or at a funeral.

I loved attending the Usher's Annual to watch our proud ushers march around the church, sometimes doing the soul train line. My niece Salena accompanied me as I sat in the library studying for an exam at the university I attended, during which the Ushers Annual was in session, and its only once a year so I dreaded missing it. Besides, when the church was open for any type of worship service held in the sanctuary, I was compelled to be there because I loved it, and I was duty bound to represent.

Sitting at the study table I said, "Salena, let's take a break and go to the church, we'll stand in the back and watch the ushers and then head back to the school."

"Ok," she said cheerfully.

So off we went. I was dressed in a nice new jogging suit but it didn't matter, we were only running in for a minute to watch by way of standing in the back. Everyone knew I was in school, studying and unable to make all events at that time.

We arrived at the church and pulled into the main parking lot in the back, where the majority enters. Leading into the vestibule from the parking area are large brown wooden double doors with full length glass windows on either side allowing visual access as to whose approaching and whose already there. As we were walking toward the doors, I could see the ushers in their traditional black bottoms and white tops, lining up to make their grand entrance as the visiting ushers processional was over, so we hadn't missed anything. "Great," I thought to myself.

As we stood there watching inconspicuously, I looked in the pulpit and didn't see Reverend. Just as I realized he was missing, he walked up behind me. His voice was relentless in front of Salena and all of the ushers. His face blew up like a blow fish, he frowned, and looked like satan, just pure evil, and he raised his voice in anger.

"Why are you here? Look at what you have on, you're representing me, don't you come here looking like that!"

"We're only standing in the back for a few minutes, we're not going inside the sanctuary, and what's wrong with what I have on?" I said it as humbly as I could, not to stir up attention, but he didn't catch on or care.

With his lips poked out and his forehead wrinkled, he barked, "You don't represent me like that!"

We left, and Salena said, "What's wrong with Uncle Hank?"

I didn't have the nerve to tell her, nor get her involved of how I was always treated, so I tried to suppress how disparaged I felt at that moment.

"Something must have happened to upset him," I told her.

That incident was years prior to the inception of the spa, and the verbal abuse was brutal on me; I couldn't stand the thought of telling my family Hank's dirty secrets. I covered the truth.

Chapter Seventeen

Reflecting back on the second year or so of our being married, I would try to have sexual relations with him, and he would always find a way to turn me down, after he walked around the house all day commando with just a t-shirt on.

The arguing was rough and he'd hit below the belt, but they only occurred maybe once a week in the beginning. I now see that he obviously tried to be on his best behavior. When and if I asked why he didn't feel like being intimate, he'd use the excuse that "We argue too much," when he started the crap. Nine times out of ten the arguments were trivial, but I hadn't yet discovered that it was modus operandi for him and that all of his arguments were trivial.

He found a way to weave my ex-boyfriend into everything, and I had no idea that I would be persecuted about *that* for the next five years. If I forgot to do something like make a phone call for him, mail a letter, order airline tickets, etc., he'd say, "I bet you didn't forget to make a phone call for so and so because that's who you love." He said that like he was singing, that's-who-you-love. Things like that would just come from out of left field somewhere. He said it so much that hearing those words and that evil piercing voice made me cringe from my gut. I thought to myself and wanted to say to him, "Giiit the F outta here, you got-damn demon!"

I'm a touchy feely type of person so after I'd get ready for work in the mornings, hustling to get that iron horse into the city, I'd lean over the bed to kiss him goodbye. He would always cover his head in annoyance, as if I'm disturbing his sleep and say, "Come on dear," good enough to say, enough, enough already! If he was standing or sitting and I went to hug him, he would grab my wrists simultaneously, then extend my arms out like Jesus on the cross, raise them over my head, then clap my hands together making me look like a standing teepee so I couldn't hug him. I laughed, thinking it was quite funny but it also made me feel bad. I realized he never wanted me to hug him.

The excuses for not touching me increased, and he would always try to lie, saying that it all stemmed from arguing. I just hadn't yet found out what he was really doing. Might I add that there's nothing wrong with me, and that I was always between a size six and an eight. Not to hurt the pleasingly plump folks feelings out there, but I wasn't fat, I was very shapely, easy on the eyes, possessing the personality and smarts to boot. I confess, beauty is in the eye of the beholder and in this case, I'm the beholder.

I could not figure out why he wouldn't look at me when I was naked. I received so many lingerie items from my bridal shower and never used them because when I would put one on, he'd look at me like I was a piece of furniture as if I didn't turn him on.

That started to wear on me but I continued on trying, not thinking of, or even entertaining the thought of another man, for years might I add. I would bend over with no panties on so that he could see all of France, using the old I'm picking up something trick to get his attention. He would make me feel so small by acting as if I wasn't even there which made my insides boil. One day, I was walking down the hallway and he was behind me, so I bent over and spread it with my hands while screaming out shouting the words, "What's wrong with mine?"

There were times in those early years when we weren't arguing, and haven't for a few days, and he'd still ignore me the same way using the "We argue too much" excuse.

Back then it was the era of the VCR and I started to find hidden video tapes with titles like "Debbie does Dallas," and "Big Booty Judy," etc. My heart sank and I was humiliated and hurt to think that after a year of marriage he got more pleasure out of a video tape than he did me. Perhaps had it aroused him to attack me when I got home, then maybe I would have reluctantly succumbed to it and it could have been our dirty little secret, but he didn't want me.

He would buy those videos nearly daily at fifty and sixty dollars a pop, and I would search them out and find them with the receipt. I felt cheated on, worthless, unloved and degraded. I would rip them apart, pulling out all of the tape and beating the cartridges with a hammer like a mad woman! Believe it or not, that didn't prohibit him from spending hundreds of dollars on those tapes so I sabotaged every VCR machine in the house. I, and my handyman self, got a Phillips screwdriver and a pair of pliers, opened the machines and ripped all of the components out and closed it back without him knowing. If you think that stopped him, he ordered satellite television after that so I gave up.

Hank was mechanically and technologically illiterate and wasn't aware that I was able to look into the purchase history and see which movies were bought on which day and what time. He'd watch that porn from the time I left early in the morning and any other time that I wasn't in the house, and they were ten ninety nine each. How did he ever get it in his mind that he needed to talk to *me* about money?

I attempted to cry out to his sisters while at a family graduation by engaging them on a walk to the ladies room prior to the ceremony. Our nephew on Hank's side was getting hooded in receiving his doctorate degree. I couldn't bring myself to tell them what their brother was doing out of embarrassment to him. There goes that pastor's wife thing again, protecting the pastor. I ended up just telling them that their brother didn't love me, and I was crying uncontrollably.

One thing is for sure, I always told him that one day I would stop asking for sexual relations, which seemed to have been a lie because I continued begging until years had passed. Now there were times that we were intimate maybe once every other week during the first year of our marriage which was deprivation to me, but toward the end of that year it had become more scarce and horrid.

Years down the line, once he realized I was no longer sexually attracted to him, nor wanted him, just like I told him and knew would happen, he all of a sudden wanted to sleep with me. After he lost all of his weight from not eating due to depression, looking like Popeye the Sailor Man without spinach, he wanted relations. Here is a person that claims they couldn't make love due to arguing once every other week in the beginning, but suddenly with arguing every day all day, is willing and able to do so. Something wasn't adding up.

I had been called so many names along with my mother, harassed, and lived in daily torment for so many years, that my insides were ripped to shreds, and I felt such an anger that my entrails would quiver at the thought of him touching me. I had no feelings, I was numb, nothing he did or said affected me any longer and he couldn't reach my lovers heart, it was in a cage. I loved him as a human being and family member only! I felt as if he robbed me at gunpoint of all my love, and there was nothing left for him.

Prior to the straw that broke the camel's back, he would get behind me and I would squeeze my pillow so tight, then tears would fall until he finished. I was frozen the entire time, and felt like I was being raped. I didn't want to say no in order to keep the peace which never worked anyway. The episode that brought this to a screeching halt, eeerrr, whether he argued about it or not, he was never touching me again, was when he finished, got up looking at me in disgust and said, "I could have gotten that from a prostitute." I laid there speechless, feeling twisted, with different emotions running from my head to my feet. I felt dirty, I wished I hadn't done it as I knew better, and I could have kicked myself. I wanted to go back in time and take it away. I felt deep penetrating anger, I wanted to scream, I clinched my teeth so hard my head shook, and I wanted to strangle him. Well that was all she wrote, the fat lady had just sung, and I couldn't find Elvis, he had left the building.

After that incident it was self-inflicted abuse just to allow him to see me naked or with my undergarments on. I felt violated and sick to my stomach at the thought of his eyes looking at me. I didn't want to entice him to ever contemplate having a desire for me. I always had a nice pedicure and I even avoided him so that he couldn't see my toes. For the last few years that I lived in that house he's only seen me fully dressed. I no longer had a home, a place that should have been my refuge. I was uncomfortable and living in constant constraint. I would only change clothes or get dressed behind a locked door. Sometimes when changing clothes in my bedroom that no longer had a lock, if I heard him moving about I would move so fast to cover up that *my* head would spin. No matter how long it took or how tired I was, I would always remain fully dressed until he went downstairs before I undressed. I no longer wore gowns unless I put a robe on over it. I wore men's flannel pajama pant sets and socks. I felt normal and comfortable with the outside world seeing me in a skirt or dress above my knees, something fitted, or a pair of shorts, but uncomfortable with Hank seeing me that way. I didn't let him see my bra strap. It made me cringe if he saw my skin, I needed to be covered at all times.

    Due to his ways of instability and flipability (one of my words) he would look at me at times and say, "You sure have some pretty skin," in a manner in which he seemingly thought would turn me on. I wanted to barf and I would silently become angry at his nerve.

    As a pastor, he should have understood 1 Corinthians 7:5, as it warns us about deprivation which in our case caused a downward spiral that was not retractable. Before all of that happened, I hung in there like a trooper for years, praying for change, regardless of the way I was being treated.

    The Pastor is well endowed, hung, a.k.a. *Mr. Hugh G. Reckshon,* but he wouldn't use it on me, before it was too late. That was hard for me to fathom because in the first year only, when it was new, we at least did it often enough to keep me silent.

    Reverend Defenbar is twenty-nine years my senior, and I bet the people in the church thought he was getting some good stuff all the time, but you never know what goes on behind closed doors. The shadow knows.

Chapter Eighteen

My mind began to wander to places it shouldn't have wandered, being a first lady and all, as some denominations consider and call their pastor's wife; but what is a girl to do when in the midst of all of her troubles a socialite infiltrates her being?

Although I didn't know who he was at the time, when I first laid eyes on him I was so distracted and had a desire to get to know him.

I was taking a business class and there he was, the instructor, tall, dark, handsome, and balding slightly toward the top back of his head in such a sexy way. At that point in my life, I was so desperate for attention that even with the opposite race, balding was sexy. The course was over a three month period, twice a week. After the first few sessions, I decided that he would most likely end up being the man to give me the affection that I was missing and so desperately needed. After all, a tongue hadn't been in my mouth in over ten years, and his lips were screaming, "EAT ME!" Shamefully, the pastor never kissed me either in an intimate way.

I had to figure out a way to tell this man that I was attracted and distracted, to and by him respectively, but in such a way that he'd have to read between the lines. I wanted to give him that open door, and let him decide whether or not to walk through it. Part of my flawed personality is that I'll openly let a man know my true feelings, which can sometimes work against me because there's always the possibility of it being taken the wrong way. I'm real, and I say it like it is with no hidden agendas. However, he did read between the lines, and very well might I add, and he graciously walked through the door.

After some time and words had passed between us, he became quite intrigued by me in the way that I conduct and carry myself. He said that I appeared to be different. I found that to be interesting, although I didn't know what he meant by it, so I questioned him. I asked him to expound upon that comment, and he did. He felt as though my being so real, extremely humorous and down to earth, yet spiritual, educated, and classy, was unusual for what he expected pastor's wives were like as he presumed they were stuffy. He and I always teased each other when getting into a sexual conversation by saying, "Oooh, God is gonna getcha!"

Be that as it may, in all reality my thoughts concerning that individual were due to what I was suffering in my home. For the record, I've never even considered talking to another man, but with that man, having to deal with him a couple of times a week, I became enthralled. Inevitably, the strong attraction shared between the two of us began at a vulnerable time in our lives, when our marriages were like hell. We were equally unhappy, and in similar situations of having to be doubly discreet due to our status in society, which made us all the more exciting to us. He also told me that I impressed him with my sticktoitiveness, intestinal fortitude and knowledge.

I believe I'm the only one that can get one of those deep down hardy chuckles out of...., well, I just call him Dr. Distraction since he's distracted me so to a point where I would've done anything for his attention, not realizing nothing would ever come to pass.

It's quite interesting how I ended up with the "Dr. Distraction" name. One day, I decided to send him an e-mail about something that I didn't give two craps about, and the salutation was "Mr. Distraction," and I proceeded with the body of the e-mail. When I received his reply and read the first few lines, my stomach was shaking because he was going on and on about my disrespect in calling him "Mr. Distraction." Surprisingly enough I was able to exhale when I read the last part that said, "NEXT TIME IT'S DR. DISTRACTION," reflecting on his PhD Degree. I smiled and was as happy as a pig in slop. In my next e-mail, I explained to him that I was very distracted by him which started this subtle complimentary e-mail ping pong that grew and grew. He let me know that he was flattered, because he sent an e-mail saying, "Flattery will get you everywhere."

He mentioned that his wife didn't make him laugh, and there was no excitement in their marriage either, only constant screaming and arguing in front of the kids. Their sex life bit the big one too. He felt as though she was thinking of another man while he was trying to get his groove on with her, and that she wasn't into it or him. He said it's been that way for a while. He lived in hell every day as I did and they also ended in divorce. Her perpetual screaming behavior showed signs of being addicted to some prescription drug or alcoholism. He mentioned that he would have left her long ago, but he didn't want to be away from his children. Well, c'est la vie mon ami, in other words, "That's life my friend!"

If the church folks knew that their first lady had a strong attraction for another man, without knowing the real story, they would have chased my you-know-what out of the country, besides the fact that I'd be the gossip of the town. My name would have been mud, but I feel justification and empowered by revealing the truth at this point in order to bring hope and deliverance to others in need, finding themselves in a similar situation.

It wasn't just a sexual attraction, but I really liked everything that I knew about him including his walk. It's not my fault Saints, forgive me, but I have feelings too, and the pastor had pushed me away through denying me sexually, mentally abusing me, calling me names, and degrading my parents and family constantly.

I would always keep Mary Ellen updated with the talk between Dr. Distraction and me, it was like a soap opera. We were so close that she thought if I sinned, she can sin too; and get this, she loves the Lord but don't let me tell her a hot and steamy story about Dr. Distraction. Before I knew it, she would be thinking wayward thoughts but never acted on them. During our girl conversations, I gathered that she was almost as much as a nympho as I remember being when I had the opportunity. Thank God all of her actions were with her husband. However, if I decided to say something fresh over the phone to Dr. Distraction, that chick would beat me to it and call her ex just to flirt over the phone too. She and I would always jokingly say, "If you go to hell, I'm going too." All in all, I was in serious need of affection, even just a simple touch from someone that cared would have helped.

Well, just like those women in the church being a fool over the pastor, I've also been a fool over who I considered to be a vainglorious socialite that seemingly thought more of himself than he should have. I've been a fool in the respect that I thought he would have been someone that I could have done more with than just talk to, believing that he would trust and respect my position as being a highly discreet one just as his was. I was hoping to feel free in being able to share by helping each other out a little bit every now and again, you know, a friend in need is a friend indeed. Instead, we never moved forward, causing me to feel as if he thought I'd say something that might lead to exposure.

After nothing physically transpired between us after two years, it appeared to me that perhaps he thought that if I got a taste, I'd become too attached, obsessed, or something of that nature. Ask me why, because I haven't done a darn thing except tease him with words as he so often did me. I can't be sure of this, but that's what I perceived from his actions, and I read people quite well. You'd think I would have known that men don't comprehend things in the same manner that a woman does. I wished he would have gotten one thing straight back then, which is that I would have never done anything to blatantly jeopardize my tired depressing marriage, and wouldn't entertain the thought of leaving my husband for him, as he had his own issues. Who in their right mind jumps out of the pot into the frying pan?

My life was so busy, that I had more than a full plate with school, church, and a full-time job. It made me so angry that I could have spit at the thought of him thinking that I could even spare a half of a second getting attached to him, or building a serious relationship. Could he have possibly been thinking that I'd be looking for him in the daylight with a flashlight?

I'd email him to suggest a cup of coffee, or a glass of wine, and he'd always have an excuse of some sort, business mostly. His emails began to become one word responses, which was annoying and demeaning as if I wasn't worth his time. I stopped all communication with him, and then and *only then*, did he try to fire things back up. I didn't speak to him for a couple of years. Our attraction towards one another was strong enough that we overcame hurdles, and remained friends, finding ourselves to a banana and a cup of coffee every now and again.

Our relationship eventually turned out to be one steamy, stimulating, journey. I didn't know how much longer I could have held out with him not becoming physical. If it would have happened, I mean had we gotten downright funky with it, and had that beginning of a relationship kind of sex, that neither of us had in years, that hot, steamy, panting, hair-wrecking sex, the boy knew it would have been good. I guess he was afraid that *he'd* get attached to my sexiness and wouldn't have been able to live without it. Yup, it never happened.

I know men, and men will do everything they can to make it look as if the circumstances are because of the woman, when it's really them. He's given me every other excuse, when his real dilemma was that he'd become uncontrollably attached. Although we never got to that physical place, he wouldn't let me go, he simply refused to let go of our so called relationship. I'm an expert on that reverse psychology malarkey. Every once in a blue moon, he felt a need to remind me that this was just for fun, but darn it he was only trying to convince himself.

Hank was too smart for his own britches, and all of those many years he harassed me about my ex's, little did he know, he should have been hooping and hawing about the socialite that I so desired, not some unthought-of-used-to-be.

I was glad to be in my f--k-it freaky forties because I finally figured out a remedy. Oh excuse me, for those of you that don't know, the f--k-it freaky forties is when a person reaches the age of forty to forty nine and they are no longer willing to tolerate stress, or anything that sets them off. Their response to things like that is usually, "F it," and the freaky part should be self explanatory. Reaching the age of forty and on into your forties is a beautiful thing, and a sexy thing, but I missed three quarters of it.

Unfortunately, I had to come to this realization through Dr. Distraction because he made me feel so sexy, which is something the pastor wasn't doing. Remember, it took years of the Pastor denying me, which brought me to this point of needing and wanting another man's affection. The pastor had years to fix it up and didn't take the opportunity. Year in and year out, I truly tried. I've prayed, cried, and wrote letters to him believing I'd be able to express myself without interruption, but the good reverend never acknowledged any of the letters, so where did that leave me?

When I heard Dr. Distraction's voice and the things he'd say to me, through arousal things started to happen to my body, and I would ache for him which was painful, but a good pain. The super intense sexual conversations between Dr. D.--as I lovingly called him at times--and me, started by my telling him that he had attractive lips. I longed to kiss him, but that for some reason seemed impossible to become a reality. That comment of mine to Dr. D. opened up an avenue of verbal sexual banter between us.

He then invited me to his office, and I believe it was to get a better understanding face to face of what was happening and to be sure that I was coming on to him in that way. Finally, I was getting some excitement in my life, and I felt alive through mind stimulation.

The three month course was since over and we would speak on the phone periodically and he'd say things to make me ache, and the more he talked, the more I wanted him. He started telling me to do things until I reached the unexplainable physical peak, and then to write him an e-mail and let him know how it was. I wasn't into masturbation at all, so Dr. Distraction tried to introduce me to taking matters into my own hands. At first I felt so terrible because it seemed as if I was being reduced as a human and forced into such acts due to Pastor Defenbar's lack, but it was all I had. There were no husbandly duties taking place, and there was no sexual contact with any man. Well, I guess my diagrammatic details via e-mail were a pleasant surprise to Dr. D., and he loved it. Thereafter, he'd ask for his happy e-mails from me, and would politely add, "I WANT VISUALS." We then graduated to late night phone sex and we would walk each other through the motions as our breathing became heavier and heavier until we exploded, and that was as good as it got. What had I been reduced to? What had Hank created? Imagine living vicariously through e-mails and phone sex, how pathetic, it had to stop and I put it to a halt. I realized I had to live and play the cards that I was dealt, and to pray for a new husband that would love me.

After I stopped that madness, I started to dream about Dr. Distraction often, and one dream in particular seemed so real and vivid. I finally had my first and only experience of a semi "Wet dream," *not* reaching a climax in which I never had in a dream. I dreamed I told him that I had something sexier than an e-mail, which he begged to differ. I went to his office with stockings, a thong, and a mini skirt on. The man took off his glasses, rolled up his sleeves, got on one knee until I ended up with my fist in my mouth, and he was like nuclear physics below. I woke up looking for him.

Dr. Distraction had to be the sexiest man I've encountered at that time in many years. After that dream which seemed so real, mixed with the fact that two years of e-mail ping pong had passed, I wanted more of him. I felt that he was well capable of giving me the satisfaction and affection that I was lacking. However, he took his time in making steps into our friendship, because as I gathered early on, he wanted to be sure that I wouldn't breathe a word of it to anyone, and neither of us wanted any strings.

I remember the first time I went to his office and he became aware that, "Yes," I was interested in him, he said right then, "You know you cannot say anything to anyone about this." If he only knew the relief I felt hearing those words come out of *his* mouth, it would have saved us lots of drama. Unbeknownst to him, I especially couldn't let a single solitary soul know about this. Discretion was of the utmost importance to someone like me having held such a position, which is what attracted me further to him because he couldn't tell anyone for his own sake. Needless to say, I was safe in seeking attention and affection from him.

I recognized the infiltration of satan, first attacking my mind with thoughts of infidelity, then he'd be able to attack my body, and being the sly old fox that he is, he did it at a vulnerable time in my life. That demon attacked the area in which I was lacking, making the struggle harder for me. I must reiterate, the bible warns spouses about this happening in 1 Corinthians 7:5, and it is worth quoting again. "Do not deprive each other except by mutual consent and for a time, so that you may devote yourselves to prayer. Then come together again so that satan will not tempt you because of your lack of sexual desires."

Chapter Nineteen

I was a young first lady in my early thirties, having to deal with a church of a large size and all of its politics. Thanks be to God, due to my upbringing I was able to handle it with dignity and represent as always, while handling a few of the sisters around there. Sunday mornings would come and the good reverend would prepare for work as he classified it and rightfully so, just as lay people work Monday to Friday. Pastors really need a pastor too because they're working through worship service and are human, having a serious need of being ministered to as well.

I'd put on my Sunday suits with all matching accessories; the hat, jewelry, scarf, gloves, shoes, and bag; but no matter how good a first lady looks, someone in the church has something to say that they feel would make the first lady's outfit look better. All the while, they're looking like who done it and why, and can we beat the person up that told them to put that on? One Sunday I spent about ten minutes trying to get a piece of my hair to lay outside of my hat in a particular way, and as soon as I walked in the church, an older woman pushed my hair under my hat and said, "Your hair was sticking out." I balled up my lips.

Certain positions are inherited by default, like that of being married to a pastor and becoming a first lady; yet, people have a hard time adjusting to that, and are still having a hard time in our churches. Back then I was of the younger generation, and they never got used to it. In any case, I was able to make final decisions regarding certain matters and they just didn't get it. I'm a no nonsense person of integrity that will say what I mean and mean what I say, which comes across in many different ways depending on the person processing the information. Wives of ministers are expected to do certain things and attend certain functions just because, yet no-one wants to support *us*, as we travail to prevail.

Pastor Jeckyl and Reverend Hyde expected certain things from me also as far as this first lady stuff was concerned, as long as we were in front of people only because I was his wife. When he became crazy at home behind closed doors he'd say to me, "You ain't no first lady, you're nothing," so I was only his first lady when it was convenient, go figure. Angry or not, behind closed doors or not, it was a travesty to hear him say that. He knew that only he and I were aware of the real truth of how strong of a first lady I've been for him.

In spite of our differences and dysfunctional marriage, I always had Rev's back when it came to opposition in the church whether it be on a local, district, or conference level. I prayed him through all tough worldly situations. Once we were behind closed doors I would exercise *my* faith and bring down the rafters sending up timber in prayer as we knelt in front of the couch. Everything always worked out for our good concerning the church but his rebellious spirit refused to kneel with me in prayer for us.

When it came to any health situation, *I* was the one he'd come to so that I can pray the prayer of faith and anoint him with oil, running off any attack of the devil. The cruelty shown to me never hindered me or caused me to compromise my obligations as a child of God. I knew how to balance my life as if I were two different people. What I went through daily had no bearing on the love of God that was within me. Hank was family, and I prayed for him regardless and protected him always, but I couldn't stand him because of his wicked ways.

Although it was never discussed between the two of us, nor asked of me, I've proudly been Pastor's scapegoat our entire marriage because I would do anything to protect him and the ministry which isn't to be taken lightly. In our denomination, the first lady is automatically the advisor over the missionaries, and I'm sure as my involvement proved, I was probably labeled a deadbeat advisor. I apologized for my disinvolvement when I did finally show up at meetings, still putting my two cents in when I felt like it, but also giving them a reason and owning the blame. I believe they were saying to themselves and each other, "The nerve of her," but I truly didn't care and always kept my head up.

The congregants expect more out of the pastor because he is the one God called to lead them. As expected I was there to back him and do what I could to make sure *he* shined. Now, let the truth be told. In one breath, Pastor would tell me at home, "You don't do nothing with those missionaries, and you need to get involved and build that organization." As soon as I'd say I'm going to a missionary meeting, or the missionaries are going to this place or that place and I'm going to go, or they're selling food let me help, etc., he would say, "I don't care, you need to take care of your husband," and he'd start a fight. I missed nearly everything they did. Once again, I was befuddled that he honestly felt he earned the right to use the title "Husband" in that manner, and only when he felt it was beneficial to him. He was no husband of mine; it was all on paper.

When it came to the parents of our church children, he'd say, "You ought to rally around the young women and do something with the youth." As soon as I started to go teach bible study on Friday nights to the youth, I had to fight about that, but the people never knew. He'd say, "They have enough people there, why do you have to be there, you just want another excuse to be out of the house." None of it was worth my living through hell all week for, so I retracted from most activities at church. I'd only see the members when at church, but had to live with Rev. Defenbar every day. It was chaos when choir rehearsal ran too late also, and I was only *in* the choir, I didn't *run* the rehearsal. Simply put, Hank never wanted me around or spending time with any other human beings. I went through it all because I loved the people so much, just to learn that they can turn on me like a venomous snake.

Behind all of the glitz and glamour of being a pastor's wife is frustration and hard work, so people shouldn't judge until they've walked a mile in the shoes of the very one they're persecuting.

I let the Jackrabbit know that I am who I am, and if he didn't like my position then he shouldn't have married me. How dare he, of all people say I'm no first lady? Hey, it gets downright ugly in the household of some pastors.

I always went above and beyond in anything I agreed to do at the church. I sang "Oh Come All Ye Faithful" one year for the Christmas program and decided on my own to sing all stanzas in Latin, "Adeste Fideles," so I researched it, and performed it well. The choir sang the chorus in English, and it was lovely.

For a season, we had a newsletter that I put out called, "The Burning Bush Newsletter." I was the editor in chief, the typesetter, the proofreader, the printer, and the distributor. Any time an organization had an event, someone would give me a report with photos from that event and it was entered into the newsletter. Crossword puzzles and advertisements were also incorporated into the newsletter which was professionally done, time consuming, and beautiful.

It's extremely common for the first lady to chair "Annual Women's Day," anyhow, Reverend Defenbar being mean spirited and vindictive would always ask others to chair Women's Day without even mentioning it to me. That was a slap in the face, so I would do all I could not to be involved at all.

Still and all, because of trying to allow Reverend Defenbar as the pastor to shine, and for the sake of the ministry, I always had his back no matter what it cost *me*. It was two years prior to his retirement that he came home one day barking at me as if it was my fault that he didn't have anyone to chair Women's Day, and it was three weeks away. I immediately had to assure Hank, so I said without hesitation "I'll do it," in a calm down manner because he was getting flustered and I didn't want to fight over something that had nothing to do with me.

That year I broke the cycle of how Women's Day was customarily run, and implemented a new system. I put an end to "Captains" and "Teams" competing against each other to see which team could raise the most money. There was no time for that, we needed to work as a unit. I pulled mostly all of the women in the church together and called them all "Angels" instead of "Captains." I organized the women to operate in the area of their gift. If they were a good decorator, salesperson, cook, etc., they were encouraged to contribute and function in that capacity. The funds raised were the funds the Angels raised as one unit working toward one goal.

I was able to get a dynamite speaker, we came up with two great events, and we raised more money in three weeks than they normally raised with having a few months to work with as unity is the key. I was not your typical first lady because I always kept it real. There was nothing within reason that I wouldn't do to help my church. One of the fundraisers for that particular Women's Day was an "Evening of Elegance," which we hosted in our fellowship hall. Much work went into the preparation of that event and it was successful.

The fellowship hall had been transformed into a dinner club sort of setting. We replaced the long rectangle tables with round tables draped in nearly floor length black cloths that my mother made. Dim lighting was used, and in the front of the room was our stage area with a keyboard for the musician. Chinese room dividers were stretched across the back of the room so that the food area was inconspicuous. The meal was plated and the uniformity of the waitresses was beautiful.

We solicited great entertainment and that's where the big surprise came in. There were selections of songs that were sung by a few choir members, we had a soloist, a Christian comedienne, and Sister Defenbar performing "The Human Train." I didn't tell anyone, not the Angels or Pastor Defenbar what I was going to do, nor have I ever shared this unusual talent of mine with him. Until that point only my immediate family has seen me perform it.

When I was ten years old, a large indoor flea market was located on the corner of forty-fifth and Broadway in NYC in the exact spot of the Marriott Marquis. I know I'm dating myself here; however, my parents had a booth there selling imported goods of the jewelry nature, and my siblings and I would always go into the basement to watch the magic show. The magician knew us well enough that he used my sister Amber as his assistant on stage in the absence of his actual assistant. Prior to the show that day, he prepped Amber on how to dodge the swords he was going to put through the box that she had to lay in. We sat in awe to watch our big sister, and that was the best show ever.

Although it seemed as if we saw the show a million times, I was always fascinated with the magician's rendition of "The Human Train," and it was my favorite part. I would go home and imitate him until I nailed it, and to this day, I am, "The Unknown Human Train." If it wasn't for that Women's Day, no-one would know this except my sisters.

Lucky for me, one of our parishioners worked as a train conductor and I was able to borrow her hat for that evening which completed my costume. When my time approached to go on stage everyone was silent, wondering what I was about to do. I walked to center stage and stood sideways, giving the view of my profile to the audience, and I waited a few seconds, then I yelled out in a loud voice, "All A-boooard!" I proceeded with a bonafide conductor's speech which I knew all too well from commuting over thirty years on the Long Island Rail Road. I started to move my feet making that chug-a-lug sound that a train makes when first pulling off, and then the speed increased, and my feet were booking. There I go dating myself again, who says "Booking" anymore? Ha! Well, one would think with the sound my feet makes that it really emulates a train at high speed. As I slowed down I would make the next stop announcement and the church members hollered and had a great time. I brought them on home making the church the last stop, and they applauded!

It didn't matter to me what my title was, I kept it real and never pretended that I was too good to be normal because of the first lady stuff. I didn't have a problem rolling up my sleeves because I know who I am.

People laughed at the "Train" and said things like, "Girl, you are so crazy," or, "You are too funny." I worked that hard for *Hank* to shine, anything to get those funds up.

There were times that Hank did speak favorably of me from the pulpit. He would speak about the faith I have, and how well I would do whatever I put my mind to. When I preached, if he wasn't angry, he would mention how well I've done my research and homework without asking him any questions or discussing my sermon with him. I was destined to represent and I did, not knowing or caring whether or not Hank was going to recognize me. I did it for the ministry. Obviously God had me there for a *reason* and a *season*.

When we would go to functions that called for music and had a dance floor, again, I kept it real unlike many other first ladies that would only sit there and watch everyone else dance as if it's inappropriate. Well, not me, I out-slid everybody when the electric boogie came on along with all of my other dance moves, and Hank never had a problem with it. I always remained down to earth. Don't let them play "Mr. Big Stuff," and "I'll Take You There." What!!

Hank still did all he could with satan's power to break my spirit. He never showed appreciation for anything I've done for him or for always being by his side and having his back till the very end. He wanted me to join him in misery and become a mini Hank. Wasn't going to happen!

Chapter Twenty

Preparing for church Sunday mornings were very disturbing and tension filled, and on communion Sundays the devil was just extra. After church, all hell broke loose; I mean the devil rode Reverend Defenbar hard like Butch Cassidy and the Sundance Kid riding horseback to escape from E.H. Harriman's posse.

I give credit where credit is due and I've learned a tremendous amount of the Word under the teachings of Pastor Defenbar. I can actually say that the majority of what I do know I learned from him, which I've told him on numerous occasions, but to hear him tell it I never ever gave him credit.

Although he speaks to the contrary, he knows that I'm well versed in the Word due to being around him. He allowed me to teach the Word once a week in the evenings to ministers, evangelists, officers, and the like for 12 years, as well as deliver the Sunday morning message occasionally.

Permission is required from the pastor for any of his subordinates to accept speaking engagements, and he also granted me that right to speak at other churches and venues. Some of the members and our choir came to support me. Three times I've been on the panel as one of the guest speakers at our spouses retreat. If he didn't trust me he would have never allowed any of that to happen.

Books were open everywhere in our house; a few commentaries, a few different versions of the bible, a concordance, the Greek and Hebrew lexicons, the dictionary, and the thesaurus; all of which were found on the dining room table, the bed, the coffee tables upstairs and downstairs, on the couch, and in his office; literally from Monday to Sunday.

Pastor Defenbar studied all the time except for the portion of each day that he drank and succumbed to other habits, which is why he can preach a sermon with just a few bullet points and not have to write or read a manuscript. In opposition, satan constantly attacked him because of it, and it's baffling as to why he didn't put all of that Word in him to use to combat that devil; rather, he acquiesced to that demon allowing lucifer to work through him.

Pastor Defenbar is one of the best preacher/teacher/administrators you can find bar none, but he is not a soldier/warrior as far as fighting satan is concerned, and that was hard for me to fathom. His excellence and skills weren't just recognized by me, but his work was known throughout the community as well. The street that the church is on was named after him and he was honored by the local government officials and the Mayor; "Rev. Dr. Hank J. Defenbar Way." It was a momentous day when the street sign went up and I was truly proud of him. We stood with the local and county officials, family, church officers, and others, taking photos and watching as they pulled the string to unveil the sign. All in all, I was empty but I played the part.

While I'd be putting on makeup in the bathroom on Sunday mornings or in the tub, he'd already be dressed, have on cologne, and pacing back and forth. While straightening his necktie; putting on his suspenders; or putting on his cross, draping it in his shirt pocket the way preachers do it, he'd stop to ask me a question regarding his sermon. It was like biblical trivia for me but for him it was having someone to share his thoughts with regarding his sermon. I would always give the correct answer but he tried his best to find a way to make my answers incorrect by rewording them, and so I'd tell him, "Oh, well that's the same thing." I pretended to be oblivious to what he was doing, and I'm not sure if he himself was aware of what it was that he was doing.

Seemingly his goal was to always degrade me, and to break my self esteem down at any cost which has proven to be a waste of his time because it never happened. He would say, "You don't know more than me, I know what you're trying to do and I'm not gonna let you do it; you're trying to upset me before church!" He would say that in such a vociferous manner that it would make one think he was talking to a person that purposely defecated on themselves and disgusted him. I would respond, "What are you talking about? I'm in agreement with you, all I'm saying is that we're saying the same thing, just in a different way!"

Mixed emotions often accompanied the feelings that ran through my entire body when he attacked me out of left field, based on either something he fabricated or that satan whispered in his ear. I felt just as sorry for him as I was angry. The sympathy was due to him being so tormented by demons that he heard things other than what I've actually said that made him angry every time we had a conversation about the bible and the Word. The anger is a result from the fact that he's a miserable person, and tried to make every aspect of *my* life miserable as well. The thought of my supposedly husband harassing me every day, especially Sunday morning, is horrific.

    I have a high tolerance for loved ones, and it took me years before I figured out he would never change. Consequently, I grew wiser and although it wasn't true, I started telling him "I don't know the answer to that, I haven't read that" or "I forgot" or just "I don't know," when he'd ask those Sunday morning questions. Every little bit helps so whenever I was able to capture an ounce of peace, I took advantage of it.

    Pastor Defenbar would do things to annoy himself and become agitated, but I'd be the one in the line of fire and get the brunt of it; therefore, I stopped at nothing to keep him as normal as possible. On many occasions throughout the years he left home without his cross on Sunday morning and I'd quickly assure him not to worry. I would drop him at church and turn around going back home to get it. Upon returning to the church I'd go up to the altar rail and he'd come down from the pulpit to meet me, and I'd drop a small velvet sack with a drawstring into his hands that contained his cross. Likewise, if he misplaced anything, I'd tell him not to even worry looking for it and that I'll find it, because the last thing I needed was for him to become flustered.

    Sunday morning wasn't out of the woods just because I conquered an evil. Everything concerning me other than financial was an indicator that he possessed a strong dislike for me. He would rarely compliment me on my outfits or anything I've accomplished as a husband would a wife; howbeit, he always complimented other women in front of me. Generally speaking, I'd much rather hear a compliment from my husband which would have meant so much more than hearing it from a stranger or an outsider. Needless to say, the majority of my compliments came from outsiders.

On one of many occasions I was dressed and ready about a half hour before time to leave for church during which I'd affix his suspenders to his pants and then put them across his shoulders, and fasten his bracelets. I was wearing a new suit that looked as if it was tailor made, a new pair of nice subtle pumps, a new clutch, and a new hat tilted in that perfect position that would make sisters holler, "You're wearing that hat girl" or "You know you're wearing that hat," but Revy Rev never acknowledged any of it, and didn't say a word.

While in the car I asked him, "Do you like my outfit, you didn't say anything?"

I tried to be as humble as I could in asking, hoping he wouldn't go off the deep end, knowing how the least thing made him flip, but he flipped in spite of my efforts.

"That's the problem with people now, they don't get ready for church they just go to church, you should have your mind on church not on how you look."

He said that as huffy as he could and it wasn't that serious, after all he was my husband, as he loved to say. There had been a few occasions throughout the years where he seemed to have struggled and painfully said, "You're looking pretty sharp there Sis. Defenbar." That was the best he could do and I accepted it and thanked him; I took what I could get.

As we arrived at the church house--I have a cousin that says "Church house" instead of "Church" and I think it's hilarious--, no sooner than we entered, a tall sister was standing there with an off-white fitted knit skirt suit on and the first thing out of Rev's mouth was, "You look pretty nice there Sis. Jesse." That was all she wrote for me, I was done, you could have stuck a fork in me.

I remained as quiet as a church mouse and didn't say a mumbling word, as my insides were twisting. After church I politely took myself to the shopping mall and picked up roughly five new name brand suits with matching shoes and paid with *his* credit card. I walked out of the mall swinging my bags with my shades on like one of those rich women, and threw my items in the trunk and chuckled to myself.

I passed the town I lived in and drove straight to Mary Ellen's house, knocked on her door, and waited for her at the car, standing directly in front of the trunk. Cell phones weren't so popular back then so she had no idea I was stopping by. It didn't matter when it came to Mary Ellen, she always had a smile on her face unlike myself when it comes to pop-ups. Heck, if someone comes by my house without notification, they'll most likely be standing outside until they decide to leave.

She greeted me at the car, "Hey! What's up girl?"

"Mary Ellen, Rev had a fit when I asked him if he liked the way I looked this morning, but he told this woman as soon as we entered the vestibule how nice she looked, so…..--I popped the trunk open and pointed--maybe out of these he might like one, and I put them all on his credit card."

As she gasped she proceeded to scream and laugh, then we went through each one.

"I did it for him, obviously he didn't like what I was wearing so I bought a few that he may like."

She knew I had to have spent a good amount of money, so she said, "He is gonna kill you!"

I replied, "Ha, nooow let's see what he says," and I drove off.

Would you know it, initially he didn't say anything because I'm sure he knew he was as wrong as two left feet, but one thing is for sure, he NEVER told anyone they looked nice in front of me again. Later on he'd bring it up in arguments saying, "You went shopping with my money and didn't ask me, I don't play with my money, you mess with my money, you mess with me!"

"Aaaw, ask me, shmash me! Bite me!" I retorted.

Jessica and Arnold, the sister that Hank holds in high esteem and her husband, were with us for a visit over a weekend and I used that opportunity to prove a point.

As we were having breakfast at the kitchen table I blurted out, "So Jessica, does Arnold ever tell you that you look nice?"

"Oh yes, he tells me every morning how beautiful I am."

I looked over at the good reverend and then back at her.

"Well, your brother said that's not important, and he never tells me I look nice."

She went on about how it's important to lift each other up in a marriage. Defenbar had nothing reasonable to say, just a few subliminal words here and there, and as expected it didn't change him. Nothing could change him.

Chapter Twenty One

    The response and comments regarding my sermons which were made to the pastor and me from the members were always overwhelmingly praiseworthy. My doing well or receiving any compliments in any area of life, not just preaching, secretly angered him and made him jealous it seemed. Only *I* knew that because I know him, and was on the receiving end of a sure cursing out after I received any compliment.

    The war going on in his mind baffled me. He'd ask me to preach knowing that the demon of jealousy was present inside of him, or whatever it was, perhaps a strong dislike. I can't properly pinpoint it, and with him not resisting the devil, he probably didn't even realize it. That demon had become so bold and prevalent, that he would follow Hank into the pulpit and only ran when Pastor Defenbar started preaching.

The word always spread before Sunday as to who's preaching if it's not the pastor. When people learned that Evangelist Defenbar was preaching, they would turn out.

The ushers lined the walls, and the church was full with people coming to hear me preach, or to hear me fail, but nevertheless they were in attendance. The altar, pulpit, and choir loft was covered with its leaders in place. The evangelists and assigned officers behind the altar rail; the pastor, ministers, and myself in the pulpit; and the choir along with the musicians were directly behind filling the choir loft ready with song.

I wore a classy size eight suit accessorized with a hat that was cocked just right--you have to cock it right if you're going to wear one—a pair of nice shoes that were saying a thing or two, and I represented as always just like the good ole reverend liked. He voluntarily paid for my clothes to make sure of that! Needless to say, I was sharp. It was one of my known traits that once I began to preach I'd remove my hat to avoid it from flying off at the height of my sermon which made some members chuckle.

Despite everything, once I enter the house of the Lord and step into that sacred place of the pulpit, I forget what color I'm wearing. It's all about focusing on the Word and allowing myself to be used by God to speak to His people. I sat prepared not having to revisit my notes prior to delivering the message and I humbly meditated and praised along with the music.

When anyone is bringing forth the Word of God, out of reverence to the Holy Spirit, it is bad protocol to interrupt the vessel being used by God as well as disrespectful to that person. You do not quench the Spirit by trying to stop someone from preaching the Word before God would have them to finish, and that is the very thing Reverend Defenbar did to me.

Reverend Defenbar would start an argument the night before I preached just as he did the night before an exam when I was in college, it was surely Lucifer himself. I'm not the type to back out from my agreed upon obligation to the Lord at the last minute so I preached all the more with vigor and much enthusiasm crushing that demon's head, and I had a good time doing it. Satan doesn't like hearing anyone preach God's Word, and I hate that devil just as much as he hates me. I get mad just talking about that no good demon! Unfortunately he worked *through* Hank on that particular day.

As I was at the height of my sermon and the true preacher was on His way, Reverend Defenbar chimed in on two different occasions saying, "Alright you need to end it," and he didn't whisper, so those in the pulpit area heard him. I totally ignored him both times as God would have me to, and although it disturbed my man spirit, it did not rattle me from the Word nor did I skip a beat. I thought "GET THEE BEHIND ME SATAN!!" Rev. Defenbar had never done that to anyone delivering the message and I know he never will, he only did that to me. I wonder if *that* was one of the nights I should have been intimate with him? I retained such a cover-up throughout those sixteen years of being the first lady that the entire congregation had no idea that I was enduring while bringing the message. Talk about I can do all things through Christ that strengthens me, I am the epitome of that scripture.

After I sat down, the evangelist sitting directly to my left who peeped the whole thing felt so badly for me that she grabbed my hand, held it tight, and as she rubbed it she continually said "I am so sorry Sis. Lydia." The tears welled up in my eyes and then fell, and I couldn't speak. Her spirit was also disturbed. It felt worse than betrayal; it felt as if someone stabbed me in my heart.

In retrospect I'm reminded of when I did my very first sermon and Hank approached me at home afterwards to pick a fight. Since he couldn't find any fault in my sermon or delivery, he fabricated something to argue about. He had the audacity to say that I didn't acknowledge him but I recognized my father and mother, so I told him to play the tape but he refused. He didn't know that I recorded my sermons. As my husband and the pastor, it's proper protocol to acknowledge him which I did immediately after acknowledging God, and before anyone else. I'm an educated woman and would never publicly and intentionally commit cultivated suicide, as I walk with dignity.

Like always, I picked myself up, dusted myself off, and kept moving like the trooper that I am. Getting out of that marriage became my main goal in life all the more, but I kept quiet about it. With my physical eye I couldn't see the light at the end of the tunnel, but I trusted God and if He loves me then He wanted me out of there too.

Reverend Defenbar would always piggyback on a guest speaker's sermon and give accolades, but that day he despised me so much that he acted as if I wasn't there. He took the microphone and proceeded to collect the offering. That was the same day someone told him after service "She's going to take over your job, she preaches just as good as you." Although they were teasing him, it was said and I know it killed him because I indeed had done a good job. I was in for a sho-nuff cursing out that day.

I went home that day and locked myself in the closet, which was a bedroom that my dad had transformed into a walk-in closet for me. My altar was in there and that's where I pleaded with God daily to get me out of that house and marriage.

Everything was made out of that white plastic coated wired shelving material. There were three shoe racks, one behind the door, and the other two nailed to the wall; two shelves adjacent to each other the length of the walls, holding labeled boxes and boxes of hats in which clothing hung beneath on long rods; and the third wall had large 14x14 cubicles stacked four high and three wide, also with hats in each cube. Two windows were on the front of the house overlooking the driveway and garage, and another single window on the side of the house overlooking the flowerbed and the main road. Under the sill of the front windows was another wired shelf that held hats on top, and handbags hanging from the bottom rod. In the center of the room was an island made of twelve white wooden cubicles, four columns stacked three high each, sitting on an oriental rug. They were backed against each other in a circle which housed gloves, scarves, and other clothing items. My altar was against a wall in the corner. I used a wooden table draped in a white cloth. On it were three crosses, one jeweled and made of brass, the other two made of wood, one from Africa and one made by the triplets in our church; my Hebrew prayer shawl; the bible; and Holy oil.

My closet was the only place in the house that I could find solace and at times I slept in there. On many nights I would find myself in there with the door locked, sitting before the altar with a grieved spirit not even able to speak. My flesh wanted to say "Eli, Eli, lama sabachthani," which means my God my God, why hast thou forsaken me! because sometimes I felt as if God wasn't going to deliver me from that place because of the time factor being years already. It weighed on me, as I suffered on a daily basis through that marriage.

Upon entering my prayer closet I went straight to the altar fully dressed, I sat there speechless and I tarried as the water trickled down my face in full understanding that El Shaddai understood my plea. Although the pain was inexpressible, through it I began to utter thanks to God for keeping me, for using me, for loving me, and for allowing me to understand that it all was a setup although I couldn't feel it or see it. I thanked Him for allowing the Holy Spirit to bring to my remembrance that God will never leave me, nor forsake me; therefore I continued to walk by faith, not by sight. You must be a faith walker in order to walk through the fire without a singe.

One word enters my mind to describe the feeling that engulfed me, and that is *oxymoron*, because I was experiencing one thing, pain and suffering; however, simultaneously believing wholeheartedly another, that I already received my deliverance. My faith in God would not allow the pain to overtake me.

Year in and year out, I had to keep believing and it wasn't easy due to the physical, the here and now. Nevertheless, one will have whatsoever one saith according to Mark 11:23, and so I continued thanking God out loud for how I wanted my life to be.

Chapter Twenty Two

Gertrude and Hank were always on the phone engaging in long conversations daily. There were many days that with my own ears, I've overheard Hank downstairs on the phone talking to her about me and my family like a dog. What I couldn't understand was, why would she entertain a conversation like that instead of cutting him off as my blood relative should have. We are first cousins and grew up together basically like sisters so I thought we knew each other, but I didn't know her. She was listening to him like she was learning something new about me and my immediate family that she didn't already know. Hank needed someone on his side, someone to listen to him. If he had someone that just seemed like they even slightly agreed with the things he'd say about me, it was satisfactory for him.

Well, his lucky day came when this woman that was as evil and as crazy as he was, knocked on our door while I was at work at the spa and told Reverend that I was sleeping with her husband, the construction worker, at my place of business.

Hank called my spa saying "Oh you're in trouble," and before I could question him she came walking through my doors as I was working with a client's pedicure. As she began to speak about her husband I interrupted and told her that she can speak to me in the basement but not in front of my clients. I hung up the cordless phone with Hank. Essie was there and because she knows me well she followed us in the basement. When she started with false accusations I was going to make soup out of her and Essie grabbed me and the woman ran up the stairs as fast as she could and out of the door and never came back. I believe Essie must have seen my lips and fist balling up and I don't know who needed Jesus, me or the woman. I knew of her from high school but we were never friends.

After that incident she had a determination to get me one way or the other. Although in opposite directions from the main Avenue, we lived about a fifteen minute walking distance from each other and sometimes I'd walk to the grocery store. She would see me in the grocery store at times and one day she gave me a dirty look and made a sly remark in the presence of a small toddler from her daycare, so I told her she better keep moving. As I walked home she had circled around my block and was driving toward me. Once she got even with me she stretched her arm out of the window as far as she could and stuck her middle finger up at me. She drove out of her way and made an effort to harass me. Having bitterness toward her past actions and with the practice of battling Hank daily, I wasn't there yet, as some would say when we're not where we should be spiritually, so I reacted instantly yelling, "No, FU bitch."

The next thing I knew, a letter came in the mail from the District Attorney's office addressed to me regarding a complaint that I harassed Marsha Stank. I immediately phoned the DA's office questioning the letter.

After hearing my side of the story of how Marsha drove around looking for *me,* the DA asked if I wanted a mediator and I quickly declined. I refused and would not appease Marsha Stank if my life depended on it! Nevertheless, I did make a trip to the DA's office to put a complaint in on her so that she also would receive a letter at home. I also suggested they watch the video tape at the grocery store.

Hank had a new kick, *the construction worker*. He took it to heart of course and went ballistic with that bogus information. He stopped eating and it appeared that he lost over fifty pounds, looking crazy, sunk even further into depression than he already was, and badgered me for years until the cows came home and they never arrived. Marsha Stank died a few years later. The Word says to touch not my anointed and do my prophets no harm; I'm just saying. It's always a bad idea to dig graves for others because the digger falls in; I read that in the book of Proverbs!

The truth of the matter is that the construction worker and I became good friends because I finally found a male that I could talk to about my marital woes without him viewing the pastor differently. Someone finally understood that Hank wasn't only a pastor but he was my husband as well. I wanted to hear from an unrelated male's point of view because women are made totally different. He also told me about his marital woes and I listened, and they were extremely similar to mine, just role reversal. We would always talk on the jobsite but our spouses were both irrational jealous people and felt that whatever the connection between the two of us was, it had to be sexual. She also had always accused him of his ex-girlfriend and other women during their entire marriage.

The irony of all of this was that Hank had a key to the spa. I gave him his key as soon as the building was rented, *prior* to construction. I couldn't figure out why he would never use the key, instead of sitting at home and accusing me of infidelity. The spa was a seven minute drive from our house.

Hank and Ms. Stank wanted to have a conference with the four of us; the construction worker, his wife, Hank, and me, but I wouldn't dare play into their sickness. I'm an adult and wouldn't slightly entertain the thought of discussing something that didn't exist, something two wackos made up. Hank said I was protecting her husband, but I told him I wasn't and that he could go over there if he wanted to but *I* wasn't going. What they needed were shrinks!

Months later Hank came to me screaming one day as usual about the construction worker again, off on one of his tangents and he blurted out, "I asked Gertrude about him and she said, 'I think Lydia thinks she's in love with him,' and that's your own cousin and I believe her."

Needless to say I felt betrayed by Gertrude. The underlying issue is that I never spoke to her about anyone, but for argument sake let's say I did, why would she tell Hank? What exactly did she have to gain? Could she have been jealous? Did she want Hank for herself? Back then I wish I knew the answers. That was definitely a kick for Hank, he literally harped on that for years, always throwing Gertrude in my face and I never told her.

In light of and in spite of my not allowing anyone to know how I was living, I decided to disregard the betrayal and give Gertrude a chance to be my sounding board. I felt that as close as I thought we were, if I told her about the dirty secrets that I kept for Reverend Defenbar and how crazy he was, then maybe she'd feel badly and not listen to him when he talks about me and my, no, *our* family. I wanted her to know what I was going through. I called her late one night after running out of the house and boldly asked her if she told Hank that I thought I was in love with that construction worker and she round about tried to say no. She seemed uncomfortable and couldn't give a straight answer, so I let it go.

In spite of that, I still began to confide in her that night and told her some of the things I had been going through, how bad I was being treated, the name calling, and that our marriage had been over for five years at that point. She was listening intently as if she cared. Lo and behold, the next day Hank told me that Gertrude told him that I said our marriage was over for five years already. There is no way Hank has ESP, and no way he could have possibly picked the number "Five." Gertrude had certainly betrayed me to the utmost, and it cut me like a knife. I never trusted her again. I didn't confront her about the new finding and I stopped talking to her for a year or so, I'd only say hi when I was right in her face at church. Clearly she had no sympathy for my sufferings and wasn't on my side, or didn't believe anything I said. She is my first cousin, but unfortunately her actions reminded me of Judas.

I could only think for her to be so cold and heartless to family, she must have believed that I was lying on the reverend, which is exactly what Mary Ellen meant about the tape recorder. I thought she knew me better, and that I wasn't a liar. Gertrude only confirmed the fact that I really couldn't tell this nightmare to anyone, not even my family. I was alone, holding it all in, and it was hard. It really hurt me that she wasn't there for me. I understood that I had Mary Ellen and Lamont, but there are many people in my life and family that loves me; however, I couldn't share my living nightmare.

Hank used her like a bat. He harassed me with what Gertrude said everyday in every argument and cursed me out hard. I had to look at her every Sunday in church and secretly inside I was beat down all week and Sunday mornings about what Gertrude said. It was eating away at me and I didn't want to look at her. What she doesn't understand is that the bible says in the book of Luke 12:3 "Whatever you have spoken in the darkness shall be heard *and* listened to in the light, and what you have whispered in people's ears and behind closed doors will be proclaimed upon the housetops." Only if she knew how Hank drilled her name into my head daily for years of how she betrayed me, and he loved every minute of it. He finally found someone close to me that joined him in degrading me. He wanted me to dislike my family so he beat *that* dead horse over and over.

After years I eventually let it go, the way Hank always mentioned her. I started a somewhat relationship back with her, and during my financial lows, she'd give me lunch, gas, and nail salon money. I wondered if it was out of guilt. I finally told her how Hank continuously mentioned daily how she betrayed me, but at that point I was already packing my bags.

Chapter Twenty Three

    The only way I kept my sanity and was able to continually function in the church and run a business unscathed after being tormented every day, is by the Word. I walk by faith and not by sight. I wrote an inspirational creed for myself to live by, one of which I had copyrighted called, "Motivational Creed for Believers." I would read that as often as I remembered just to keep myself focused. I realized that the hell I was living through was superficial because the name calling didn't define me, and that wasn't who I was nor who God made me to be. I'm the Michelangelo of my own life, and *I* paint my own picture.

    I would go to the weekly class I taught on Wednesdays and would draw strength from my lovely students because I felt lots of love there. Gertrude was actually a part of the class, but I had to keep everything in perspective and couldn't be biased. In my position I had to play the roll I was currently in; be it first lady, teacher, evangelist, choir member, missionary, family, or friend; and cut all else off like a faucet. I couldn't allow things in my life to overlap. I didn't see her in any other way other than a student in class. They thought I was helping them but they were actually my breath of fresh air, and was helping me. We were supposed to have an hour and a half class, but it turned out to be a three hour class and at times longer because we'd share stories, thoughts, and ideas together, oh yeah, and eat! They had no idea how I was really living. People besides my students would call me individually to pray for them, and I would at the drop of a dime. Besides being strong for myself, I had to remain strong for the people because as a first lady that's what we do, well, that's what *I* did.

From the pulpit Pastor Defenbar would tease all of my students in front of the entire congregation saying how we would have class all night and then eat, and some would laugh. What went unnoticed was the fact that I actually got cursed out and harassed about going over time. I didn't allow it to hinder me or my class because if it wasn't that, it definitely would have been something else that I would have been harassed about. I decided that if I was going to get cursed out, let it be for a good cause. Just let it be.

Sometimes when I would be in the house alone when Hank was away, usually on and around my birthday--in the last seven years or so of our living in the same house he'd always leave at that time but I didn't care, at least I could enjoy my birthday--I'd just sit on the side of the bed knowing first that I could exhale for a few days. Then I'd reflect upon the cards I had been dealt in that part of my life, and the compassion I still showed Hank; and how in the midst of chaos God gave me strength to carry on and be the first lady, helping to lead the people. With melancholy I began to sing my version of "Let it Be," in that famous melody as the tears from my heartache fell: *"When I find myself in times of trouble, Jesus*

Christ He comes to me, speaking words of wisdom, let it be; And when I'm really feeling lonely, there's the Light of Christ that shines on me, shine until tomorrow, let it be." I take that and move on in faith, so I would pick myself up once again and keep it moving, exemplifying strength and no-one knew my plight.

I sang in the choir and had my solo's that were solely dedicated to me, as did others. Once you're given a song, it's yours for keeps until you are no longer in the choir. Whenever I presented my renditions the people loved it, and I always exerted much energy when singing in the choir, solo or not. I love the Lord with all of my heart, my being, and with everything that I am; therefore, I can't hold my peace when praising Him. If I can cut up on the dance floor, as I can, then I'm certainly going to go crazy for Jesus. I done did -- no grammar correction necessary -- yes, *I done did* the "Cabbage patch" in the choir loft, I rocked the "Side look" up there and I did that one all the time, and I just had a good time in the Lord, heck I felt like break dancing. I would have rocked the "Running man" if I could have. Under the worst of circumstances, I praised my way through. Not a day passed that I ceased to give God praise, and ultimately that's how your change comes.

My love, appreciation, and relationship with the Lord is so profound that I stand weeping, praising, and sometimes shouting in thanksgiving to God. I publicly become lost in the Word, worship and praise week after week. I can't hold my peace. My momma always said that I had the loudest mouth in the church; that's her story and she's still sticking to it. My dad agrees with her and says "Can't (kaint) nobody out-holla Lydia, they try." No-one realized why tears always flowed down my face when I worshiped but I was so grateful that God brought me through another week of turmoil and I knew firsthand what His love felt like and the meaning of being blessed.

I sat in the first seat on the third pew which has been designated for the first lady of that church, positioning the majority of the congregation behind me. When the Word is preached, or lyrics to a hymn gets good to my soul I stand and began to rock from side to side and after many years it had become known to everyone. My mother told me that she would always say to my dad, "Lydia is getting started, there she goes rocking." She also told my sisters that lived out of State about my rocking and that I had the biggest mouth in the church, she just didn't know that I had a lot to be thankful for and to shout about. Life is so funny; we just don't know what others are going through.

We had a "Fun Night" in church one evening and played charades and someone started rocking from side to side and everyone yelled out "Sister Defenbar!" I'm not ashamed to express my love for God corporately as I can't hold my peace anyway, He's been too good and I don't care which church I'm in. That demon was *not* going to get the best of me, nor was he stealing my praise, or getting any glory; the glory belongs to God, *my* Father, always.

Chapter Twenty Four

Proper protocol is very big in the organized church. There were times when we had special guests whereas I was duty bound as the first lady to sit with that person or persons and/or their spouse, so I didn't sing on those days. In my case I didn't sing on the days that I preached either. It was my obligation to entertain persons such as, the mayor's wife, the bishop's wife, the elder's wife, other minister's spouses, and certain female dignitaries. I loved what I did, I did it well, and no-one could refute that lest they should lie. If we had a female guest speaker, I would sit with her in the pastor's office prior to service and then I would proceed to the choir loft once service started.

I was clever about my actions in the church, and with the wit I possess I was always a step ahead of everyone. Most times I pretended to be oblivious to situations and the actions of others while reading them the entire time. Although not a rule, nor an obligation, it's expected of the first lady to smile at everyone and to speak to them which was never a problem for me because I loved everyone in spite of themselves. Unfortunately, it would give the impression of naivety toward those that didn't like me, was jealous of me, or couldn't stand to speak to me. I smiled and spoke to those that smiled and didn't mean it, those that only spoke because of accidental eye contact, and the ones that had no choice because they were standing too close not to speak. I knew them all. At any rate, there were some genuine people there too. I have to admit, it was fun to make some of them squirm, and I'd do it on purpose.

I have the gift of discernment which is something I've only shared with a handful of people subliminally, family included, and I never expounded upon it. I can see through a person like a piece of glass.

There was one woman that couldn't stand me because she wanted to marry Reverend Defenbar and she never seemed to get over it after all of those years. I caught her downstairs in the hallway one Sunday and wouldn't let her get away. I kept complimenting her, first on her outfit, then her shoes, then her handbag, and boy was it killing her. She was trying her best to get away. I was tickled and went on about my business.

The younger women in the church in my age category had a rapport with one another outside of the church, thereby growing comfortable calling each other by their first names. On the contrary, I met them *in* church, only saw them *in* church, and all of our dealings were *about* church. I called them all Sister A, or Sister B, whatever their last name was, or whatever they told me they preferred to be called. I wasn't only doing it out of respect, but also that's the norm of what we do in church and I've done it all of my life.

One day a Sister called me Lydia and I politely in a loving and friendly way, so I thought, asked her to call me Sis. Defenbar, Sis. Lydia, or Evangelist Defenbar, and that I wasn't used to being called Lydia, it just didn't feel right. I saw that she silently took offense to that although she didn't want it to appear that she did, but I saw it. Her face and body language was screaming, "Who does she think she is? Is it because she's the pastor's wife?" I thought to myself, "Oh boy, here goes one of those petty church issues."

I guess she thought she'd convert me without my realizing it. The next encounter she quickly called me Lydia as if she didn't realize she even said it, giving the appearance that it was so natural and just flowed out. I saw through her, and she was just being disrespectful and rebellious. I politely wiggled it in the conversation and mentioned it again.

After my persistence, some of the younger women stopped speaking to me, and through discernment I knew it was because they spread the word amongst themselves that I didn't want to be called by my first name in church, so they assumed not to call me anything. I couldn't see the big deal, as long as I was giving them the respect I requested for myself. Isn't it modus operandi to call a person what *they* want to be called, and not what *you* choose to call them? I mean, who does that? Specified church folks, that's who.

There are some people that just roll with the gossip, and if the gossip isn't favorable toward the person being talked about, then they don't like that person; not because of an experience they've had with them, but only because they heard something. In that church, I know who those persons are too and I know that character. One of my own students did that and stopped coming to my class in which she always loved, and I felt sorry for her being only a follower and haven't a mind of her own. She also wouldn't speak any longer if I wasn't directly in her face. Get this, my class was based on divine healing, and she was listening to a house full of sick people, diabetics, high blood pressure, fibromyalgia and everything else.

One demonic woman stopped speaking to me after I attended a cook-out that *she* invited me to, and to this day I have no idea what her problem was, or why she became angry. However, I haven't missed a meal, or lost any sleep behind it. She has an evil spirit that rubbed off on her poor little husband and most of the folks don't like her. I'm also disliked by the lady that literally has a foul body odor and she smells that way by choice. She has a house, water, and a job just like everyone else, and she can buy soap and toothpaste. I've never done anything to her, never had any dealings with her, and am clueless as to what her problem was other than jealousy. The majority of the people at church don't like her either, they just tolerate her.

There was a mother/daughter team that tried to duck me at a conference when we were out of town so as not to have lunch with me, and I pretended to be oblivious to that too. It tickled me.

Those sorts of things went on for years, actually all of the years. I would immediately tell the pastor about someone and he'd say, "Oh that's a woman's thing, you just don't like that person." What he failed to realize was that I call a spade a spade, whether it's a good spade or a bad spade, and I give credit where it's due. It doesn't matter what my personal feelings are. Lo and behold, months or years down the line Hank would always come back to me and say, "You were right," and I'd just look at him and say, "Uh-huh."

I never let anyone inside or outside of the church know that I was aware of their little situations or feelings about me, but I know immediately from the giddy-up what people are about. I see right through them, especially those with little teeth that claim to have loved Pastor Defenbar so much and always doing for him; all the while hugging him with one hand, and stabbing him in the back with the other, there were a few of those too.

The job of first lady wasn't difficult for me, it was right up my alley, it was just extra with Hank and all, and don't forget Scooter.

For years Reverend Defenbar liked to tell the people that I didn't know how to cook, and I wouldn't correct him, I played along with it and would tell the ladies that liked cooking for him, "Cook enough for me," and they would. Honestly, with a chef-dad like mine from Texas, and a Mac-n-cheese, banana pudding momma like mine from North Carolina, what, what, what made him think I couldn't cook? I rolled with that one for years, shoot I was benefitting. I don't *love* cooking, I'd much rather be catered to, but shucks I can out cook all of them. Well, that's *my* opinion, but I believe Hank will agree.

Chapter Twenty Five

Reverend Hank Defenbar isn't just an ordinary preacher, he is also a PK of a PK. For clarification, to those not familiar with church lingo, PK is the acronym for "Preacher's Kid." With that being said, Hank has had a front row seat and is well aware of what it is that I was going through in my role in the church. In having that knowledge, it's unexplainable how his compassion toward me has failed him terribly. Other than to be a thorn in my side, why would he compound that which was already being aimed at me from a select few of the members?

In comparison to my role, his involvement as the CEO is magnified one hundred times, and even with my not being a PK, I understand that. I tried my best to show compassion toward him which should have been a two way street. Case in point, in our earlier years, one day I came in from working in the corporate world at my nine to five and I felt like my world was caving in on me. As I walked into the kitchen, I dropped my bags right where I stood, started to wail, and said to Hank, "I need a hug, please hold me, everything is going wrong." He looked at me without the least bit of sympathy, didn't hug me or even come near me, nor had a kind word to say. What he did say in an unconcerned way was, "Well who's gonna hug me, nobody cares about me!" He didn't even inquire about what my problem was, although after his comment I would not have told him anyway. I felt like a piece of garbage, so I stood there and had to man-up. Our home should have been our sanctuary, but instead it was our battlefield.

The way Hank treated me in church I'm sure had to be evident to some because he didn't try to camouflage his actions.

The beautifully shellacked wooden altar rail with balusters is forty to fifty feet long. The ends turn inward toward the pulpit resembling half of a hexagon, forming a vertex with an angle of one hundred and twenty degrees. On each side there's a swinging gate about five-feet long for entering the pulpit area. The altar rests on roughly a five and a half inch tall carpeted platform and sits about eight inches from the edge, leaving a lip for kneeling only, not to be stepped on at any time.

During service, if someone must speak to the pastor, usually an official, they'll walk up to the railing, get the pastor's attention, and wait for him to come down from the pulpit which is on an even higher platform about three steps up. Pastor Defenbar would lean down over the altar positioning his ear closer to the person's mouth to prevent loud speech. It wasn't often that I needed to say anything to him during service but when I did, he would come down and instead of leaning over the rail toward me, he would back-up with this cantankerous look on his face not yet knowing what it was that I wanted or needed to tell him. That was hurtful and bothered me dearly. It burned inside that he would treat everyone else better than he treated me, and I would feel so embarrassed. I so desperately wanted to walk away and say forget it, but I pretended not to realize it in hopes of throwing others off. I was always being watched, as all first ladies are, and people are so nosey that I'm sure they were looking every time I made a move. I wondered if anyone noticed his behavior.

I never had a first lady mentor if you will; however, I do believe that God ordained me for such a position because I was divinely compelled to move in a particular manner for the sake of the ministry, regardless of what befell me in the process behind closed doors. Certain things come with the territory without having to be said or told, usually called an "Unwritten law."

I did everything I could to avoid having to speak to him during service, but if there was something he needed not to forget, or something he needed to know immediately, I made sure to tell him so that *he* would shine in spite of the fact that he treated me like I had the plague. Because of the flesh I wanted to say "I'm not telling him anything since he acts ugly, let him look bad and not be reminded of certain things," but I couldn't and wouldn't do that. It appeared that he took me for granted out of arrogance because he never showed appreciation for the way I watched his back and fully had his back. As a matter of fact, there were many times during arguments that he would say, "You don't have my back, I wouldn't trust you for nothing." That was just downright demoralizing. In my dictionary, money isn't appreciation, respect is.

In the denomination that we were in, on New Year's Eve we celebrated and had what is called a "Watch Night Service." The church would be packed out, filled with the regulars and those that only attend church three times a year; Mother's Day, Easter, and Watch Night, as if they're going to get brownie points from God for that. When I see people like that, my mind tends to direct me to the scripture in the Gospel of Luke 13:22-27, where the Lord says, "I don't know you."

Watch Night Service starts on December thirty-first at ten o'clock at night. At around 11:50pm, Pastor Defenbar would call everyone to the altar for the welcoming in of the New Year in prayer. Watchmen, those that kept the time, would be placed sporadically around the church and nearing the midnight hour would take turns in answering the call. The designated person would call out in a boisterous voice, "WATCHMEN, WATCHMEN, DO YOU KNOW WHAT TIME IT IS?" Another would respond, "IT IS ELEVEN FIFTY FIVE AND ALL IS WELL." They did that until the midnight hour approached us. That was my favorite part.

The "Call" is and was extremely emotional for me as God had seen me through another year, and counted me worthy of seeing a new year. He kept me once again through my trials and tribulations, and I would began to get full with emotions and weep in gratitude.

I would be standing at the center of the altar right in front of Pastor Defenbar who was behind the altar rail, and he would instruct everyone to hug someone, so people would be kissing and hugging all around the church and saying "Happy New Year."

Years prior to my day spa and throughout the entire marriage, every single year Hank would disregard me, even if we weren't at odds with each other for that moment. Hank would turn away from me, kissing and hugging everyone in his path except me. I would try to get his attention and he'd ignore me. One year I grabbed a hold of his robe sleeve before he could turn away and with no embrace he barely touched my skin to kiss me. He had that standoffish kind of attitude toward me which made me feel so horrible. I have no idea why he would even think *not* to kiss his wife first or at all for that matter, regardless to what problems he felt we may have had. God had allowed us to see a new year and had given us another chance.

After years of that I eventually changed, and in the last few years I would walk away so not to give him the opportunity to ignore me. What did I do after that? I continued to protect him and let *him* shine. That in and of itself was enough to know that I had to be ordained by God for that mess, because I would have liked to have put him in a yoke hold on most days if it were up to my flesh. The flesh is weak.

Once a month on the last Tuesday we had an evening service called "Love Feast," in preparation of Holy Communion which is on the first Sunday of every month in our denomination. Love Feast was an indication that the partakers of communion were in love and charity with their neighbor and in right standing to receive Holy Communion. Our belief is that communion shouldn't be taken if there is strife between you and someone in your life.

The stewardesses were there according to the board that was serving that month, dressed in their white uniforms with the little white hats which reminded me of the Pillsbury doughboy. Their job is to prepare the Love Feast which consists of small pieces of sliced white bread and water in the communion cups for each participant. We the evangelists, would start devotions with prayer, song, and scripture, then the pastor would give a lesson, and afterwards we'd share in the Love Feast.

Everyone would line up around the church shoulder to shoulder across the altar and overflowing down the side isles. Pastor Defenbar would stand in the center isle facing us and explain the meaning of Love Feast, and then we would all drink the water in unison with the pastor. Afterwards, a stewardess walked around with a lined basket to collect the empty cups. The bread is held in the left hand for others to take from, and with the right hand we take a small piece of our neighbors bread placing it in our left hand on top of the bread already there, and then extend the right hand of fellowship with a kiss, hug, or just a handshake, and move on to the next person. The bread is a symbol, not for consumption.

The pastor started by breaking bread with me and the ministers, and then we would follow him to the end of the line to start with the first person. Pastor Defenbar was the first to shake everyone's hand, and as we broke bread with each individual that person would get on line behind us and follow until everyone had been greeted by everyone.

When Reverend Defenbar would break bread with me he would always back off and not kiss me. As I followed him, he kissed every woman there with a holy kiss but wouldn't kiss me, he'd just shake my hand. Sometimes I'd tug on him a little as he's shaking my hand to make him kiss me, and he did reluctantly. There didn't have to be an argument at all, he just needed to be mean to me. I don't know if anyone ever noticed how yukky he was towards me but I felt very bad. There had been a few times that I'd miss Love Feast due to the fact that Hank was just extra in his evilness, and when that happened he'd carry it over into Sunday, which by then there would be a new argument anyway.

During communion service the first family and the officers would commune first and then the congregation would follow. If I didn't go to Love Feast, Reverend Defenbar would say "Today the first to commune will only be those that attended Love Feast." Many officers and officials were always absent during Love Feast but he only made that announcement if I didn't go. I never acknowledged or mentioned to him that I recognized what he was doing, I totally ignored it. Seeing that he didn't get a reaction from me, he eventually gave up on that tactic. No one knew what he was doing and it was so childish, I didn't even care. He worked so hard at being evil.

Our worship services were structured, and we followed an outlined program in our weekly bulletin except when the Spirit would have Reverend Defenbar to move differently.

One Sunday morning Pastor began our service with testimonies to give people a chance to share their stories of how good God has been to them. It makes a powerful witness when one corporately tells of God's faithfulness.

People weren't rushed, interrupted, or hindered from telling their story. Some were lengthier than others depending on who was speaking. There are those that you can't give a microphone to, and would you know it, I'm labeled as one of those persons. At any rate, my mother had been attacked by anaphylactic shock that week and almost lost her life. I was tearfully witnessing how merciful God had been and how thankful I was to Him for saving her life. I spoke of how my father was sitting near the nurse's station unaware of my mother's condition, thinking the doctors had everything under control. God had me at her bedside at the right moment and I began to see her vital signs and her strength rapidly failing, and I screamed out to the doctors, no, I hollered, "Help, help, she's going, she's going, she's going" and they ran over, kicked me out, and began to work on her to revive her. That was the very moment anaphylactic shock was diagnosed.

As I told my story that demon rose up in Hank and he interrupted me and said "Ok, ok, that's enough," before I could finish. He has never publicly disrespected anyone else like that. Witnessing serves the purpose of helping others to believe all the more in God's Word, so in essence, Hank was disrespecting God, and that was nothing but the devil. It was so unexpected and took me by surprise to hear this voice cutting in from the pulpit that I immediately became discombobulated. I was already crying, choked up and emotional in telling the story alone. I then turned to look at

Rev. Defenbar in disbelief, wondering if he was serious. I then looked back to the congregation. I felt so embarrassed and violated that I stopped talking out of respect to the pastor and I sat down without finishing my story. I was totally humiliated to say the least. He then allowed others to proceed uninterrupted.

With Hank knowing he had ill feelings toward me, although I didn't warrant any of it, he would ask me to do certain things because he knew I was very capable. I was asked by the Friends and Family Day Committee to do the welcome one year on the Annual Day in which the pastor had already approved of prior to my being approached. Friends and Family Day came and went, and I carried out the welcome address with enthusiasm and great articulation because I'm a natural at it. When we arrived home that day, he started one of his fights and told me that I embarrassed him in giving the welcome address. He said that another woman was better than I was and would have done a better job. Besides the fact that he was clearly fabricating the whole embarrassment thing and that anyone in that church could have done a better job; he then tried to further insult me by picking someone that actually sounds like a man when she talks and she couldn't stand the ground that I walked on because she was envious of me and he knew that. If he thought I believed him or that he could probably damage my self-esteem, then I could have sold him the Golden Gate Bridge for five cents! If my mama didn't do anything else, she made darn sure that I had some powerful and deep rooted high self-esteem along with some Wushu skills, so I'm glad he didn't push it.

Yes, I have been to and through Hades and the weird thing is that up until the last moment, if anyone tried to harm Rev. Defenbar in any way, shape, or form, I had his back. Please do not hurt the reverend. I hoped that no-one would have spoken ill of him in my presence either. I loved him like family, he *was* my family. I'm grateful that God gave me armor to protect myself, and the Holy Spirit reminded me of what I had in my possession to block those evil darts. I was able to keep on the breastplate of righteousness, the shield of faith, the helmet of salvation, and the sword of the Spirit, or I wouldn't be here delivered and living in peace today.

There was a song we would sing on Communion Sundays and that I would sing on almost any day, that brought me through so much pain and disappointment, and it gives me strength to this day. This song was and is always apropos for me when I'm hurt by family, when friends betray me, and when life disappoints. The truth and realism of the lyrics invoke such a deep appreciation and gratitude for God's expression of love for me, and the power He has given me through the shedding of Jesus' blood, that I weep and praise Him uncontrollably when I hear it. The emotions are so deep that it feels like a hurt, like a pain that grips the soul when your heart is broken or you've been shaken to your core, only it's an inward expression of exaltation and thanksgiving. The lyrics are a constant reminder that the blood shed by Jesus gives me strength from day to day, it reaches to the highest mountain, it flows to the lowest valley, it soothes my doubts and calms my fears, it dries all my tears, and it will *never* lose its power.

I'd like to end this chapter with a scripture for reference sake, to enlighten those that may not be familiar with it. The Word of God boldly states in Ephesians 6:14-18, "Stand therefore, having girded your waist with truth, having put on the breastplate of righteousness, [15] and having shod your feet with the preparation of the gospel of peace; [16] above all, taking the shield of faith with which you will be able to quench all the fiery darts of the wicked one. [17] And take the helmet of salvation, and the sword of the Spirit, which is the word of God; [18] praying always with all prayer and supplication in the Spirit, being watchful to this end with all perseverance and supplication for all the saints."

HALLELUJAH!!!

Chapter Twenty Six

I'm well aware that all things work together for good to them that love God, to them who are the called according to His purpose, as stated in the book of Romans 8:28. In remaining prayed up, I've seen God's Word at work in that catastrophe I called "My life as it was." I could never understand why God allowed me to go through such turmoil and how that could possibly be working for my good but I believed it, and I began to see the light. It's hard to see when you're in pain.

I had the authority to pray over my spouse's life as we were one flesh whether I liked it or not, it was like praying for myself. One of the reasons I believe God placed me in Hank's life was to save him from self. Hank has been the epitome of self destruction which only seems to take place when he's in a marriage because he's fine alone living single, and appeared to have coped well. He took pride in telling me over and over, even before we married, that he was supposed to be alone and that some woman told him that God wanted him to Himself and that he wasn't supposed to be married. Hank believed and confessed that wholeheartedly, however, he said it in an effort to hurt me but it backfired. Unfortunately he didn't understand the Word of God or the law of attraction. Hank spoke his future not realizing he'd have what he say.

I was a substitute teacher at the local high school and every day during my lunch break I'd call Hank and talk about my day, what we'll have for dinner, and what time he should be there to pick me up. Some days I drove, and other days he would drop me off, as he did on this particular day in question. When I called during my break, Hank started the turnaround game designed by Hank Defenbar and began to take the conversation left, mustering up an argument. He proceeded to tell me *while* I was at work, that I didn't have a job, I didn't work, and that I was nothing. Go figure, don't ask me. I was so outdone that I decided to walk home that day.

The school was approximately a mile and a half away and it was a nice day out. As I neared the twenty-four hour coffee shop on the corner that Hank and I frequented due to it being a five minute walk from our house, I thought to stop there. After all, that was my refuge when I would run out of the house at any hour of the night as late as two o'clock in the morning to escape constant harassment. I would sit there and have my usual cup of coffee, medium with skim milk and two sugars, and I'd begin to say a breath prayer and write down what had just taken place.

As I was walking by the coffee shop I saw that no customers were inside, no lines, and all of the tables were empty and God knows I wasn't ready to go into that tension filled house. I thought to stop and stay there at least for an hour, and immediately a war literally started in my mind. The entire time that this war was going on, my feet never ceased to continue toward home, they didn't lose a beat, not one step. I was consciously thinking "Stop," then I would think, "No, go home and put on your sneakers and then come back." Then I'd think, "That doesn't make any sense, why go all the way home just to get sneakers, and come back, I'm here now!" Meanwhile my feet were still walking toward home, it was like someone was pushing me. Again, I thought, "You're here now, so stop," then just like before, something said, "No, go home first, get your sneakers, then come back." I was baffled in the natural and clueless as to why this battle was going on in my mind, but I was compelled without a question, and was pushed all the way home. Although the will of God was only in my subconscious mind at that time; looking back at the incident I could really see God moving and ordering my steps.

When I opened the front door the smoke billowed out of my house, I couldn't see and I was afraid because both of Hank's cars were in the yard, and the adrenaline set in. The first that I could see was my then fifteen year old cat that I raised from three months old sitting at the top of the stairs laying low for air, so as he ran down to me I grabbed him and threw him outside and ran straight downstairs to Hank's room. His room was filled with smoke and he was lying there asleep as drunk as he could be.

I screamed, "Hank, Hank get up! the house is burning!"

I was telling him to get up and get outside but he wouldn't, he said he didn't care. I then ran upstairs but I couldn't breathe so I grabbed a towel out of the linen closet and wet it, and then covered my face. I went right into the kitchen to find that Hank had burned some food on the stove. I threw the pot into the sink, put water in it, and then I went throughout the house opening every window and door. The ceiling and walls everywhere were blackened and covered in soot and our clothes were smoke damaged. The house was on fire without the flames. I had to call the fire department and the insurance company. The insurance company paid for everything and connected me with a local outfit that cleaned fire damaged homes. Hank was still downstairs in his room acting as if he could give two cents about his own life, so what could I do? I left him there and stayed outside until help arrived.

There could have been another contributing factor to Hank's "I don't care if I die" attitude but I had no way of knowing, I couldn't smell anything on him.

One weekday while Hank was at the church I was cleaning the house and he had just returned from Philadelphia a few days prior. Being the thorough cleaner that I am, I went through his room and was emptying his bag to put away his clothes and BOOM-SHAKALAKA-BOOM, there it was underneath his belongings. I found a plastic sandwich baggie full of big cannabis clusters, weed, marijuana, Mary Jane, trees! I was furious to say the least and disliked him even more. I started searching after that. I found pipes and would smell them and bingo! I never found any papers; I guess he didn't know how to roll. I decided not to mention it to him because I was so embarrassed for him so I didn't say a word I just watched. I couldn't even blurt it out in an argument, no matter how nasty he was to me.

He would never smoke so that I could smell it when I got home, so he had his secret time and place to do it. He would always have a new batch after a Philadelphia trip. Dude was probably drunk and high and didn't care about a fire. I finally found out after years, that Scooter was getting it for him and they blamed it on Hank's being diagnosed with glaucoma. I know Hank and it was used as a vice, a coping mechanism. Had it been a glaucoma remedy why hide it and keep it a secret from me?

The cleaning company came and cleaned everything, from shampooing the carpet to washing walls, cleaning windows, ceilings, washing dishes, cleaning inside and outside of cabinets along with its contents, bagging smoke filled clothing and bedding, etc. They cleaned literally everything in the house, it was like new when they were done. All of the bagged clothing was sent out and cleaned. Although that was the result of one of Hank's depressed pity parties, he refused to get involved and the burden was on me to get everything back in order. In the living room upstairs as I was talking to the manager of the cleanup company Hank came up and yelled at the poor man and said, "Why are you talking to my wife? I'm the man around here and you should address me not my wife."

Well I could not have been more embarrassed in my life. I lip motioned to the man and said, "I am so sorry." I kept apologizing to the man and he told me "That's ok," but I felt so bad.

Hank wasn't just acting crazy, he looked crazy. I'm not sure if the man was afraid or confused. The house was nearly completed and he hadn't seen Hank during the entire process, he only had me to talk to. Who did Hank think the man was supposed to talk to? I can imagine the man wondering, was he supposed to walk into this house and question the woman as to whether she's married, who her husband was, and where he was? Really Hank?

There was a similar situation with a member of our church that Hank hired to do some small jobs around the house. Brother Fields was a handyman, you know, a jack of all trades-master of none. As he was working upstairs, Hank remained downstairs by choice. Later, Hank decided to come upstairs to wolf-off at Brother Fields making him feel inadequate or as if he was up to something shady because I was upstairs with him, so he left. Again I was beyond embarrassed.

Had God not pushed me home that day, Hank and Butterscotch, my cat, would not have survived. Another hour would have claimed their lives all because Hank's depression lead him to carelessness for whatever reason on top of drinking and getting high, and having no regard about his own life. Hank had a praying wife on his side and thank God he stayed in the Word if he didn't do anything else. They that dwell in the secret place of the Most High shall abide under the shadow of the Almighty, taken from Psalms 91.

Typical of Defenbar, he fought me that night after God used me to save his life. Every argument following for the next few months he'd say, "You love that damn cat more than you love me, and you got him out of the house first, and then came for me later." Whatever I said to Hank was always used against me; he was in an unconscious state and only heard my recap of the story. Butterscotch came down the four steps when he saw me as he always did so I didn't have to look for him. I was down to Hank's room in a super flash; it was a simultaneous action, not to mention the fact that he didn't come out of his room and said he didn't care if he died. He may not have loved his life but I loved it for him. If he was a "Thing," I would have entered him into "Ripley's Believe It or Not," because up until the very end he would tell me "You don't love me, you love that cat more than me, you're just waiting for me to die, and you only wanted me for what I can do for you." If I wanted him dead, I would have taken my cat and let Hank suck smoke for dinner, he was already asleep. I could have easily said, "Go on and take your rest," and collected the insurance money.

I've had my share of close encounters of the third kind and surely Hank was the third kind, but the close encounters were of a different nature. I don't know if Hank was trying to scare me or what with this next incident, but I'm not the one to ask questions and run later, because when you wait around thinking "Oh, he or she won't do that," that's when it's too late and you're dead. I run *now* and ask questions *later!* Although true, I use that as a metaphor because I didn't actually run, but I immediately took precautions.

Our furnace had given out one winter and it was a few days before we could get it fixed. We purchased a kerosene heater to heat the upstairs, thereby having to purchase kerosene from a gas station two towns over. My mother was always very afraid of kerosene heaters because as a child in North Carolina she seen one explode from a distance and her home was gone.

Upon entering our high ranch, the choice is to either go upstairs or downstairs from the platform. I arrived home one night at approximately eight o'clock and as I opened the front door, Hank was standing there with a t-shirt on pouring kerosene all across the threshold and the rest of the entire floor landing; he had been drinking and I began to scream.
"What are you doing? Are you crazy, that's kerosene!"
His slightly slurred response was, "I'll burn this mutha fucka down!"
Well who had he been arguing with? I wasn't home. Most arguments started that way out of nowhere and that's why I would say he always had conversations with satan. Was I supposed to start singing, "The roof, the roof, the roof is on fire?" No, I did ninety getting the cat litter, I mean I thought fast as the adrenaline set in and I poured cat litter all over the floor to soak up the kerosene. At that point my mind was saying, "Ok, dude is crazy for real, barricade yourself in the bedroom tonight Lydia so you can sleep with both eyes closed." I don't think I argued with him *that* night.

The fortune five-hundred company that I was employed with as an executive assistant for many years would give out catalogs every year for us to choose a Christmas gift from. It was set up into category "A," that allowed two gifts, or the more expensive section in category "B," that allowed one gift. Everyone was ordering beautiful items except me; I was silently using survival skills thinking of my life. I selected a chain and ladder that you can hook over a window and climb down, if need be.

Ordering the ladder was when I first realized he was crazy which was years prior to both the kerosene incident, and my day spa.

After soaking up the kerosene, I put my life into God's hands and slept soundly, but I barricaded myself and Butterscotch in the room and placed my chain and ladder under the window. The bible says to watch *and* pray in Colossians 4:2. I guess God said, "I'll help you, but you got to do the running."

I pushed the huge dresser drawer against the door and then I jammed the bed between the dresser and the wall, not to be moved like a tree planted by the rivers of water. How is *that* for a close encounter?

Yes, we went to church that Sunday too and no-one ever knew. I, as usual, gave God all the praise; and Pastor Defenbar, as usual, preached his heart out. Somehow he would pull it all together for Sunday worship service and resurrect himself, straight-laced and not depending on any vices.

I always walk with my head high in the air, it's my trademark because I'm a Soldier in God's army and I will fight that demon toe to toe, eyeball to eyeball, and I *will* win, I've won every battle!

I wouldn't let anything get in the way of my responsibilities as a leader, even in the midst of getting cursed out in a heated screaming match. It's as if a hypnotist snaps a finger to instantly bring me out from under hypnosis. I have received phone calls for advice, prayer, or just ordinary church business, and I'd answer the phone like everything was peachy keen and jumped right into action on the request.

I always had a laugh, or a smile. I've been asked to pray at the close or opening of choir rehearsal; I've been asked to give a lesson at the spur of the moment at a conference because the minister scheduled for that morning's meditation didn't show up; I've been in many "Be ye also ready" moments, and I had just been cursed out, but it had no effect on me or my deeds because I know who I am and whose I am.

Things were so covered up that a woman a few years older than myself came to me one day in the fellowship hall and said, "You and Pastor Defenbar are the perfect couple," and I simply smiled. I personally wondered how she could make that assessment from seeing us once a week for three to four hours, if that. The truth of the matter is that most church goers make assumptions like that regarding their pastor and his wife. To this day, people will say to me, "Oh, I know my pastor and his wife, they have a wonderful relationship." I just shake my head and think "Yeah, the exact same thing has been said about us."

I personally know of a pastor that up until their last day of marriage would speak extremely favorably about his wife from the pulpit. He'd always refer to her as his brown sugar this and his brown sugar that and they were admired as a loving and powerful couple. Well they had one of the nastiest and most scandalous divorces known to man. They have children and grandchildren but he shockingly married his mysterious mistress that no-one ever knew about.

Not only the Defenbars, but there are some pastors that give true meaning to the saying "You can't judge a book by its cover." I'm just saying.

Chapter Twenty Seven

Our denomination is categorized into 19 districts, each being under the auspices of a bishop. Every district is broken down into conferences, and then further broken down into sub-districts if you will, all according to demographics. Annual conferences are held for pastors to give an account to the bishop and conference of the church's progress they've been assigned to. Churches are ranked by membership status and dollar amount raised. Our church has been ranked second, then third on our sub-district out of roughly twenty-five churches or more.

Every year, Hank would give me money to shop for new outfits complete of gloves, shoes, hats, and handbags for each day of conference week. I needed certain colors for specific days which will always remain unchanged. Each organization had its day, and besides opening day and closing day the majority of people went according to their association other than the delegates who had to be in attendance every day. I wore red on Monday for the evangelists; white on Tuesday for the missionaries; and the first ladies, minister's spouses, widows, and widowers were supposed to wear black with a red, black, and green sash on Wednesday for the official opening day of conference. Hank was excellent at his job, and he had the rank to go with it. If it was the last thing he did, he was going to make sure we dressed the part. He would not have anyone look better than me, stating that his father did it for his mother.

The opening and closing day was when the first ladies and minister's spouses really showed out with hats and their best outfits. We all sat in one designated area with signs posted at the end of roped off pews that read: "MINISTER'S SPOUSES." We all were seated on the side of, and behind the bishop's wife. All of the brown-nosers wanted to sit close to her. All I cared about was an end seat, so I'd get there early because I didn't like crossing over people. Everyone would look to see how the spouses were dressed, and I always received compliments, it was like a big show. I wore the large brimmed hats with rhinestones sparkling all over, some that cost Pastor Defenbar three hundred dollars but he didn't care and sometimes he didn't know.

When it was time for the pastors to read their reports, the bishop would call their spouse down to stand next to her husband in front of the entire conference while the report was being read. I stood proudly, as Pastor Defenbar always had a meritorious report, and the people applauded as they did for everyone anyway.

During offering the bishop would call the contributors by categories; pastors, delegates, conference officers, etc. When it was time for the spouses he would say, "Alright, where are my hats, come on spouses." As we approached him, he would call our names as he did the pastors. Everyone would watch us parade around, and if your hat really stood out the bishop would comment about it. There were a couple of times when

Hank would put my one hundred dollar offering in for me, so when he gave the two hundred dollars for both of us the bishop would say, "Ok Rev. Hank Defenbar, that's for you and Mrs. Defenbar," and when I'd hear that, I'd shout out, "Hallelujah, thank you Jesus," and people would just crack up laughing.

I never let that spectacular week of dressing change me, as I was the church van or bus driver on Missionary Day, depending on which vehicle was available. We'd meet and load up early in the morning at our church in order to get to conference early enough for breakfast. I'd pray once everyone was on board, and we'd take off to New York City or wherever conference was being held that year.

As we rode along I'd always keep everyone laughing; I was as jovial as ever. I would say subtle things about Rev. Defenbar and they'd laugh saying, "Leave my pastor alone." We'd talk about church, and have a good time. We were all dressed in white as was the other thousand women there. All you could see was a sea of beautiful big white wide brimmed hats.

Because I had to be at conference, the church always gave me a stipend at the beginning of the week for expenses. Perks did come with the territory. Every four years for the Quadrennial Conference, directions would come from headquarters explaining that a particular suit was needed for our district to look uniform in which the church paid for mine, as well as hotel, airfare, and food. That was the life people saw, but they didn't see *my* life and what I had to go through to maintain what I had. I deserved everything I ever received, and some.

Chapter Twenty Eight

There were terrible and embarrassing scandals in our district regarding pastors, just as there are in other districts and denominations. I'm thankful that Hank wasn't a philanderer, homosexual, pedophile, murderer, child abuser, and/or one to send naked photos to boys and men, have children incarcerated, or children selling drugs because that would have been trouble on top of trouble. Unfortunately, there are some that preach in churches having those problems, so who can start throwing stones at my story? Don't let Jesus start writing in the dirt. To those that find themselves making decisions about the status of anyone's relationship, please stop saying how happy *your* pastor and *his* wife is because you don't live at their house. Although it may well be, what it looks like isn't always what it is. If you don't know you don't know, so unless you have ESP, speak not! Remember what one of our members boldly told me, that Pastor Defenbar and I were the *perfect* couple. A first lady in Tennessee that had three little children shot and killed her active pastor-husband because of the extensive abuse; remember, they were *perfect* to their parishioners too. I quote from the news report, "We're grieving, this was a *perfect* family," church member J.T. said. You couldn't tell them any different, just like no-one can tell most people any different about their pastor. I mentioned that because looking on Facebook, website forums, and attending meetings and conferences; the first ladies who are directly affected act as if they're oblivious to their husband's misdoings, or as is custom we cover up well. Their husbands may be the scandal of the church and they won't say anything about it at our monthly meetings as I didn't speak about my woes. Once, I indirectly tried to at a spouses retreat and I could see the agreement nods and expressions of familiarity but no-one dared to delve in, so neither did I.

A few of the first ladies ended up divorcing their husbands and one in particular with a very large church asked me privately how did I do it? She explained that she was tired of having to be so perfect and phony. I told her that she should have never allowed anyone to change her and that she needed to be herself. She held a high position in the minister's spouses organization and was always flamboyant, but from the first time that I met her I was able to detect her phoniness, it was so perceptible to me. There is a need for change; a support group would be great and is necessary.

There is one couple that always look tremendously happy, nothing but smiles and teeth to this day. They have three or four children, yet had to be moved to another State due to the pastor having impregnated a young lady in his church. One pastor was caught kissing a teenager in his church but his wife is still first lady all mighty. Another pastor is the child of a bishop and was caught having intercourse in the basement of the church with someone that wasn't his wife. There was a pastor on the news in handcuffs on national television begging forgiveness for his criminal act. It goes on and on, however, we don't support each other and talk about it, we hide it to protect our husbands. I know, I did it. I can only imagine what their sex life and life in general was like at home.

In defense of a few, there are those women that had more guts than I did and left their pastor-husbands right smack dab in the middle of his active ministry. In the case of the first lady in Tennessee, she just went on and killed hers. Hank should be thanking God for Grace that I didn't cut'em.

On the contrary, there are those pastors, bishops, etc., that actually talk the talk and walk the walk, living the life they preach about, and their fruit bears witness. May God continually bless them abundantly!!!!!

Chapter Twenty Nine

When things were indescribable and incommunicable I didn't know what to do other than to get Mary Ellen or Lamont on the phone to listen. I'd put my Bluetooth in my ear so that Hank wouldn't recognize my being on the phone. One night I had Lamont on the phone and I hadn't said a word to Hank, he was drunk and appeared delusional. He came upstairs, fell in the middle of the living room floor and started wailing with a long drawn out heavy scream as if he was being tormented by demons right before my eyes. He would stop for a second and then do it again. I was afraid that he went off the deep end and I'd have to get him admitted. I stood there starring at him and whispering to Lamont saying, "Oh my God, do you hear him?" Lamont said yes and he was also very afraid. Hank eventually stopped and laid there. I asked him what was wrong but he wouldn't speak.

Mary Ellen has also heard him over the phone going off and cursing me out for naught; he even cursed her out and she heard it. She suggested I call his sister, she said, "At least let her know his condition before he kills himself." I would have been blamed for knowingly having watched him deteriorate without notifying his family, and if they didn't act, at least I reached out for help.

After closing hours one evening at the spa as I sat at the reception desk, I called Jessica to enlighten her on Hank's status and the physical effect it was having on him. I also pleaded with her to allow me to call her on any given day including that day when I got home so that she could listen to her brother for herself, but she adamantly refused, saying she didn't want to hear it. Well that ended that. I have no idea if she ever spoke to him about it but she acted as if that conversation had never taken place.

Mary Ellen is very respectable and would never interfere with a situation that doesn't pertain to her. As we were riding from Manhattan to Long Island in the car with Hank one evening, of course he started a fight. I was driving and eyeballing Mary Ellen through my rear view mirror. Whatever the conversation was at that time, Hank and I had the same take on it, only I worded it differently. He fought me as I continually tried to convince him that we were on the same page, but he kept argumentatively challenging me as if I were wrong on the subject at hand. It was so ridiculous that Mary Ellen couldn't hold her peace and she was compelled to interject. She finally said, "Hank you guys are saying the same thing." Hank got quiet but had an attitude and I didn't want to go home with him, I dreaded that night. I needed to find an ice breaker and thank goodness we were passing a great delicatessen on Queens Boulevard and I knew that a bologna sandwich would make him happy. We stopped, got the sandwiches for dinner and he was all better, the fire was defused with a bologna sandwich.

Our rare semi-good days didn't even work well. I was preparing dinner one evening and simply asked him if he wanted broccoli and he went off again. He started screaming, "I'm your husband and you don't even know what I like," and he snowballed from one subject to another until the argument was explosive.

I refuse to be defeated by anyone or anything, so I may as well be called little Apostle Paul, or better yet, Pauline. My woes may not have been as great as Paul's were, but I still stood as Paul did no matter what my tragedy. Paul should be every Christian's example when going through rough weather, and a reminder to never give up, stay the course, and God will see you through. In spite of everything, Paul still wrote most of the New Testament.

The "Message" version of the bible is basically in street language in order to be clearly understood by anyone. From the "Message" Paul writes to the people at Corinth in II Corinthians 11:12-33, saying: "12-15 And I'm not changing my position on this. I'd die before taking your money. I'm giving nobody grounds for lumping me in with those money-grubbing "preachers," vaunting themselves as something special. They're a sorry bunch—pseudo-apostles, lying preachers, crooked workers—posing as Christ's agents but sham to the core. And no wonder! satan does it all the time, dressing up as a beautiful angel of light. So it shouldn't surprise us when his servants masquerade as servants of God. But they're not getting by with anything. They'll pay for it in the end. 16-21 Let me come back to where I started—and don't hold it against me if I continue to sound a little foolish. Or if you'd rather, just accept that I am a fool and let me rant on a little. I didn't learn this kind of talk from Christ. Oh, no, it's a bad habit I picked up from the three-ring preachers that are so popular these days.

TELL THE TRUTH AND SHAME THE DEVIL!

Since you sit there in the judgment seat observing all these shenanigans, you can afford to humor an occasional fool who happens along. You have such admirable tolerance for impostors who rob your freedom, rip you off, steal you blind, put you down—even slap your face! I shouldn't admit it to you, but our stomachs aren't strong enough to tolerate that kind of stuff. 21-23Since you admire the egomaniacs of the pulpit so much (remember, this is your old friend, the fool, talking), let me try my hand at it. Do they brag of being Hebrews, Israelites, the pure race of Abraham? I'm their match. Are they servants of Christ? I can go them one better. (I can't believe I'm saying these things. It's crazy to talk this way! But I started, and I'm going to finish.) 23-27I've worked much harder, been jailed more often, beaten up more times than I can count, and at death's door time after time. I've been flogged five times with the Jews' thirty-nine lashes, beaten by Roman rods three times, pummeled with rocks once. I've been shipwrecked three times, and immersed in the open sea for a night and a day. In hard traveling year in and year out, I've had to ford rivers, fend off robbers, struggle with friends, struggle with foes. I've been at risk in the city, at risk in the country, endangered by desert sun and sea storm, and betrayed by those I thought were my brothers. I've known drudgery and hard labor, many a long and lonely night without sleep, many a missed meal, blasted by the cold, naked to the weather. 28-29And that's not the half of it, when you throw in the daily pressures and anxieties of all the churches. When someone gets to the end of his rope, I feel the desperation in my bones. When someone is duped into sin, an angry fire burns in my gut. 30-33If I have to "Brag" about myself, I'll brag about the humiliations that make me like Jesus. The eternal and blessed God and Father of our Master Jesus knows I'm not lying. Remember the time I was in Damascus and the governor of King Aretas posted guards at the city gates to arrest me? I crawled through a window in the wall, was let down in a basket, and had to run for my life."

Looking at that scripture, Paul's issues cause mine to appear as minced meat, and I serve the same God that Paul served. God is no respecter of persons, and I will never give up.

Chapter Thirty

I always had to encourage myself around Hank and I did so because he'd put me down at every chance he got. He would often tell me that I let myself go and how fat I was in order to make me feel bad about myself, although I never exceeded a size ten. He would also say, "No-one would ever want you, and that's why none of your boyfriends ever married you." Thank God none of his repulsive tactics ever worked on me. They were all lies, and *his* pretentious assumptions. How did Hank forget about my first husband? He spoke as if he married *everyone* he dated, well he tried; I was his third wife!

Hank was very good at playing the dozens although laughing in our house was a rarity. When I went natural with my hair, he told me that it looked like one thousand little men with their fists balled up.

Hank wanted me to be a puppet and do only as he said, when he said, although he didn't literally say that. We had a revivalist to preach at our church during revival week some years back, a nice looking younger gentleman from New Jersey, and I thought his message was good. I sat in the audience and said my Amens, my Hallelujahs, and I stood at times as I always do when the Word is going forth with clarity. I had no idea that Hank was going to curse me out about it. Getting cursed out because you agree with God's Word, no matter who's preaching, is scary and of the devil.

When we left the church that night and were in the car on our way home, Hank said to me, "I saw you clapping for that man, standing and saying Amen, and he wasn't any good, what were you clapping for?"
Hank didn't say that to reflect on the speaker; he said that out of jealousy, selfishness, and just another reason to dig at me!
I responded, "I enjoyed the Word, how could you tell me not to say Amen?"
Then he said, "No, you were clapping for *him*."
I was perplexed to say the least. At that stage in the game I still wanted to try to make Hank happy and thought I could, so for a while I said Amen to other speakers with trepidation. I watched to see if Hank clapped before I would clap until I fully realized that my worship wasn't about making Hank happy, it was about giving God praise.

Hank just went along life's journey and would pop-up with new crap that would be meaner than the crap before. Sitting in the choir loft, we were behind Reverend Defenbar, and like sitting anywhere else in the church I'd respond to the Word as is normal for anyone agreeing to the message.
One Sunday after church he told me in his nasty way, "Don't be talking during my sermon and interrupting me!"
I said, "What, when did I do that!"

He replied, "Don't be saying 'Amen,' 'I know that's right,' and 'that devil is a lie.'"

At first I couldn't believe he was saying that junk to me, and then I remembered, its Hank. I paid him no mind and never stopped saying Amen, or anything else. Now *that* devil, IS A LIE!

To make matters worse, Hank tried to control what I watched on television, and had the nerve to get crazy, although that didn't work either.

A year prior to my building a spa I was hospitalized a few days for surgery due to a benign fibroid having to be removed which resulted in an incision from my navel down to the edge of my hairline. Two of the main post-surgery directions were not to walk stairs, and not to drive. The surgery was extremely successful and removal of the staples took place in the doctor's office seven days post-surgery.

Upon arriving home, my brother-in-law Wilfred, Essie's husband, and my dad were there to meet me in order to carry me in a chair up the stairs outside and inside the house. It was like the bride and groom being lifted in chairs at a Jewish wedding reception.

Hank was helping by changing the dressing on the incision with my instructions, because I can't look at a cut, even if it's on my own body. I would hold my head in the air, looking in the opposite direction while saying, "What does it look like, what does it look like?" He also prepared and served my food, helped me in and out of bed, helped in getting me dressed and undressed, etc., and everything seemed fine on day one and two of being home. On day three, Hank stormed in the room and started cursing me out about what I was watching on television.

He said, "All you watch are those stupid talk shows."

In the midst of my being tantalized he started to snowball. He went on talking about things that happened before we met which he knew not of, and I couldn't believe it.

I said to him almost tearfully, "What harm have I done to you on my knees?"

Hank continued on in a very bad way, he went crazy, cursing and all. This was a year or more prior to his latest gig, *the construction worker*, so that wasn't the underlying issue. I hadn't been anywhere, I hadn't done anything, so why was he harassing me? I still don't know and never will.

    I could barely walk at that time, my steps were baby steps, and it was painful and difficult for me to move. Bending was nearly out of the question. Needless to say, I had to get up with staples in my stomach and struggle to get dressed. I inched down the hallway which seemed to take an hour, slid down the inside stairs on my butt, then crept down the outside stairs, climbed into my SUV and drove which was all a no no. I went to the park so I could sleep in peace and get some rest. I cried and cried before calling Mary Ellen, and she was very upset about that.

She said, "Oh no, Lydia."

    Hank was so evil that he didn't try to stop me or ask where I was going, nor did he apologize or anything. He didn't stop screaming at me about how stupid I was for watching talk shows. He was well aware that I was getting out of there because he was harassing me, I couldn't take the stress, and I wasn't feeling well. I couldn't even raise my voice because my stomach would hurt just as it did when needing to cough. I was instructed to press a pillow against my stomach when I needed to cough so not to burst the staples and to prevent the accompanying pain.

    I was too embarrassed to tell my parents or my sister that Hank was treating me that way on my third day home. I leaned my seat all the way down, and slept in the park with staples and bandages for about three hours. I cried myself to sleep. The remainder of my recuperation was okay, he didn't do that again during post-op.

After being home a couple of weeks, I finally went back to church which was a wonderful outing for me. I walked down the side isle slowly with my donut shaped pillow to sit on and Hank would watch me to make sure I was ok, and he didn't want me standing too much during the music. He was caring in front of people, and in his own weird way, I believe he meant it.

Chapter Thirty One

When I love someone I give it my best shot, and in love relationships my love is in overdrive and overboard, nearly unconditional. I have a high tolerance level toward my significant other so although there's poor treatment, my heart won't allow me to accept it. I continue to believe that the person is a good person and that their nasty behavior will pass until I realize it won't and then I'm out. I had to be beaten over the head to finally accept and understand that our marriage wasn't going to work and that it was what it was.

After years of verbal and mental abuse, Hank would do something funny while in one of his good moments like break out in a dance move right quick, knowing that he moves like a toy soldier. I would laugh and try to hold on to that moment thinking that "if he can remain this way, we can make it." When I'd see him in the pulpit with his robe on, and listen to the intelligence that came from his mouth, I felt so proud and I tried to cherish that moment holding on to it thinking again, "If he can just stay like this, we can make it." There was always a glimmer of hope for him but without failure, before that day was out, he'd give me a reminder that it's not going to work. There was never twenty-four consecutive hours of peace before he'd be cursing me out and degrading me again. One day he told me that I had cum running through my veins instead of blood. I would say to God, "Ok God, I know he isn't going to change, I know I must leave," and then before I knew it, that glimmer of hope again. I was a glutton for punishment. It was a vicious cycle until one day I accepted the fact that the glimmer of hope had ended. I needed to change my environment, saturating my marriage and home with my absence. I tried to create peace and happiness by becoming a thermostat and changing the environment but the atmosphere was destroying me.

I wasn't living *my* life, I wasn't able to be the person that I truly am, and it was evident to those that know me. Those that I only communicated with via phone that know me, could hear the stress and change in me because I'm an extrovert, and I enjoy being in the company of family and friends. That was all taken away from me in living with and trying to please Hank, although the adjustments I made didn't make one bit of a difference.

It was a trying life as I endured bumps and bruises from all angles. Friends and family would take my behavior of being aloof at times out on me, and I would allow it. It was crazy because I preferred to have taken the heat than to expose Hank while he was an active pastor. I didn't want anyone to dislike him for my sake, if he didn't do anything to *them*.

One day I went to a bookstore to have time to myself and he literally said to me over the phone, "How dare you want to spend time alone." At that point he had become unrealistic so I hung up on him and made sure to close out the bookstore, and I left at 11pm.

Hank never wanted me to visit my parents for whatever reason, I don't know. I believe he was jealous of my time. He wanted to be my entire world so he could curse me out and degrade me every moment of the day. A normal person's life consists of more than one person; there is family, friends, business acquaintances, co-workers, church family, etc. However, just to have the peace of one less fight, I'd do anything although it hurt to do it.

The times I did go to my parents house I had to lie and tell Hank that I was going to the mall, he preferred that because I was alone although that too angered him. Anytime I was out, on my way home Hank would call me or I'd call him to see what he wanted me to pick up and bring, if anything. I would tell my parents and whoever was there to keep a quiet background so that Hank wouldn't know where I was, it was sad but I never told them why I asked them to be quiet. I could never stay any length of time, I was always on the run and I took the blame for that too. My parents would complain and make me feel bad by saying, "You never come to visit, and when you do come you're always in a hurry." I know they felt terrible about it but I never put it on Hank. I took the bumps on top of the bad treatment I was already getting from Hank, but I still praised God. The same went for my friends.

I got hit hard from another angle and that was from my sister Silvia, one of the three that lives out of State. She was a true piece of work, but I can't really blame her because it was due to my silence regarding my suffering. Unfortunately, people judge you by what they perceive. I took more bumps and bruises along life's journey not understanding and wondering why me?

I don't get to see my sisters as often as I'd like because we're all scattered throughout the United States. When Silvia would come to town I would never invite her over, I'd meet her at our parent's house and when I had my spa I met her there. My house was tension filled, not tidy, an unhappy place for me, and I risked being embarrassed by Hank. There have been times when he wouldn't come out to speak to my parents or my sister Essie who lived near me, but they would yell downstairs and say hello to him through his closed door anyway. Hank would also argue with me in front of my parents, sisters, relatives and friends. They've all witnessed arguments that Hank started out of the ether for no reason and they'd look at me like "Whoa," and I'd be so embarrassed. I eventually stopped everyone from coming over. My visitors and I were never able to speak freely, it was just very bad there and not a good situation for company. *I* didn't want to be there so why would I want to take my loved ones there?

There were many times when Essie, my parents, or one of my girlfriends would pull up to my driveway and I'd run outside to meet them at the car, not inviting them in, and I'd make up an excuse for it. I wouldn't show it or tell them, but I was hoping to end the conversation as quickly as possible because I knew I had to go inside and fight like hell because of it. However, I would never rush them although my insides were shaking. I wanted to appear as normal as possible. Hank didn't want anyone visiting me, clean house, spotless house, untidy house or not.

Prior to my ceasing all travel with Hank, we would go to our second home in Florida and I'd be able to see two of my sisters, at least once a year. Hank would argue like a madman because I rightfully wanted to visit them but I would leave him and go visit anyway. It was a rare occasion to succeed in persuading him to join me, and when I did, it was a fight. Did he really think I would travel that far and not see my sisters who literally lived on the same street? Same street or not, it was a sick thing for him to think that way. I would have never entertained a thought like that if it was his family, I'd want to see them myself!

I was able to convince Hank to have dinner with us; the three sisters, and our three husbands. We had dinner on the harbor one night in Miami and we were all at the table laughing and having a good time. I, like always, being the life of the party, was telling them stories about my boss on the job and they were rolling. All of a sudden Hank broke in from nowhere and screamed at me, scolding me like a child. His face swelled up like a blowfish and he looked evil and said, "Eat your food, stop talking so much, nobody cares about what you're saying, eat your food!" My sisters and brother-in-laws looked in amazement good enough to say "What?" Out of shock and bewilderment we all grew quiet. I was humiliated and didn't speak to him for the rest of that evening. He surely killed the mood for everyone and it was ugly, nobody wanted to talk to him after that.

Upon graduating college my friends and family attended the ceremony. When it was over I walked out very proud and happy with my degree, cap and gown, and a smile. My friends immediately ran to me to take photos. When Hank approached me he screamed at me in front of my family and friends saying, "I'm your husband, and you're taking pictures with them first?" His face was swollen again like a blowfish looking evil, and I was extremely mortified. Did he want me as a grown woman to tell them, "Hey get away from me, let me find Hank first for a picture?" He just couldn't be happy for me, so he stormed off and went home. I was aghast. Once again, everyone was stunned and couldn't believe it.

If those individuals hadn't witnessed it for themselves they would have never known because I wouldn't talk about Hank to anyone other than to the two faithful; for crying out loud he was a pastor!

I didn't have the nerve to tell Silvia the truth about what I was enduring, so she talked about me with her daughters, and her stupid friend, saying that I, Lydia, thinks I'm better than everyone else. I know she said it because she told me; and my niece, the younger of her two daughters agreed with her. She had no idea what I was protecting her from by not inviting her to my house while she was in town. I thought she knew me all of my life. On our wedding day, Silvia and her daughter Tabatha stayed the night, but unbeknownst to all of us Hank most likely didn't want them there. Hank didn't start cutting a fool yet in that area. Why they thought my love would change toward them is beyond me. If it's up to me, family is always welcome. Silvia was kind enough to drive Butterscotch eight hours to her home in Virginia so that she could babysit him for the two weeks we were on our moon.

One of my aunts on my father's side passed away and we all journeyed to Philadelphia for the funeral, but Hank did not go. Silvia and her then new husband Lester were there. I didn't know Lester and he didn't know me. Immediately I saw Lester's arrogant approach toward me and I said to myself, "Un huh, Silvia was talking about me to him too." Personally as an adult, I don't base my actions toward a person on what someone else tells me about them when both parties are outsiders. However, when it comes to family, every relationship should be individualized. For me, if an outsider comes up against family then they have to come up against me too. Lester would move any time I was next to him as if he didn't like me. He didn't want me near him without even knowing me, other than what he had heard. With Lester being oblivious to my being on to him I chased him all over the church. I stood next to him every time he moved, and I was tickled on the inside pretending like I didn't know, and he just kept running, and I kept following him. I stood next to him at a little take-out next door, I tried to sit next to him for the repast, and he had no clue that I had already peeped his card. I didn't like him very much after that.

My niece Tabatha got married and requested her Uncle Hank to perform the ceremony, but as always Hank wanted to hurt me, and didn't even attend her wedding let alone perform the ceremony. He gave the excuse of having to be out of State at the bishop's meeting, but he could have gotten out of it if he wanted to. Hank paid our driver to take Salena and me to Virginia for the wedding and back the same day. My niece ended up with a pastor that reminded me of Jerome from the sitcom "Martin," but the venue was absolutely gorgeous.

    I was so happy to see Silvia and I didn't care what she thought or said about me because I love her, but only she can do that, not her husband, and not her stupid friend. My sister cannot divorce me and she will get over it. I could have told Silvia how I was living, but I continued to take my lumps and be beat down by the world around me and by Hank. Obviously I put on a good front for my family too. I actually felt less fortunate than my sisters, let alone to think I'm better than they are.

    I was walking down the hallway upstairs in Silvia's house and I crossed paths with her friend, so Tabatha said in introduction, "This is Lydia," and then Feefee, I believe that's her name, said boldly, "Oooh *this* is Lydia." Now wait a minute, did that tramp think I was born just the day before? What the heck was the meaning of that? "*This* is Lydia," so what had she heard? It was Silvia badmouthing me again. I was going to turn Silvia's house out but it was my niece's big day so I sucked it up. I truly would have knocked Feefee. That was like talking about me to me, she could have had more tact about it. Just the simple fact that she thought I was stupid and couldn't pick up on her blatant innuendos, I wanted to reach out to her. I never told Silvia what Feefee said.

    Up until now if my mother is sitting on a couch or sofa chair, I will wedge my way down behind her with my feet balled up underneath my buttocks so that I'm comfortably squished between the couch and my mom. Well to prove a point to Lester and Feefee, I did that same thing to Silvia when I was there because she's *my* sister, and she can do what she wants to do but they can't. I got behind her on her sofa chair or whatever it was and squeezed myself in just to grind it in for those two. I wanted to say, "Ha ha ha, I'm sitting on my sister and all of that talk she did meant nothing, she is still *my* sister."

My life wasn't easy; I caught hell outside, from family and friends, then I caught hell at home; but I kept my head up, and with all the pain I still continued to praise God.

Silvia would come back home to the New York area, not say she's in town, and stay with Feefee, claiming that I didn't want her at my house. I finally told Silvia "You are welcome, the next time you come please stay here with Hank and me." That would have fixed her; I bet she would have never come back!

Chapter Thirty Two

I'm not sure if the term "Opposites attract," only goes for humans, or does it relate to professions as well? I pose that question because Hank doesn't like people, but strangely enough he's in the people business. As pastor and first lady there were many events throughout the years that we've attended, and before we could even get there he'd be in the car talking about how he's getting out of there as soon as he gets a chance. We didn't have fun at home and he refused to allow us to have fun anywhere else.

We would walk in dressed to the nines and smelling good, but we were empty shells. I was like a beautiful box with nothing inside, as far as possessing the components of a marriage were concerned. Hank and his rude personality stripped all of the wifely feelings for a husband that I had toward him away, leaving only the love for family and mankind. Thank

God that within I'm happy by nature and I've always possessed an unspeakable joy that will never cease.

I always drove to all of the functions. Once we were there, whether or not I was enjoying myself, talking to someone, or eating, he would rush me. If I took another *five* minutes, literally speaking; he'd get loud, blow up his face and say, "Give me the keys, I'm leaving," and he would do that in front of whoever was standing in earshot. I could never understand how he could instantly get fiery mad at me just because *he* wanted to leave. He wanted to rush home because he had a standing need to withdraw from society and retreat back to what was familiar; going in his room, smoking, drinking, and slumping right back into depression mode; that was his life, and he wanted it to be mine too.

Years prior to Tabatha's wedding, Hank and I drove out of State for Silvia's oldest daughter Brandy's wedding which was on our wedding anniversary, and he made me leave there early too just as the dancing portion began. My entire immediate family was there but I had to leave which was terribly upsetting. He was as nasty as he could be for no reason. I pretended in front of my family to be in agreement with Hank and that we had to leave for whatever reason, when in actuality I was being dominated by his depression and evilness. Silvia thought that was another one of my "I'm better than everybody" acts.

Making sure that he wasn't a part of my family and that I wasn't a part of his was Hank's favorite past time. He would always repeat what he said to me to Gertrude over the phone saying, "I told her your family isn't my family, I don't have anyone here in this area, I'm not a part of your family, and you're not a part of mine, you're no Defenbar, you're a Bonner." He wanted me to hate my family, and I presume, thought he could accomplish that by constantly talking bad about them.

When I was working a nine to five, speaking to Hank and my mother every day was the norm. One day in a conversation, I mentioned talking to my mother every day from work and Hank lost his mind. He couldn't believe that I spoke to my mother daily and thought he could stop me from speaking to her, but I stood my ground.

I said to him, "It's not even on your time, you're not at my job with me so why do you care who I talk to from there? And if it *was* from home, how dare you tell me when I should and shouldn't talk to my mother!"

Well that was a big fight, and he said, "I should have moved you away from your family so that you wouldn't have anyone, because you will never be anything around them."

What a cruel thing to say to someone. Does he not know that all that I am is because of my family? If it wasn't for my strong family and upbringing Hank would have had me in the crazy house believing all of that crap he was slinging. He purely did not want me to have a family, and he despised it.

Here's the kicker, Hank would always brag about how wonderful and nice the relationship was between his secretary at church and her daughter who lived in another State. He'd tell me constantly of how they spoke on the phone everyday and touched base. Was he serious? He'd then speak about how he admired the closeness of some of the families in the church. Really Hank? He is one twisted brother. That's it! I have yet another name for him, "Pretzelman."

I also named him "DIP," and only the lady that sat next to me in the choir and Sis. Arletha knew what it meant. I would only use it if I wasn't happy with Hank. They thought it was love taps because I appeared to be so calm about it, but they had no idea that it was knock-down drag-outs and that I meant it when I called him DIP. I would say,

"Here comes DIP," and one of them would respond, "What did he do now?" I'd just laugh. DIP is the acronym for "Devil In the Pulpit."

It was automatic and a sure thing that I kept my marital anguish far from members, but for laughs I would insinuate at times when we were at odds. We would be leaving the church and I'd look back at someone and lip motion, "Help me!" and we would crack up laughing and Hank wouldn't even know why. When around others I'd always try to make light of the situation.

Chapter Thirty Three

I'm a heavy sleeper and when I was younger my father used to say that someone can knock the house down and I wouldn't know it. I told Hank about this long ago, therefore he was well aware of my sleeping behavior.

I was buffeted with evil from can to can't which is pronounced, kin-ta-kaint, meaning, from the time you can(kin) see, to the time you can't(kaint)see. An argument didn't have to be in session for Hank to harass me; I believe my existence upset him and he'd be angry with me as I slept.

"Lydia!" Hank screamed from the top of his lungs and it nearly frightened me to death. His intentions must have been to give me a heart attack screaming me out of my sleep like that so early in the morning. My heart was pounding so fast and before I could get it together he was barking at me with such anger, "Where is the other cordless phone, this one is dead?"

I handed him the phone without saying a word. I was so angry that he was capable of being extremely evil to another human being, especially for such a minuscule situation such as a phone needing to be charged. That wasn't the only time he did that. Another time he screamed me out of my sleep in the same manner trying to cause me to have a heart attack was to ask me in a ruthless tone of voice, "Does the garbage man come today?" It was after a holiday, but he seemed to have been mad at *me* because *he* didn't know if the garbage man came that day.

 Although absolutely nothing warranted that behavior, in giving him the benefit of the doubt of not having a prompt, I assumed that he had to have been annoyed that I was on the phone the night before with Lamont, but could that have been the issue both times? Hank only argues, yells, and barks at me; yet, he had the audacity to complain that I talked to everyone else more than I talked to him. Uh, duh. When Hank initially started complaining that I talked to others more, it was a lie. He only said that in hopes of making me feel guilty so that I wouldn't speak to anyone else at all especially my family because that's the type of nasty person he was to me. However, it manifested to be true because you *will* have what you say besides the fact that he had become unbearable to talk to on any subject. He would fight me on the bible. I learned and made an effort to not talk to him which took time because it's hard for me not to talk to the only other person that lives in the same house as I do. Being normal I'd find myself talking to him, then after he would start a fight in two minutes is when I'd remember *not* to talk to him.

 I took Hank's crap as much as I could before permanently putting any particular activity on the list of *"Things to never do again in life with Hank."* The top three answers on the board were: never go on vacation with Hank again; never go to the movies with Hank again; and never have sex with Hank again (as the term "Making love" had ceased many years prior.)

Each time we'd go on vacation, Hank would be arguing before the plane was airborne. I would still grab his hand and pray out loud prior to takeoff and that was one prayer he never rejected. There's something about an airplane that will cause a person to accept prayer. On and off throughout every trip were arguments about any and everything, but I still wouldn't give up and would go on the next trip until the deal breaker.

We went on a 10 day vacation to Aruba and didn't speak the entire time. It was horrible having to share a room with him but at least I was smart enough to book double beds. I carried on in activities alone trying not to ruin my time. Every day I'd go outside the hotel, catch a crowded banana bus for one dollar and ride downtown to the mall. The entire bus was a crayon box; it had replicas of large pieces of fruit on top, extremely colorful sides with no glass in the windows, and it was so packed with natives that I had to squeeze on. I'd go into the internet café and pay hourly to use the computer so that I could talk on IM to Mary Ellen and Essie all day. I had spa treatments, browsed the mall, and also went to the casinos.

On a trip to our second home he became so angry that he actually went to the airport and caught a flight back to New York without telling me. I thought he went to the store or something just to get away. The next thing I knew, I received a phone call and the caller ID displayed the number from my primary residence in New York and it was Hank. He actually got on the plane and left me. THAT WAS THE DEAL BREAKER!!

Nothing could be done in peace; being around Hank had become burdensome. I pushed and pushed, exhausting all of my Godly means to be nice. I nonchalantly tried to extinguish fires when I saw one starting, and also attempted to do activities that would make him happy rather than him feeling depressed.

I would suggest for us to go out to see a movie and would have to practically force him into going. One time I was able to get him to consent but I lived to regret it.

The theatre was a multiplex and it was crowded with people from all walks of life. Being in the positions we were in, we never knew who may have seen us that knew us or who we were, although we may not have known them. However, there were times we saw those we did know.

Our first stop like most people was to the concession stand for popcorn and soda. We then walked over to the self help butter, salt, and napkins station and I proceeded to butter the popcorn. I put a little butter and salt then bounced the bag on the counter to shake it down and repeated those steps until satisfied. A few popcorn kernels spilled as always because they fill the popcorn higher than the bag.

In a crowded lobby with people everywhere, Hank started screaming at me and making an evil face saying, "Look at you spilling popcorn, what are you doing!" At first I thought he was joking because it was way too many people there to be acting out like that, and what was the big deal? Sometimes it appeared as if he didn't know who he was because he had no problem being very conspicuous. It mystified me that he didn't care if someone saw a pastor acting that way. I would always try to shush him in public in such a way to remind him that people may see him and he's a pastor, but he never cared at all and would get louder. Out of embarrassment I didn't look at anyone and I quietly asked Hank if he wanted to go home. He became louder and said, "I'll go home!" He wouldn't take a hint, nor be quiet or stop, so I just started walking away from him fast, then up the stairs toward the theater and he followed me. THAT WAS THE DEAL BREAKER!!!

There was another unforgettable incident at a large church during the opening of an Annual Conference where there were many people everywhere resembling that of being on a New York subway. Hank shouted at me and blew up his face and I was so embarrassed because everyone knew who we were. Thankfully I was standing right in front of a set of stairs and I just took off running down them, hoping that no one paid any attention.

I don't know if it was amnesia, Alzheimer's or what, but many times after those unforgettable events he'd say to me in an argument as if to guilt me, "We don't go on vacations anymore like we used to, we don't go to the movies anymore, we don't do anything." I became speechless every time I heard him say that and I refused to remind him of his behavior from the last deal breaking incident. He's a grown man and should have known exactly what he's done. I let him talk all he wanted to and still wouldn't go anywhere with him. I just refused to explain as I no longer had patience for him.

Contrary to popular belief, Hank's favorite food is steak, not pig's feet, so I took him to a prominent steak house for his birthday one year and he started an argument at the table. The bad thing about him is that he gets loud so everyone can hear, maybe he was *trying* to embarrass me, I don't know. He would do that at every restaurant and make a scene, sometimes getting up and storming off. His behavior was always abnormal and I could have crawled under the table. One night after he cut up, I walked home from a Chinese restaurant that was two towns over. On his way home he drove right pass me and didn't stop. I made it home hours later in the dark but it was peaceful.

Another time when we were out of town, we went to a large grocery store with my parents and one of my sisters, and Hank showed out. Right in the parking lot with many other shoppers Hank started screaming at me and stormed off like a maniac. He then turned back around and started pointing and yelling at me. My family didn't say a word; we were terribly embarrassed. Although we were married, there still should have been a level of respect in front of my parents and the public. He could have shown couth, at least waiting until we were alone, but by then he would have forgotten what it was about because it was so small. It was either about the space I chose to park in or my suggestion of what was next on our agenda for the day. Hank showed no sense of tact. He was working very hard and diligently to murder our marriage.

Chapter Thirty Four

There are some people in the ministry that simply *went* rather than having been *sent* by God. My personal experience in being called is when God sets you on a path to do something that you ordinarily in the natural wouldn't do and have no desire to do if it were by choice; yet, you are compassionate about it and compelled to do so.

I was called into the ministry to teach Christians about God's Word on divine healing. I would teach once a week with a determination to get people to understand that God's Word still works today and will work forever more. The thing about ministry is that it's not based on your personal feelings, being selfish, or biased. If you want one person saved or healed, then you should want all people saved and healed.

Regardless of what was going on in our personal lives, I wanted Hank healed and would pray the prayer of faith over him anointing him with oil against any infirmity that tried to come against him. I would lay hands on Hank from anything as small as the common cold to a tooth ache along with any medical diagnosis that he may have received.

    I teach from what I know, not from what I think. I was diagnosed with having a fairly large cyst on one of my ovaries, and was told that surgery was necessary for correction. I prayed the prayer of faith, spoke with my mouth, and believed; after a month or two it disappeared. The doctor couldn't figure out what happened, so I told her and everybody else in that office *exactly* what happened. As a result of teaching that class I've seen lupus, asthma, and arthritis healed.

    My ministry is a tough one because it's very difficult to get people to believe opposite of what's been ingrained in their minds for centuries that man deems incurable, like a cancer. It's when you can get pass that and truly focus, believe, and have faith in only God's Word, that your healing manifestation will take place by way of just claiming the Word. There are also other ways to receive healing, but my focus was an in-depth study of receiving it through speaking the Word.

    I believed that Hank could be healed from depression and alcoholism, but he would have needed to admit to being hindered by those things. Hank's addictions became worse after he felt that he had someone on his side from my family no less, to agree with his accusations concerning me. Once Hank believed Gertrude's words in saying that I thought I was in love with someone else, he stopped eating, started drinking more, and smoking weed not caring about himself. What Reverend Defenbar believed Gertrude said nearly killed him. For years he didn't handle it well constantly throwing Gertrude's name in my face every day, which is why people should mind their own business. If you don't live with a person, then you don't know the person or how they would handle a particular issue and it ends up doing more harm than good. Hank's body weight was zapped and it embarrassed me, thanks to a bunch of no good talking and stinking thinking.

Upon arriving home one night I discovered that Hank hadn't eaten all day as was the case on many days, and I felt obligated to help him. He reeked of liquor and cigarettes, looked like a skeleton, he hadn't shaved, and white whiskers were everywhere. I suggested we go to the diner, at least he could get something to eat. It was late night and as we sat in the diner I was hoping no one we knew would walk in, seeing his condition. Wouldn't you know it, within minutes, in walked two pastors that we knew well and I said to myself, "Oh God, oh God." Each of them hugged Hank and I wanted to go under the table. Hank was as drunk as a skunk, his eyes were red, and he looked troubled, foreign, and zoned out. Hank was literally bones with skin attached. I was no-where near as close as a hug and he reeked at a distance, so I can imagine how they talked about him. Those guys were huge and it must have felt like they were hugging a broomstick. They stood there talking and Hank wouldn't give them direct eye contact. I just wanted them to leave and get away from us. I don't think I've ever felt worse and embarrassed beyond belief.

I was always too sympathetic to talk to Hank about his condition, even at home. I didn't want to embarrass him about his problem, and it would have just been an argument starter anyway because he didn't think he had a problem. We never discussed the diner incident as I always wanted to make him feel normal. My goodness if the tables were turned he would have delighted in dogging me about my condition.

I did everything I could to not add fuel to the fire by trying to avoid doing things that Hank didn't like whether or not I felt he was right or wrong. Hank hated me talking on the phone to anyone. He has yelled at me about talking to my sisters, my mom, my friends, and my cousins. I have never said one thing to him nor did I care who he talked to on the phone, or for how long. I didn't see what the big deal was. I didn't want to hear any fuss if I could help it, so I'd always whisper when I was on the phone and if I heard him coming I would stop talking.

I was on the phone with crazy Lamont, and Hank was coming up the stairs thinking I was asleep, so I whispered quickly and softly, "Here he come, here he come, here he come," and Lamont whispered back, "Play dead." It took all I had not to laugh at "Play dead," and so that became our thing. I would get quiet all of a sudden on the phone at times because light-footed Hank would sneak up on me before I could warn Lamont so he'd be on the other end saying, "Hello, hello," and I would say as low as possible, "I'm playing dead." It had become the norm, but who lives like that?

Chapter Thirty Five

I have visions and goals in life, and I see a bright future with an expected end as promised in the book of Jeremiah 29:11. Years ago in the midst of my trials, I put together a vision board with photos of tangible items on it and the intangible desires were written. I continually thank God for both the intangible and tangible things I desire in my life even if they haven't yet manifested. I've been thanking Jehovah Shalom for peace in the midst of hell, not *asking* Him for it, but *thanking* Him for it.

Surely God had to deliver me from that place that I was in mentally, spiritually, and physically because nothing was coinciding with His plan. As an entrepreneur it's impossible to succeed playing dead all the time, not wanting to get up to use the computer because I had to pass by Hank, not wanting Hank to know I was awake in order to capture a moment of peace, walking on eggshells, and not expressing myself or being who I am just because he'll turn anything into an argument. I only have one life to live, and I'm determined to accomplish my goals. The aforementioned issues were holding me back from working which was a contributing factor to the deal breaker. Gotta go, gotta go, as a comedian used to say.

It was inevitable that Hank and I separate, divorce, end it, because he had been saying he wanted a divorce literally for the entire time of our marriage. He'd say it during insignificant arguments which would throw me off. He threw that 'd' word around as if it meant nothing, but I knew better. In the beginning I would always tell him not to say that because he will cause it to manifest; but after years of pure hell, I welcomed it, knowing that the more he said it, the quicker it would happen.

Hank came upstairs as I was multitasking; cleaning the house, folding laundry, and typing emails to clients interchangeably and I said, "Hank I have the pants to the jacket you're wearing, I'm folding them for you."
Hank loved wearing jogging suits. If it wasn't a fly pant suit, it was a jogging suit with shoes and dress socks.
Hank went all in, somehow he saw that as an argument and said in his oh so familiar hateful manner that pierces through me, "You're trying to move me out, you're trying to get rid of all my stuff."
That was one of those "Buck my eyes" situations that Mary Ellen would have asked what was she missing, and I would have bucked my eyes at her because my guess was as good as anybody else's. I didn't say anything so he went back down to the dungeon, well it was the dungeon for me, he had turned it into one.

Before I could exhale good, Hank was on his way back upstairs. Every time I would hear him heading my way, I cringed and thought, "Oh God, here he comes, please don't let him say anything to me." Well, that breath prayer didn't work, and neither did my lips. I let him talk because what he was saying was nothing more than unnecessary badgering, not worth a response.

He proceeded, "Lydia this isn't a marriage and it's bad for my health, I'd rather be alone and you need to be alone, you don't need to be married. You need to go back to the niggas you were fucking and spent time with." He then went back downstairs. Only if he knew the burning desire I had for those words, "I'd rather be alone, and you need to be alone," to come true. He actually said that as if to give me some rude awakening. I guess I was supposed to wake up from being this horrible whore of a person that didn't love or care about him and straighten up so that I wouldn't lose him. He was in denial thinking I probably still wanted to be married to him.

Being irrational was Hank's personality, he would bite his own nose to spite his face. He'd get angry with me and not eat. His favorite thing to do was to pile up all of the jewelry I'd ever given him, including his two wedding bands, and put them all on my dresser as if what? Was I supposed to cry, or feel bad, or say, "Oh no, not the jewels?" He did that for years, and by the time Sunday would roll around he had taken everything back. I never touched his jewelry when he'd do that and I never mentioned it, I just ignored him and left the jewelry there until he decided to collect it. I guess the fact that I always ignored the jewelry, provoked him to leave a note one day as well, it was so kindergarten and juvenile that I had to laugh to myself.

Also on my list of "Things to never do again in life with Hank," is not to ride any length of time with him in a car, alone or with people, it didn't matter; it could be church folk, kin folk, or any folk. I should've had one of those automatic talking things put on his cars that would remind me and tell me, "PLEASE BACK AWAY FROM THE CAR." However, I didn't think five minutes would be a problem but I've learned that one minute was a problem. Hank had to bring up something controversial so that he could fight.

In the town next to ours about five minutes away is a large fishing dock and we'd go there to eat or either purchase fresh fish at times. On our way there one day, he got ugly and told me that his secretary and others wanted to know why I didn't ride to church with him. He didn't know that church was too far for me to be getting into his vehicle, it was like ten minutes away, much too much too far.

I never mentioned, discussed, or told Hank due to his irrationality, that there was a "Do not do with Hank" list. No matter what he's done to me over all those years, I wouldn't knowingly hurt his feelings. Besides, his temper had him extremely unapproachable and he would just turn everything on me and start an argument. The simplest things couldn't be discussed.

Although it wasn't their business, I was protecting Rev. Defenbar from being exposed as to why I wouldn't ride with him. I let him know that I would tell them it's not their business, and he knew I would because homey don't play that. Of course he turned it on me and started a fight. He tried to tell me--when he doesn't know because obviously he was pastoring a church in a different city --that the previous first lady rode with her husband. I quickly reminded him that there was a parking space designated for the first lady and proceeded to ask him whether or not it was for an invisible car. Obviously she drove at times. Might I add that I don't care whether or not she drove, rode, walked or ran, I was *not* riding with Rev. Defenbar!! Unfortunately, there were unavoidable occasions that I ended up riding with him in spite of my efforts not to.

When we returned home he took the fish he had purchased for me back like a kid. I had been inundated with Hank's insignificant, malicious, and premeditated arguments and I refused to be subject to his harassment that night, so I decided to leave and I slammed the door as I left. I went to my girlfriend Myra's house and stayed there until twelve midnight drinking coffee. I always skimmed the surface with her about what was really going on because she's one of those judgmental Christians that lives in a glass house, but I loved her all the same. We have to learn to meet people where they are. Myra put sixty dollars in my hand one night just because, and it was a blessing, she had a good heart. We had become like sisters and would do anything for each other.

I arrived back home and Hank started again. Out of frustration he hit my laptop, but I honestly don't believe he realized it was my computer that he hit. He actually pushed me or shoved me when I walked by him, but I didn't do anything except to keep walking. I told him that if I hit him I'd kill 'em. He had become feeble, and I on the other hand don't miss a meal. I'm full of collard greens and all, me eat me spinach. When I went into my bedroom Hank had his pile of jewelry on my dresser with a note that said "THE END," and that tickled me so much. I then realized that he took the telephone, so I went to the twenty-four hour pharmacy and purchased a cordless phone for ten dollars. When I returned home I barricaded myself and Butterscotch in the room, then slept peacefully after talking to Lamont until three-thirty in the morning and watching funny YouTube clips together.

There is a gold refinery practically around the corner from where we lived where you can sell gold and get paid the market price on the spot. Well I put an end to Hank piling up his jewelry on my dresser. I broke him out of that crap and he never did it again, no matter how harsh the argument. That time when he eventually collected his jewels back he noticed a missing bracelet and asked me had I seen it, and I said no. He knew I sold it but couldn't say a word because after all, he gave it back; therefore, it was mine. I bet that fixed him. Gold was at an all time high and I got around seven hundred dollars for that one heavy bracelet. Now *that* was the end! You couldn't pay Hank to put his jewelry on my dresser again.

Hank had started a great regimen of going to the boardwalk to meditate early in the morning to get a little exercise. He said it helped him. I must confess that looking at the vastness of the ocean that God created was indeed serene.

The next morning I got up early and left to get my coffee around 6:30am before Hank returned from his walk. In my meditation, God spoke through His Word in the book of Romans 4:13-25. This Word encouraged me to go on in faith and that my faith was not going unnoticed by God, but that He keeps His promises. I know that regardless of what I see, feel, hear, taste, or smell, I am gloriously abounding in and reaping God's promises. Never ever give up!

Chapter Thirty Six

My love for the Word is sincere, and it's only about the Word. Regardless of the arguments on Sunday mornings or Saturday nights, I would still go to church because I was compelled to do so and it was a part of me, of who I was and still am. Hank would say things like, "I wish you would find another church, don't come to my church, and if you come I'll embarrass you." I didn't care what he said. As far as I was concerned, the church is God's house not his; and I wasn't missing the Word, although coming out of DIP's mouth. Had I stayed home angry, I would have *never* been in church.

Sometimes Hank would get in the pulpit and preach about himself, he preached against the very things that *he* did. He goes into depth about how in Christ we're a new creation, that old things are passed away and how satan will bring up your past; yet, although he knows nothing derogatory about my past because there is nothing, Hank would tell me about what he thought I used to be and curse me out as soon as we got home. It was obvious that he didn't believe anything he was saying because he wouldn't have married me, he just stopped at nothing to try to offend and hurt me. Unfortunately he was unable or unwilling to live by what he preached.

I hold the sanctuary in the highest regard, fully understanding that even the parking lot is Holy ground but the sanctuary is the sanctuary. Hank doesn't respect the sanctuary at all when it comes to being mean to me. One Sunday, I was truly shocked at the words he whispered in my ear.

On occasion my parents would miss church for whatever the reason, and every time without failure I would get cursed out by Reverend Defenbar when we got home. Neither of us knew why they weren't in church until I called afterwards. However, Hank would say, "They don't support me," and he'd go on and on disrespecting their character which provoked me to defend them causing a mega fight. He thought it was about him and it wasn't, people should go to church to serve God not the pastor. I would tell him I'm not responsible for them coming to church, they're grown, and why was he worried about what they did? He tried to use anything he could to turn me against my parents. I believe he thought that if he badmouthed them I wouldn't like them. At times it seemed as if he thought I'd agree with him but I never did and never will. I always told him that it's between them and God and that it wasn't any of his business. He would say it *was* his business. Needless to say, I had to fight every time they didn't come to church. When I didn't see them I'd think to myself, "Oh God, why didn't they come to church?" I would secretly always try forcing them to church when I knew beforehand if they weren't coming but I wouldn't tell them why. I only felt that way because I knew I had to fight. Unbeknownst to Hank, during service I would go to his office as if I was going to the rest room and call my parents to see why they weren't in church. I wanted to have an answer ready for Hank, hoping it would be good enough for him not to argue with me. Early on I was still on this thing about trying to please Hank.

After years of that and the worse our relationship grew, I finally just told him off and said, "If you want to know why they didn't come to church call them and ask them dammit, and if they don't want to come to church they don't have to!" He eventually left me alone about that in our last year or so of being together in the same house.

My mother isn't one to run down to the altar if and when there's an altar call, or one to stand up on every little thing, she has her own inward way of expressing her love to God. My parents sat a few rows behind me and because I don't turn around in church I never knew what they did or didn't respond to. Pastor Defenbar would always tell me, "Oh your mother didn't even stand up, I don't know what's wrong with her, and she never has an expression on her face."
And……he was telling me that because……..?

My dad on the other hand would join me at the altar for altar calls or prayer etc., but that didn't make me love my mother any less nor is there anything that can. Everyone shows their expression in different ways. Hank would proudly mention from the pulpit how *his* mother stood in one spot and shouted quietly in her spirit. First of all he has no idea what was going through his mother's head while she stood there quietly, she was a first lady, hello.

Four months prior to Hank's retirement he allowed a layperson to bring the Sunday morning message, and he sat on the front row next to me and things between us that particular morning were quiet for the most part. After the message was delivered, Reverend Defenbar commented on the speaker and asked all parents and children of all ages to come to the altar for prayer, so my father came up with me, but my mother chose to remain seated. It didn't bother me because that's mommy and I love her tremendously for who she is. Every individual has to work out their own soul salvation. Was it possible for Hank to think that I wouldn't like her or love her after that?

Pastor Defenbar looked dapper like any typical preacher; you could've picked him out of a line-up. He took his seat next to me after the altar call. Cocking his face up to the side and speaking out of the side of his mouth he audaciously whispered to me at least three to four times with his fist in front of his face to deter anyone from reading his lips and he said, "I wish I could beat your mother." That was outrageously unethical and he didn't say it in anger toward me that time, he was looking for my conformity.

I was devastated, I wanted to tell her, I wanted to tell my father, I wanted to punch him in his face right on the front pew, I wanted to scream! I sat there and smiled like the first lady and no one knew what that demon said to me in the sanctuary during worship service. How did he think he could tell *me* that he wished he could beat *my* mother, did he really think I would have agreed with him? I didn't want my parents smiling at him or talking to him, but there was nothing I could do because I didn't tell them. They didn't know how he always spoke poorly of them and it really hurt my feelings something awful. I didn't phone my sisters to tell them either, I kept it all in. I never said anything to Hank about it, how it hurt my feelings and how I didn't appreciate it because he was already a lost cause. Little did I myself know that God had a plan, and I would be gone out of that relationship in eight months.

Four months down the road, had my parents not showed up at his retirement dinner, Hank would have lost it and claimed how hurt he was by their not supporting him, claiming that they don't recognize him as family. It's only always about him. He is a good one to be able to dish it, but he can't take it. When he called me a name, especially in the beginning of that relationship, and I yelled back and called him that same *exact* name, he would go bananas. For instance, he would say, "You stupid bitch," and I would say to him, "You're a stupid bitch," then his response was, "Did you just call me a stupid bitch?" He said that as if he was surprised. He was like that with everything, he could dish it out but the same exact thing he couldn't take, and I called him everything he called me, plus some.

Anytime I made a subtle comment around my parents insinuating that I can't stand Hank or that he's crazy, my mother would always come to his defense and say, "Oh well, all old men are crazy, just be nice to him." She never got it because I never told her. Mom is from the old school anyway, of staying with your husband no matter what.

Hank allowed satan to work through him and use the church as his playground. I could imagine hearing the devil saying, "Lydia thinks she's going to get away from me because she's at church?" The only thing Hank didn't allow that demon to do was *curse* in the church house.

Hank was nasty as well to officers and clergy that were his subordinates. They saw that demon rearing his ugly head too at times. One Sister told me that he got so nasty with her in discussing an issue that she thought he was getting ready to curse. Another came to me and said, "I don't know how you do it." Mind you, they were saying that from what they saw at church only. I personally witnessed Hank in his office yelling at an elderly clergy woman after service in a reprimanding fashion for having corrected him in the pulpit during a secular announcement detail that he got backwards. I was very embarrassed and angry, but I waited until we got home and lit in on him like never before. That time the abusive verbal consequences wasn't a factor, I didn't care what his response was going to be, so I set him on fire metaphorically speaking, and told him not to ever speak to someone like that again.

My niece Salena gave my father her white SUV because she got a new car. At one of my bumps in the road I was without a car and my father allowed me to use his SUV for a day or two. That truck was a sure blessing although when on the highway I couldn't drive it under forty or over fifty miles per hour to prevent it from malfunctioning. One Sunday when I arrived at church the secretary was parked in my space as she often did when she assumed I would be riding with the pastor. I would park my car perpendicular to hers directly behind her, blocking her in, and I'd take my time after service as usual, and she couldn't leave until I left or until someone came and found me to let her out. I did that to anyone that parked in my space although it rarely happened. She was a sweetheart about it however, and she started to call me on Sunday mornings to ask if I'll be riding with the pastor or not.

On the Sunday that I had my dad's SUV, I parked behind Pastor Defenbar due to a guest speaker utilizing my space, and Pastor Defenbar was in nasty mode that Sunday letting the devil use him. My intentions weren't to block Pastor Defenbar in, it was where I parked instead of on the street. I was running late that Sunday and it was understandably assumed by Rev. Defenbar that I wasn't coming. After service I immediately went to move the SUV and Hank was already in his car. He saw me in his rear view mirror getting into the truck and before I could pull up, he backed into the passenger's door of my dad's SUV hitting it on purpose disregarding his own car as well. I was livid. Thank God it didn't damage my dad's car. My parents weren't in church that day so I went to their house to tell my father what happened and he grew angry and said, "Shiiit, he can't be backing into *my* damn truck because he's mad at you!" I was able to calm him down only because there was no damage. God was on Hank's side that day. I went to Myra's house too after church that day and told her about it. I wonder if any of the members had watched that happen.

Oft times I'd walk in the house and Hank would be sitting on the couch downstairs just staring, seemed like into space, and smoking cigarettes. The television would be on a music channel with a black screen displaying the composer's name and song details in the corner. I know how he likes to feel sorry for himself as on many occasions he has shouted and said, "Nobody gives a damn about me, and never has; and you Lydia, don't give a damn about me." I never responded to that, I couldn't change his mind anyway. When I would see him on the couch like that is when I began to realize that when he wasn't studying the Word he just sat in pity, thinking hard, meditating on everything negative like what could he complain about, what could he do to be mean to me, and why he hated his life. His face looked lost and sad. It was almost like I could see satan whispering in his ear. He would always admit openly from the pulpit how satan always messed with him telling him this and that. My only concern was, if he knew it was satan, why in the world did he listen to him? Personally I don't talk to the devil, I curse him and that's about it. I would try to explain that to Hank, but who was I and how dare I entertain the thought that I could tell him anything; after all he's the theologian, which is what he'd always remind me of, and it would end up in a fight.

One of those couch and staring times he said to me, "I told my secretary that she can have that parking space on Sundays because she parks there during the week and she's the secretary, not you. My secretary should have somewhere to park, not you."

When he said that it actually was degrading and it hurt. It's bad enough to belittle and disrespect me at home, but he went way too far and displayed his disrespect toward me to his secretary and whoever else she wanted to tell. He was abusing his authority as the ultimate voice on decision making at the cost of stripping me of who I was and the title I held by default of being his wife. I felt embarrassed but yet I handled it in my own way and in less than a week he changed it back.

I made sure to drive to church alone that very next Sunday. I parked across the main street which was in front of the church, instead of the back parking lot that was always full. I went down the block that was perpendicular to the front doors of the church, got out sporting a big fancy hat, and walked to the church. Everything went according to my plan and of course either before or after service someone saw me and asked why I parked down the road. Right in front of big time Reverend Defenbar I got loud and said, "Oh, the pastor gave my parking space to his secretary so I have to walk and that's where I'll be parking from now on." Boy oh boy did that embarrass him and he switched it back that same day. Did Hank really think that he was going to play the player? Child BOO!

Chapter Thirty Seven

Anything I ever did had to have a suspicious motive behind it, as far as Hank was concerned. I mentioned to him that I was going to lose weight, like any woman mentions to her husband, especially when he always says how fat she is, or in this case how fat I was.
His response was, "For who?"
"For myself and my health, besides, everyone is looking nice and fit at the events that I attend."
I had begun to network with the rich and famous, frequenting their homes, castles, and penthouses through meeting the right people and making the right connections. I made friends that touched my heart and we became close due to their sincerity, realism, and genuineness. I had to start working on what it was that I wanted in life, and I needed desperately to make a way to get out of that house away from Hank. The only thing that was down the road any further with Hank was more

mental and spiritual beat downs that I'd have to continue combating to my grave. *The devil is a lie!*

Hank responded, "I'm not jealous! When I start going to the football games and looking good, I'll be around a lot of women."

Ok, he said that as if I cared, wow, denial, denial, denial.

I said to him, not as a question but as a matter of fact, "Ok, so you're going to gain weight."

My honest opinion was that if he intended to look good, it was obvious he'd have to gain weight. That conversation ended and went well so I thought. About ten minutes later I was working on my laptop in my room minding mine, and here comes that buster out of nowhere, I guess he had a conversation with the devil again.

Hank didn't realize that his lack of confidence overshadowed the guilt he was attempting to bestow upon me, and through falsification he responded, "You know you're always putting me down, and talking about how I look, I knew you were going to start doing that."

"What did I say? I never put you down."

Hank wanted to fight, but I honestly didn't know where he was coming from, and what he was talking about.

He then said, "I know you're waiting for me to die."

I was so tired of his perpetual pity party and refused to play into it any longer, so I said, "No, wait until I get insurance on you, then die."

He finally walked away all depressed. He seemed to never learn to stop messing with me because every time he would get his feelings hurt. He's the one that ended up behind a closed door, mad, depressed, hungry, losing sleep, and pouting while I was going about my daily routine, and yes, eating and sleeping. I may have been barricaded, but I was sleeping.

I don't want to be misleading on the barricade issue, there are roads that took me there and one road came about in a horrendous manner, almost in inches of my life. When he would argue and start snowballing I'd go into the master bedroom, which was eventually designated my room, and I'd close the mirrored door and lock it. Thanks to Scooter we had locks! I'd turn the volume up on the television as loud as it would go and let him stand out there in the hallway talking to himself where I couldn't hear him.

Being that the master bedroom had become my domain, I used a thick magic marker and wrote in large lettering on the mirrors encouraging words to myself, scriptures that I didn't want to forget, and a list of the names of God. I wrote things like, "Faith without works is dead," and "I will not procrastinate, I will be productive today," so that I would be reminded that I needed to work no matter what, in order to generate funds so that I can leave. Next to each of God's names I wrote the meaning, i.e.; Jehovah Tsidkenu, The Lord our Righteousness; Jehovah Rapha, The Lord that Healeth; Jehovah Nissi, The Lord our Banner; and El Shaddai, God Almighty; etcetera. There had to be about twelve names in all which enabled me to call on El Elyon, The Lord Most High as needed in an appropriate manner.

We were in a screaming match one night so I closed and locked my bedroom door as had become custom and Hank was going crazy banging and banging. I turned around to face the door and as I did he kicked it in and the entire glass trim broke and a huge piece of glass fell in toward me about a half inch from my chest, dead center. Had I been less than an inch closer to the door it would have went right through my heart, but JESUS!!! Oh, they that dwell, they that dwell, they that dwell. Had the glass on the back of the actual door itself fell, then I would have been a goner for sure. The lock was busted out completely, and has never been repaired, hence barricades! Hank did not apologize or anything, he kept on arguing after seeing all of the glass on the floor, and I told him that it almost killed me. I still protected Hank and told no one.

Although that was a scary and very sad situation, I had to wonder was it on purpose or did Hank forget that there were mirrors everywhere and glass on the back of the bedroom door.

I prayed and tarried before my altar more than ever, continuing to keep a smile on my face. I desperately wanted out of that marriage and out of that relationship being totally away from Hank. I wanted and needed to experience life without Hank. In the last couple of years living in that house, the stress started to set in and I would get tight, and I don't mean the slang word "Tight," I literally mean my neck, shoulders, and back would just tighten up. It had gotten so bad that my physician had to prescribe ten milligrams of muscle relaxers to me. It's not worth compromising peace to the mind, body, and soul, for anything or anyone.

While the hope of *ever* getting out of that marriage seemed to have been fading at one point, I had to consciously cast that imagination down because I was determined to never let my hope fade. I had to focus more on the truth, which is God's Word. All I had was my faith. I didn't have the funds necessary to move, nor did I want to start a scandal and leave while Hank was still pastoring which was synonymous to Hank's request. For a season I started to watch only Christian channels around the clock listening to the Word of God in order to stay strengthened and encouraged, I even forwent Lifetime and LMN.

God knew that my spirit was grieved and that I had become weary over the fact of feeling trapped, seeing no way out; so He started to send me the strangest signals that everything was being worked out on my behalf and was going to be alright. I have experienced this phenomenon lying on the bed, sitting on the couch, standing in my bedroom, walking down the hall, in my prayer closet, and crossing the threshold of my bedroom. Never having heard of this before, my spirit immediately knew it was a sign from God letting me know that He's watching me, He hears me, didn't forget about me, and that He was on the case. It always comforted me and gave me that extra strength that I needed to continue in withstanding the evil that lurked in my house. I thought it was an Angel, perhaps an Angel of protection, but now I understand it could have been God Himself.

It happened just about every day, multiple times per day, but only in the house wherever I was. The first time it happened I was lying on the bed when this beautiful fragrance, seemingly a mixture of perfume and a flower, would move pass my nose and vanish as fast as it arrived. I would jump up smelling all around in the air, then I'd sniff the blanket and pillows, lift my clothing to smell them too, and I couldn't find it anywhere. My first reaction was to say, "Thank you Lord, you sent an Angel," because my spirit immediately knew it was heavenly. When I'd walk through it going into my bedroom, I'd quickly back up thinking I'd back into it, but it had disappeared that fast. Sometimes it would be ten minutes later and there it was again. Likewise when walking through it down the hall I'd back up right quick but it was gone. That happened for the duration of my stay which ended up being another two years during a very dark time in my life dealing with Hank. I asked Hank if he ever smelled it, and he said no; I didn't think he did but I asked anyway.

I shared this with my students in the class that I taught at church. The minister there told me to say, "Yes Lord, I am here," the next time it happened so I did, but nothing other than the usual took place. I told Lamont and he said it must be a Guardian Angel to fight those demons that Hank brought in, which was a relevant hypothesis. I used to watch "Snapped," and thank God I was always safe. I always felt safe no matter what because I know that *NO* weapon formed against me will *EVER* prosper, and in the end I was delivered out of that house.

God always stepped in and made things happen, albeit seemingly always in the nth hour, a.k.a. "On time." When I didn't know what to say or how to approach the issue that I was finally packing up and shipping out, the perfect situation was presented to me along with the right words, all initiated by Hank. It only happened as easy as it did because I relied on, believed and trusted in God, and endured by faith.

At any time Hank would arbitrarily mention divorce and leaving, and I should've known that his mouth would be my ticket out. God had it all planned, but out of anxiousness I wasn't factoring in Hank's daily cruelty. Case in point; one evening I was in the kitchen preparing a meal and everything for that moment was quiet but nothing was ever fine because Hank lived in turmoil creating havoc for me, but that particular moment was quiet. Out of my peripheral vision I happened to see Hank coming up the stairs and immediately upon entering the kitchen he said, "Lydia, just let me say this." I knew it was controversial and trouble so I inwardly said, "Oh Lord, here we go." I hated every second of standing there, I hated breathing the same air that he did, I hated the tension, and my insides quivered at the sight of him and the sound of his voice.
He then said, "All I'm asking is that you just stay until I retire, I don't want another divorce in the church."
Ok, first of all I never spoke divorce to him as he did me, although I secretly always prayed for it, and we weren't even having a conversation so I was speechless and didn't respond. Hank is the only one that spoke negativity toward anything concerning us.

Once reality started to set in and there was only a year left until he retired, he got on the retirement kick. Every argument he would hammer me and say in his funkafied way, "After I retire, I'm leaving and getting a divorce." He put so much emphasis on that "l" in leaving and that "d" in divorce, that I thought his teeth was going to come out. He said it as if I was supposed to get scared, but rather I was expressionlessly elated.

I should have known that all I would have to do is to piggyback on his next outburst of saying he's leaving, but I was too nervous about finally leaving that I couldn't think that way.

Chapter Thirty Eight

There were many things that contributed to my mental and emotional state towards Hank, which strangely enough, he didn't appear to be aware of which was evident by listening to him talk.

There was never a reprieve for me to heal from a verbally abusive battle because before I could come up for air, I was hit with another verbally abusive battle. They were one after another; layer upon layer; day in, day out; month in, month out; and year in, year out. It was like someone holding me down with their foot on my neck as I'm struggling to scream, "Let me up for air, I can't breathe!"

I had become so immune to verbal abuse that I learned to keep my guard up around my heart, thereby still having enough stamina and human compassion to take care of Hank's health because *he* didn't care about his health. It didn't matter what he said or did to me, if it was in my power, I would do what I could in order to prevent him from getting sick as I was always concerned about his wellbeing.

Little did I myself know that time was winding down on that relationship. I was soon to be delivered, living alone in peace far away. God knows I was ready, as the marriage had run its course. God is so good that He sent me to a place that I knew not of, making it impossible that I could have remotely had anything to do with it.

I had no idea how many more years I'd have to go through being a silent sufferer, or how close I was to deliverance, but it didn't matter, I drew a blank of all abuse when it came to Hank's wellbeing.

Reflecting on yet another infamous day in the life of the Defenbars it started off on a normal note. Hank went for our morning coffee as he did the majority of the time, unless he was so upset and depressed that he didn't attempt to leave the house not even for coffee. Afterwards, he was picked up by our driver to be taken to the dentist in New York City. I took that opportunity to clean the house and then I drove to my office. I called him on the cell phone after his dentist appointment and told him that I was leaving the house but I did not tell him that I had cleaned.

He said in a surprised voice, because the hour was late for me to be leaving for my office, "You're just now leaving the house?"

"Yes, I'm just now leaving, on my way to the office."

He must have been acting in front of the driver because he started calling me "Sweetheart," joking around and laughing which was all unlike him. Then he called me "Sun," and told the driver, "I call her Sun not because she's mine, I call her Sun because she shines." Granted, he did say that dryly on occasion when he was okay, but at that stage in the game I was like, "Whoa, eew," to myself.

He then said to me, "I'm getting all of my doctor appointments out of the way today, so I'm going to my general practitioner now."

I said, "That's good, ok, I'll talk to you later."
Everything appeared to be going along fine, he bought coffee, he was kee keeing in the car and calling me pet names, etc. I waited a few hours and then I called him from my office to see how it went at the doctors.
He answered the phone, "Hello?"
"Hi Hank."
"Yeah, hi Lydia," he said all in a funkafied way.
I thought to myself, "Damn, he's all messed up, what now?" I started to get tight. Ignoring his aggravation, not to feed fuel to the fire I said, "So what happened at your doctor's appointment; what did the doctor say?"
He hesitated, then said with a nasty tone barking at me, "Uh, he asked me if I wanted to die."
I was as curious as ever because whatever it was, the doctor presented it as if it was Hank's fault.
I said, "Why did he say that, what happened?
"Because my blood pressure is where it was before, it didn't change, my blood pressure is very high, and he told me that I lost eight more pounds."
He barked every word of that to me as if it was my fault. I found out later that he was indeed trying to blame me for his condition, but it was his thoughts, beliefs, and what he listened to that ate him alive.
"So did he give you any medicine?" I asked.
"He knows something's going on, and *we* know something's going on."
I can read Hank like a book and I know him like I know the back of my hand, so I knew where he was trying to go. He was about to flip it on *me*, and at that point trying to get him off of that route was not going to be successful. He was going there, come hell or high water. He was setting the stage to make it seem like he was all jacked up over such a miserable relationship because of me and my misdoings, whatever the devil told him that they were.

Getting back to the subject at hand, I repeated my question, "Hank did he give you any medicine?"

"Yeah, and he told me to come home and lie down, so I put my prescription in and I have to go back and get it."

He didn't tell me what his blood pressure was, so I said, "Ok."

"And I don't like being here, this is a problem," was the next thing I heard. Of course he's talking about living in the house with me, and he started going crazy. He tried to get me into a conversation about that dumb marriage. He couldn't guilt me into liking him with a pitiful doctor's story, especially when he was intentionally not taking care of himself, that wasn't going to work. He was trying to put his illness off on the relationship when it was his depression and inability to cope. The truth is, he fabricated stories and created his own problems, and his condition is due to his personal demons and others feeding the situation by agreeing with and appeasing him.

As far as I'm concerned, once a person presents themselves undesirable in all aspects and nothing likeable is left, continuing to behave inappropriately, then trying to guilt someone into wanting them, is in and of itself a turnoff. Hank did that constantly which to me made things worse.

So Hank takes another dig at it, and repeats, "He knows something is going on."

He said that in the vein of a teacher warning a child that their parents will be notified on some wrong that they've done. Was I supposed to be afraid of the doctor?

"Hank, if your blood pressure is high and you didn't get your medicine from the drug store yet, why are you upsetting yourself and making it go higher?"

I didn't yell at him nor raise my voice, but I was extremely annoyed that he was so thoughtless of his current circumstance that he would still engage in a topic that would be upsetting to him. How is it possible that I cared more about Hank than he cared about himself? I just simply hung up the phone on him.

    I left my office around ten thirty that night. Even though I hung up on him hours earlier I still called him on my way home to see if he wanted anything but he didn't answer the phone. So I went home, put on my pajamas and went downstairs.
I said, "Hank, how do you feel?"
"I'm alright."
"Did you eat?"
"No, I haven't eaten anything."
My initial thought to myself was obviously an expected one, "Didn't the doctor just tell this man that he lost eight pounds? How much smaller could he get? He's going to be the incredible shrinking man!" I thought he had a death wish.
So I said unbelievably, "You didn't eat?"
"No, I didn't."
"Do you want me to fix you something to eat? There's some fish upstairs."
Not eating had become the new normal for Hank, so all I wanted to do was to help him. He would say he didn't like eating alone, but he didn't like me either, so who did he want to eat with, and was it worth dying over? If one doesn't eat, one dies. Also, he was notorious for not eating when he was upset and he never made it through a meal without arguing with me and then walking away from his food. He was much better off eating without me.
"Well, I guess I'll take some fish and grits," he said.

Hank refused to eat fish without grits; and with high blood pressure or not, it must be fried with the fish grease poured on the grits and then he adds salt.

It was late at night and he had picked up the medicine a few hours prior, so I asked, "Did you take your medicine?"

"Yeah."

I went upstairs and fried him some fish without adding salt, and the first thing he said was, "There's no salt in it."

"I'm not giving you any salt."

Hank was calm since I cooked him something to eat and he finally decided to tell me, "I have to go to the doctor tomorrow morning at nine o'clock, he wants to see me."

"For what? You were just there today!"

"I don't know."

"I wonder why whatever he's going to do tomorrow, he couldn't do today?"

"I don't know, my blood pressure was two-something over two-something."

I screamed, "What!"

"He told me that I should be put in the hospital but I didn't want to go, I wanted to come home, so he made me sign a form that states he told me to go to the hospital and I refused."

Hank actually signed the form and went home; he seemingly had a death wish for sure.

I blurted out, "Two-something over two-something? Check this out, I'm going to the twenty-four hour drug store right now to get a blood pressure machine."

I use the old fashioned one that you pump and put the stethoscope in your ears because I learned how to use that one in biology class in college, reading systolic over diastolic. The one I had was broken.

I told Hank, "I don't know what your blood pressure is right now, but if that medicine didn't work, and it's still two-something over two-something, you're going to the hospital or I'm calling nine-one-one." Nobody will be dying on me or stroking on me, freak that!

Before I walked out the door he said, "You can eat your fish first."

I had cooked some for myself as well. I can't believe he thought that I'd eat before going to get the blood pressure machine.

"No, I'll be right back."

He didn't tell me any of this over the phone earlier that day or I would have gone home instead of purposely staying away at the office until ten thirty at night. Anyway, I jumped in the car and flew to the drug store. I went in my pajamas and ran like somebody was chasing me. When I got back home, I took his blood pressure and it was one ten over seventy.

"Thank you Lord its normal, that medicine worked like a charm, now you have to eat." I was reiterating the fact that he needs to eat everyday to survive.

"There's nothing here to eat," he snapped.

"Hank there is always something here to eat."

"Well, there's nothing here, so I don't eat every day."

"So you sit here while I'm at work and won't go get anything to eat if there's nothing here?"

"I'm not going out to buy nothing to eat, I don't have money to buy food, and I have to pay these bills."

Un huh, he was trying to go somewhere else with that but I played it opposite and said, "Oh, so you rather die by not buying food and just pay the bills?"

First of all he lied about not having money to eat but nevertheless, that's what he said.

I continued on saying, "Ok Hank but you have to eat, can you finish your fish? You're eating like a bird."

Again he said, "It doesn't have any salt on it."

"I'm not putting salt on it," I repeated.

He didn't want to finish it and I was tremendously worried about his health.

I humbly pleaded and said, "But you have to eat your food."

What happened next shocked me as it would have anyone. Hank jumped up from the table, left his food, and started walking so fast he was almost running, the kid did ninety down those stairs and shouting back at me he said, "Lydia, I'm going to kick your fucking ass."

I asked him, "Well how are you going to do that?"

By the looks of it he wouldn't have been able to kick a mosquito's butt let alone my big collard green eating one. "PLEASE BACK AWAY FROM THE BLACK CLOTHES AND SNEAKERS!"

    I would get cursed at on a whim about the darndest things. In the sixteen years that I worked at my last job I would go to the company outing every year, sometimes driving the church van and taking some of the children from church. Hank was always invited but only participated once, and he was miserable being there. Every year he would get angry and fight about my attending the company's outing and curse me out. I would tell him every year, "You may as well start fighting now for next year because I'm going to the outing again and will always go until my employment ends."

    I never pitied myself or wallowed in what had befallen me and my compassion always went far beyond Hank. With our track record, only

God knows what I probably went through with Hank on a particular morning that I had to be strong for mankind.

One morning in New York City as I exited the subway station walking toward my job, I had to cross an Avenue filled with cars, taxis, buses, and pedestrians everywhere; I saw a filthy homeless man that looked as if he passed out from the heat, lying with his head hanging off the curb. A bus stop was a few feet away and the buses would ride right up on the curb nearly scraping it, and I was afraid they would run over his head. People were passing him like he wasn't there. I didn't have time to think of any problem of mine, I had to pick that man up.

I was dressed in my business suit, makeup and hair done, and this unfortunate man's hair was matted, his nose was dripping, and his white skin was black with dirt, but my heart didn't see what my eyes saw. For starters I'm totally afraid of other's bodily fluids, but again, my heart didn't see that. I actually have a booga phobia, I'm seriously boogaphobic. Everything I see that's unidentifiable on anything is a booga to me, and I say to myself "let me move!" Continuing on, I bent down as men-folk passers-by watched and I put both my forearms under his armpits and was lifting him as if a mother would lift a car singlehandedly off of her child, and then and only then did men start to help me. We sat him against a building and I offered him food. Something strange happened at that moment, he refused the food, but looked me in my eyes and with a sober voice he said, "Thank you." I walked away with a full heart and cried. Hank didn't exist at that moment, but a life did. I went back shortly after to give the man money, but he was gone.

Chapter Thirty Nine

Believe it or not, I did the math before walking down the aisle and I knew how old Hank would be in respect to my age every year and it didn't bother me at all. Hank looked great for his age and dressed impeccably. However, as I witnessed Hank's personality behind closed doors beginning to dwindle, I would assure him time and again when he was cutting up that his behavior would land him living out his old age alone. I would say, "You really need to stop because you're going to be an old man by yourself." His response was always, "I don't care, I'll be by myself, I don't want you, you ain't nothing and I wouldn't trust you with my life." He had a propensity to say that, and with a hurtful intention. He tried to devalue my character as if I'd purposely hurt him or put him in harm's way in his old age. I never let that bother me at all because that's not who I am and his words don't define me.

The inevitable happened and now that he's alone he doesn't like it. As long as the earth remains, there will be seedtime and harvest as far as Genesis 8:22 is concerned. It doesn't matter what type of seed you're planting, every word out of your mouth is a seed, and it will produce a harvest of its kind. Birds give birth to birds, cows give birth to cows, roses give birth to roses; and seeds of curses, lies, misfortune, and bad health, gives birth to curses, lies, misfortune, and bad health. The law of reproduction doesn't change. The difference between your seed and harvest, is expectation. I've heard so many people say, "I knew that was going to happen!" Exactly, they were expecting it.

Hank had a defiant attitude when it came to me regarding anything I said or did no matter how infinitesimal, good, bad or indifferent, or what the subject was. Whether it was hurtful to me or not was a non fricking factor. The old cliché "If you give a person enough rope, they'll hang themselves," was obliterated by the fact that Hank never even handed me the rope so I don't know why he was so belligerent toward me from the beginning, he had no just cause. He argued on our *moon*, some people classify it as a honeymoon. Maybe he was taking out all of his worldly frustrations and prior relationship woes on me. I tried everything to straighten out that crooked road, but nothing worked.

Hank was good for vacillating often. He would complain like crazy that I didn't do one big grocery shopping every so often, so I did it his way to appease him. When I came in the house with a boatload of groceries topped with all of his favorites; ice cream, bacon, Swedish fish, Cheez-its, grits, salad, fresh sliced fruit, ginger ale, t-bone steak, collard greens, etcetera; he cursed me out.
He said, "Why did you spend three hundred dollars on all of these groceries, only you and I live here."

A huge argument started and I was so outdone that I didn't even entertain the thought of wasting my time and energy in reminding him of what he always complained about. I stopped talking, shook my head and put everything away into its rightful place, but that was the last time I did that kind of shopping.

It didn't stop there, it was the same with the cleaning of the house. When I cleaned around him he complained, started an argument and ultimately cursed me out. When I didn't clean, he complained, started an argument, and cursed me out.

My sister Lele was in town and I hadn't seen her in a year, if not more. Hank actually *suggested* that she and I go to the mall or something in order to spend some time together, and we did. When I got back home, it was Armageddon up in that piece. I was damned if I did, and damned if I didn't.

I tried speaking and rebuking the devil in the form of a soliloquy when Hank would act out, thinking he would feel foolish that I didn't address him per se, but instead I addressed that demon in him, but it only backfired. When he would go off I would walk away from him and start saying things like, "Satan I rebuke you in the name of Jesus, leave this place." That demon would rile up in Hank and he'd say, "You're satan, and I rebuke *you*," and off we went. I needed to unearth another tactic that would possibly defuse Hank's daily outbursts thinking something had to work, not knowing or realizing that nothing would ever work.

Prayer, that's it, prayer changes things is the thought that entered my mind. Once again I was hopeful that I had reached another solution that might work, so when Hank would get started, no matter how much the flesh part of me didn't want to, in the midst of an argument I'd say, "Let's pray," and the pastor would say, "I don't want to pray." Eventually I walked away from that too because you can lead a horse to water but you can't make him drink. However, when he tried to compare other marriages to ours in hopes of magnifying our dysfunctionalism he'd always add in, "We don't even pray together like husband and wife." Okay, woooowwww!

As I reflected on the reality of my life as it was, I became cognizant of the mediocrity of anything Hank had ever given me or has done for me, be it out of obligation or gifting due to my inability of being able to count how many times he asked for everything back. In my opinion, and this is *my* life, a person should give and do from the heart, not in order to gain something in return. Hank would use the gifts he bought for me as ammunition when in an altercation. Money was the only thing important to Hank and by him constantly throwing all he'd spent on me in my face took away from the meaning of what was done or given. That's a scar and a void in and of itself that can't be undone.

In this day and age wigs have become an accessory, and like most women I have a few in different lengths, colors, and textures. Hank would get angry and go down his list saying, "Give me back my mink coat I bought for you, give me back my hair, give me back my food, give me back my jewelry, and give me back my money, car, and vacations." I was appalled that he would term it "Give me back *my*." How was it still his after he'd given it to me? Those were the things that took the meaning away from everything that he's given me, leaving me feeling empty and hurt. I always purchased great items for him also during the days of our buying things for each other and I never went back at him with the "Give me back my," because it was preposterous. What I would say was, "I'm not like you when you give back all of your jewelry that I have given you, piling it on my dresser, and I'm not giving you a damn thing back." Also, I would never ask for him to return any item back to me that I've purchased for him.

I don't know what Hank looks like through the eyes of his family members and best friend, but it would be interesting to know if they were aware of his true character. If Hank wasn't lying, he was embellishing. He did that when he was talking to *me* about me, so I can imagine what he told *them* about me. Truthfully at that stage in the game, I can't say I cared.

On numerous occasions Hank professed to paying my way through college when in fact the fortune five hundred company that I was employed by at that time paid not eighty like most companies, but paid one hundred percent for my tuition. Hank may have purchased some of my books and that was it, but don't let him tell the story.

Prior to locking the doors of the spa, I did all I could to try and salvage it. Hank was the first person I approached, and I lived to regret it. With the permission of Reverend Defenbar and the generous consent of my mother agreeing to sign for business purposes, we were able to refinance our property and I was grateful to both of them. Sitting around the closing table were my parents, Hank and me, the two attorneys, the representative from the title company, and the bank. I was flabbergasted to say the least, to learn that Hank went about claiming that he knew nothing of the refinance. He actually said that he didn't attend a closing which insinuates that someone forged his signature a thousand times at the closing in front of six witnesses, is that possible? Hank was so interested in trying to make me look bad that he gave no thought to what he was saying. I brushed it off as him being the old nasty and evil Hank that he was. There were many days that Hank said, "You and your mother can have this fucking house, I'm getting out of here," although not relevant to the argument at hand.

I recently found out that he truly doesn't remember being at the closing and that he really doesn't even recall the incident ever happening although his signature is all over the papers. It is repugnant and dehumanizing for him to think and always say that my mother and I would plot against him to steal a house that's already half mine, and it shows that he doesn't even know me or the character of my mother. If he doesn't remember he should say that, and not that my mother stole our house. She didn't even want to sign, but out of the kindness of her heart for me she did. The thought alone of Hank even entertaining the idea that my mother and I are capable of doing such a thing is ethically impugned and damaging.

I never allowed Hank's evil ways to rub off on me so I still tried to do right by him, thinking I could make him happy, even if just for a day. He was a miserable person and I felt sorry for him.

Midway through the marriage I planned two milestone birthday parties for him at wonderful venues in spite of all situations. One of the venues was on the top floor of a building in New York City overlooking the East river. Each party I planned was a surprise, and I would never break the silence and tell him. As we neared his birthday and he didn't hear of any plans from myself or the women at the church he would get angry and say, "I don't want anyone to do anything for my birthday." I would say, "Ok," and he would proceed in picking a fight mentioning how no-one gave a damn about him, especially me.

On the day of one of the parties I had to cry and lay in the floor in order to get him to get dressed so I can take him out for his birthday. We argued tooth and nail but I wouldn't budge and tell the secret. I went to the extreme, and whatever I thought it would take to bring even just a moment of happiness into his life I'd do it. Finally, I won. When we arrived and he saw the people from church, his sister and family from New Jersey and Philadelphia, my sisters from Florida, and friends that also travelled from afar, along with the beautiful classy atmosphere of the venue, he was happy for those hours. He sincerely thanked me and told the story to the people. Unfortunately, the next day or maybe even later that night at home he would revert back to what was normal for him. I finally realized that it was beyond my control to make him happy or to make him treat me nicely.

Chapter Forty

In his most pleasant and distinguished voice, Reverend Defenbar would get on the phone and talk so nicely to some of his officers and members which was how they perceived him for the most part. I wasn't going to expose my husband so I let the perceptions remain the way they were. Being on my end it was just like a slap in the face listening to him speak so nicely to others, deeming them more worthy of his kindness than his own wife and that was wounding to me.

As always the house was filled with tension whereas Hank and I weren't speaking. The phone rang and it was Sis. Deluth from the church, a woman that wished she was the first lady. Hank spoke so kindly to her that I wanted to wring his neck and tell him to curse *her* out and call *her* the names that he called me. I felt that way when he spoke to anyone in that nice manner; be it his family, male, female, or whoever because if he knew how to speak nice to people then why did he choose to always bark at me? He showed no respect for me as a human being, I'm still baffled by it and unaware of why.

As he answered the phone he was trying to fix the answering machine and it ended up recording the entire conversation.

Finally, Reverend Defenbar says, "Hello?"
"Hi Rev."
"Ah yeah yeah, so I'll be there tonight for love feast."
"Right, right," said the voice on the other end.
"They were telling me you had some information on the calendars?"
"Right, un huh."
"Ok, ah, I told the secretary to tell you he needed to know ah…, what we wanted uh, on the calendar."
"Yeah, he needed to know the color..the uh (a little humph laugh) the ink color, what kind of binding that we want..what kind of finish, and so forth."
"Yeah," he said absorbing the information.
"Um.."
Before finishing her thought he cut her off, "Have you spoken with the Treasurer?"
"Nah, I left a couple of messages for her, she hasn't gotten back."
"She's still at the church, she….at least she was a half hour ago," he said.
"Oh, ok."
"Uh, because we had uh, spoken of…..of ah, including anniversary dates of organizations?"
"Right."
"She said that she could get that together, I think she was working on that today."
"Ok."

"You know what to add, so uh, see if you can ah ah, reach her, and ask her if she will ah, you know, meet with us before love feast."

"Ok, what time?"

"Uh, I'll be there at 7."

"Ok."

"And so uh, we should be able to, you know, to go over it by that time."

"Ok, great."

"Ok, alright, I'll see you then," Hank said before he changed the conversation. "Ok, need you to do me a fa-vor!" He sings the word "Favor."

"Sure."

He laughs, then she laughs, and he said, "Remember you said 'sure,' ah ha ha ha (a subtle flirtatious bull crap laugh.) Ah, I had asked umm, uh, name went out of my....my my, ah, President of the Usher Board."

"Mildred."

"Mildred," he said in agreement.

"Un huh."

"I had asked Mildred to be, ah, since she was the Queen last year, I had asked her to serve as the Chair for Women's Day."

(They both laugh together at that.)

"I need for you to represent the Missionary (he laughs) for Women's Day, and I need you to, I want you to do that."

"Ok, alright."

"Okay?"

"I'll do my best."

"Okay sweetheart, ha ha, I'll see you tonight. That was easier than I thought it would be." He laughed, then they laughed together. He then said, "I'm going to set up a meeting next week, with the uh, Commission on Stewardship and Finance."

"Ok."

"So we can um, start dealing with these ah, seed jars and all."

"Alright."

"Ok hun."

"Talk to you later Rev."

"Talk to you later."

"Bye bye."

"Bye bye," and they hang up.

I've never had a pleasant conversation like that with Hank. Me *and* my momma would have been called God knows what, after a phone call of that length.

It goes to show with that conversation being in our earlier years of marriage just how long Hank has been overlooking me for heading Women's Day just to be mean and spiteful. He's always had a demeaning gesture toward me. I just observed his actions over the years and took note, hence "Tell the Truth and Shame the Devil." The flirtatious undertone in that conversation didn't move me not one iota.

As soon as he hung up the phone the switch in his head flipped back and he was in depression mode instantly and not speaking to me, but nice and humorous to others.

Chapter Forty One

The expression "You can't see the forest for the trees," has never been more true to me. Due to my retaliation and my "I ain't no punk" syndrome, hitting every ball that came my way right back at Hank, I didn't realize that I was verbally and emotionally abused until I stepped out of the situation and looked in.

I recall riding with Hank locally in the car on the parkway and I was driving as is the majority of the time, and a left fielder came right at me. Hank decided to bring up Morris, my ex, from one hundred years ago as if he knew anything about him and he snowballed from there. I wanted to jump out of the car. Going back many years, literally, is bad enough, but to add on talking about someone you know nothing about is atrocious.

It would be safe to say that Hank must have been sitting in the car thinking about my not sleeping with him without considering how he treated me. I'm not sure what percentage of men along with Hank doesn't understand that women are emotional beings. Therefore, once he damaged my heart, feelings, and psyche, I couldn't do it, wasn't happening. There wasn't a hint of attraction. He based everything on money spent which in no way could repair the damage done. As previously mentioned, the money Hank spent holds no weight with me because he threw it all back in my face as if he did me a favor and I owed him.

In referring to the apartment I lived in before I married Hank he would always say things like "Morris could come over there at twelve o'clock at night and say 'I want some,' and he can't even compare with what I have done for you." Just for entertainment purposes my response to a comment like that would be that Hank was so blinded by ignorance, materialism, and evilness that he had no idea that being nice and respectful to a woman far outweighs material things. However, two plus two wasn't equaling four in this case because where would Hank get that information if I didn't tell him? It's not rational that I would mention anything of that nature to him. As time went on Hank increasingly appeared to be nothing more than a fabricating liar. When it comes between Hank and anyone I've ever dated there is no comparison, Hank loses. He was the most nasty, hateful, and trifling human being I've ever met.

He then reached over to turn down the radio and I tried to change the subject by saying, "You can turn it off," pretending to appease him although I knew he was turning it down to make sure I heard his crap. He said, "I don't care what you do."
As I reached over to turn off the radio I said, "I turned it off, why did you roll down the window?"
"Don't worry about it," he said.
I was trying to remain calm to hopefully put out that already burning fire and as the driver I gently said, "Yeah but the noise is irritating."

"I don't give a damn whether it's irritating you or not Lydia, it ain't irritating me! I gotta do something because it irritates you? You irritate me!"

I got quiet, as it was clear he wanted to fight.

He decided to roll up the window and repeatedly said, "Now you know what it is to be irritated."

I told him twice "You can put it back down," in a tone that let him know I'd rather hear that noise from the wind than to fight about it.

He decided on a short monologue saying, "Why did you tell me it irritates you? Your going around enjoying my comfort and so forth irritates *me*; your driving my cars and so forth irritates me; your using my money irritates me; your thinking you don't have to be agreeable, or pleasurable with me irritates me, and that irritates me more than anything; and you think you don't owe me nothing? You owed Morris, you owed Taye, you owed everybody else, but you don't owe me? That's because they wouldn't take your shit."

I remained silent because that was more than sick and idiotic. Since I wouldn't feed into what was being said he started on money that I supposedly owed him, and switched the subject just like that, presto!

"I really don't care if you don't give me the six hundred dollars back, just deduct it from your mothers rent. They can have the house, I don't care, she can have it."

My parents never lived with us, and vice versa. Also, we never paid rent to my mom, we paid a mortgage to a bank; and get this, my mother in no way, shape, or form wanted that house, so he just made that up all together.

There were times when Hank had to be out of town for mandatory meetings, thus when he returned he always brought back barbeque ribs from his favorite place bringing enough for me. During one of those trips I overlooked paying my cell phone bill which resulted in my services being disconnected, but of course I had it put back on in hours. It so happened that during the transition of getting it turned back on Hank was trying to reach me via cell phone. The day after he returned from that out of town trip, in another car ride to the store gone wrong, Hank had been drinking and he said, "You went out of town yesterday." From that comment alone, I knew the argument was going to be a bad one because he started off concocting something. I could not and would not go out of town with having a business to run and he knew that all too well. When Hank asked me what happened when he was unable to reach me via cell phone I told him, and his response was, "Oh that's bullshit, you turned it off so you could drive around and not talk to me." Although he got on my spare nerve and it was a good idea to *never* talk to him, I always took his calls.

In lieu of my cell phone there was a landline at my place of business and a landline at our home, therefore, I could have been reached. He continued on in another one of his infamous monologues while I'm stuck in the confined space of a car with him and he began. "You didn't owe the phone company, you had the phone turned off, you're a crook, your whole fucking family is a crook. You had your phone turned off and you were out screwing around and had your mother at your business, and I knew exactly what you were going to say tonight. You intentionally had it turned off and asked your momma to cover so you can disappear. I haven't heard from you for four hours. You know what you did Sis. Morris, you encouraged me to get out of town. You did the same thing when that man was working at that fucking business and nobody could reach you. Your daddy and mamma told me they couldn't reach you."

As always, he needed to reiterate the fact that he doesn't like my family and that they lied for me. He said my parents were in on helping me to sleep around with everybody, and that I slept with everyone.

Listening to him I wanted to throw up. He reeked of liquor, looked stupefied and wasn't making any sense. Every time he would get mad and wanted to dig at me, he would call me "Sis. Morris," or Sister whoever my ex was. I never retaliated when it came to Hank's attempt to always scrutinize my past relationships. I didn't throw his ex's in his face because they were irrelevant to our situation; I couldn't even think or remember to talk about them. He would do or say anything if he thought it would hurt me. When he would go off, I didn't even stop him to interject the truth and point out all of his made up lies because I had enough, I was mentally drained.

Hank's entire monologue was falsified. Prior to his going out of town he told *me* he was going, so how was it that I encouraged him to go? Then he said he went that far out of town just to buy me food. Really? Also, since when can a customer ask the cell phone provider to turn off their phone for a couple of hours and then put it back on? I didn't even know how to address something so bizarre if I wanted to so I didn't respond.

In the midst of his offensive melodramatic behavior he asked the most unimaginable question that nearly blew me away. He asked me if he could be with me intimately. I nearly passed out. I think I wanted to spit! I was nauseated. H-E-triple L-NO!!! I didn't say a mumbling word to him. The only thing I cared about was driving his intoxicated self to the store to keep him safe.

There was an incident when he drove under the influence as he always did, but this particular time in question he drove the car into the garage. Our garage had little square windows across the top of the door but he didn't worry about the consequence of possibly popping the glass out so thank God they remained intact.

Upon arriving home from the office one night, I pulled into the driveway and the house was as dark as I'd imagine a hell hole to be, and the Cadillac was pressed into the garage door so far that the door was concaved. He didn't even back up off of it, he left the car there. Now that's some foggle-noggle bullcrap right there if I ever saw any. I went inside the house, got the keys, and moved the car off of the garage door. I then tried to pull on the garage door with my hands to straighten it out. That was one of those nights he obviously spoke to the devil and got mad at something that I wasn't aware of as I wasn't home. I was fit to be tied, hot under the collar, done! How is it possible to be in such a state of anger that driving into your own house with a practically new car that *you're* paying for turn out to be beneficial? That is a sign of weakness, and I wasn't with it.

There are many times that I necessitate referencing the spa because Hank would say that our troubles started after the spa and the construction worker. We were married eight years prior to the spa and I've lived in hell for seven and a half of those eight years, which is why I had to sleep with a recorder in my pajamas and carry it everywhere starting in year two of being married, as was suggested by Mary Ellen.

Everything was taken to the extreme and becoming unrepairable. There isn't a line that exist that Hank wouldn't and didn't cross. There was one point in time, years before the inception of the spa, in which the church recognized Pastor Defenbar with a "Pastor's Appreciation Day" for all that he'd done, and he was presented with a beautiful memorabilia book. That book contained letters to him from many people whose lives he'd touched inside as well as outside of the local church. Being his spouse, my letter was in the front and I meant every word I put on that paper, listing only the positive things about him. In an effort to hurt me, Hank tore that letter out of the book and destroyed it during one of his episodes. He left the book open on the dining room table to be sure that I saw it, but I never mentioned it because at the end of the day, it was his loss.

When we were newlyweds I had not yet picked up on the fact that Hank had a vendetta against me and wanted anything or anyone out of my life if it or they brought me joy. I secretly and honestly have always believed the reason Hank denied me of sex from the inception of the marriage and constantly blamed it on arguing is because he wanted to make certain that I didn't get pregnant. Thank God for Hank's miraculous unintended wisdom because that would have been a lifetime attachment which I'm sure he regrets now, but it worked out for my good. What man meant for harm, God meant for good. However, he knew I would have loved that child like crazy and he refused to allow that type of happiness in my life.

Butterscotch was around two or three years old when Hank and I married, and Hank said that I'd have to declaw him prior to joining our lives. Out of love and respect for Hank, I did so thinking he sincerely made that request for the safety of the furniture. Seeing that it was my pleasure to make him happy and the fact that I immediately declawed Butterscotch, defused his evilness. He saw that I wasn't the least bit hurt by it, but I didn't recognize his intentions.

Hank observed the love and affection I displayed for Butterscotch and would tell people at the church, "If she had to choose between me and Butterscotch, she would put me out!" When Butterscotch turned four, out of the clear blue Hank said to me without explanation that I had to get rid of him, and again although it hurt like crazy I concurred.

I put an ad in the newspaper for the adoption of a beautiful red tabby. A family of three travelled long distance to adopt him and Butterscotch bit all three of them. Butterscotch was always smarter than the average bear. Way back then Hank was downstairs in that bedroom listening to all of the confusion through a closed door so he came out grouching at all of us saying, "Just leave the cat alone, he doesn't want to go." I was very happy and I also concluded that Hank was only trying to hurt me, his new wife, and I was perplexed by it. Then and there is when I decided that Hank would never tell me a single thing about Butterscotch again!

Chapter Forty Two

I had been inundated with Reverend Defenbar's rudeness and disrespect toward my parents, family, and me, that I was overwhelmed with bitterness toward him. I no longer could stomach his voice, his facial expressions, to watch him chew, to watch him walk, or to merely just look at him.

It was inconceivable how he kept me separated from his family and then would turn around and say that I don't talk to any of his relatives. He would tell me things like no one in his family liked me, and how he told them all about me, meaning all of the bad things he perceived about me. His main thing to say was, "You're not a Defenbar, my family is not your family, and your family is not my family." He always said that his family was better than my family, and that his sisters didn't like me, but in that same breath he'd say, "You don't give a damn about my family." He was adamant about making the distinction between me and his family and that

I wasn't a part of it. Hank kept us separated and then blamed me for not having a relationship with them. I can't count the number of times that I've eaves dropped over the banister and heard him badmouthing me to Gertrude, his sisters, his son, other family members of his, and his close friends. Was I expected to think that his sisters and others wouldn't believe the things he'd say? I can only imagine what his family thought about me over the years. Hank was so evil and selfish that he not only robbed me of a relationship with his family, but he robbed them of a relationship with me.

When it came to my family I never entertained the thought of robbing him of a relationship with them, I tried to promote it and I wouldn't entertain the thought of badmouthing him to my family. I protected him across the board. He tried his best to say on many occasions, "Your mother and family don't like me, and they don't give a damn about me." He may have said that but I wouldn't allow it. I would stop him in his tracks and refute his words only because my family *did* like him and never said a bad word about the good reverend. He would purposely make himself an outcast and not attend certain family dinners or holidays so that he could convince himself that my family didn't like him. Who does that? I always gave a deceitful excuse out of embarrassment as to why he wasn't there.

One thing Hank succeeded in doing was keeping me away from his family. Did he really think I'd want to talk to them after he hammered it into my head that they didn't like me? I'm not the one, never have been, and never will be. My mother always taught me that if someone doesn't like you then don't like them back, all I have to do is love them. So it was see ya, love ya, bye, when it came to his family.

It wasn't easy for me to sit around people when everyone was looking at me like I was crazy and have been taking advantage of their brother, father, and uncle. He told *me* a million times that I married him to take advantage of him, and that I never loved him. Did he *surely* tell them that? You think?

When they visited or we were in the same place at the same time, I was always cordial but secretly wanted to get away from them. When his nephews married, all of a sudden their wives were his nieces, and his sisters' husbands were his brother-in-laws or referred to as his brothers, but I was isolated. They seemed to be nice people but Hank made them look horrible in my eyes because he said they didn't like me when I've never done them any harm or treated them unkindly.

I was introducing Hank's niece to someone at our church and I told them pointing to Hank's nephew that, "He's Pastor Defenbar's sister's son," and pointing to his wife I said, "This is his wife." Well I saw her countenance fall immediately as she didn't see the point in the explanation, she just should have simply been Hank's niece. She never verbalized an issue to me about it but I knew from her reaction. She did try to retaliate by doing something similar to me during our next encounter but I didn't care, I was used to it from Hank. The only reason something came of it was because of what I picked up from her right away, otherwise I would not have realized it because it was normal to me and I meant nothing by it. I have a habit of explaining the relation when I introduce people. With her only knowing what Hank said about me behind my back to them, I'm sure she thought I did that with a purpose.

For Hank, there was one goal regarding me and the outside world around me inclusive of friends, Butterscotch, acquaintances, church family, co-workers, relatives, and in-laws, both far and near; and that was to divide and conquer. He wanted to divide my relationships and conquer me with his abusive insults as he emphatically hurled them at me.

I had to walk on eggshells just to feed Butterscotch. Hank would argue when I returned home from my nine to five if I took one minute to open a can of cat food to feed my baby before I cooked an entire meal for him. I'm sure with being home and around the church, Hank ate something during the day when my cat didn't. He would be evil and scream "You're going to feed that damn cat before you feed me!" In the beginning I tried to please him not knowing he was totally bonkers, and wouldn't feed Butter until after I cooked an entire meal. However, when I caught on I stopped that and took a second to open a can of food for Butterscotch first. Hank was jealous of my cat too, the only child I had.

Hank liked to taunt me, so he thought, but I had become immune to his abuse and didn't give a care about one word that he spoke. I kept my head high, always walking with pride and dignity. Speaking of the church folks he would say, "Those people know who you are," to insinuate they've had discussions with him and told him that they knew about my dirty little past. Really? Give me a break! Was I supposed to believe *that* lie, knowing that they only knew me from church?

Hank was really a piece of work, a devilish piece at that. I honestly believe that if Hank and I were stranded on Gilligan's Island he would fight about why in the world did I choose to go on a three hour tour rather than a two hour tour, and that the millionaire and his wife didn't like me.

Some people may view me as a battle-ax, and I really thought Reverend Defenbar was one of them, but obviously not. When he made his daily derogatory accusations about me, he thought he could threaten me with them and would say, "I'm gonna tell the church." He was so adamant about it as if I had done some wrong to him and the church was going to protect him, almost like "Oooh Lydia, you're in trouble." Were they supposed to kick my butt or excommunicate me? I was so infuriated that he remotely could have thought that I was scurred and all I could say was, "Who gives a fuck, tell the church, what are they gonna do?" I guess he never did it because he was blowing hot air, or knew it would have backfired. First, he would have been lying in God's house against one of God's children, also he would have gotten it right back from me and I would have told the truth and shamed the devil, hello!

I am happy with how God created me, I'm an unusual being and there is no-one on planet earth that I admire so much that I'd like to emulate or to have what they have. What God has for me is for me, and it may be more than what someone else has so I'd be limiting myself to want anything other than what God has for me. For some strange reason this elementary piece of information didn't permeate the good reverend's thoughts and he assumed he could make me jealous over what others were doing.

He would point out pastor and wife teams that have excelled in the ministry and say things like, "See, they work together, and do things together, and have the same mind," and blah blah blah. He would compare our relationship to the lowly and to the prestige. He went as far as to compare our tired, abused, broken down relationship, to our President and First Lady of the United States saying, "Look how they work together." Was he kidding? I don't believe the President calls his wife a whore every day. Did he think that would encourage me to have a desire to work with him? Eeeew!! I didn't give a flying flipping whistle about that either. I love being me minus him, and it's nothing short of amazing how I got to this point of actually *being* me without him.

I know it's done by irrational abusers, but it's still hard to digest how a person would degrade their spouse publicly as well as privately whenever given a chance, then complain and expect a flourishing fruitful relationship? I can't and won't ever forget the torture I lived through, or the experience although I forgive Pastor Defenbar.

One of the outlandish ordeals that Hank has perpetrated against me was at a seafood restaurant during another appreciation dinner in his honor, approximately in our fifth year of marriage. The church had a section of the restaurant blocked off for the occasion and we sat at a table with one other couple and everything seemed to have been going just fine. We were pretending to be happy as always for the sake of the people. I wasn't thinking that anything would go awry but as we talked and laughed Hank came out and said to me, "As long as I get my money back you can leave." I thought, how did that possibly fit into the small talk that was going on?

I felt awkward as did the others at the table. I was embarrassed for his ignorance, and hurt that he would do that to me. No one responded, pretending not to have heard it, forcing it to be a subliminal comment. Those were the days that I only went to my job, to school, and back home. He always said that to me but I never thought he would say that in front of people. That was a clear indicator that the only thing that ever mattered to Hank was his money, not me.

The very thought of Hank being capable of inflicting such pain and humiliation on another human being reminds me of a painting he told me about. The painting had a little Caucasian girl poking a pin in the hind parts of an old African American man to see if he had feelings. Well I have feelings and it's a shame that they weren't taken into consideration by my husband. I refer to Reverend Defenbar as my *husband* only at times like that which mattered due to the principle of it. Hank liked to throw that "Husband" word around like it had pull and tried using it to guilt me into sleeping with him, or wanting to spend time with him in spite of his behavior. Instead, he should have thought when he used the term "Husband," that he shouldn't have treated me the way that he did.

Instead of Hank pretending that all of his problems started after I opened my business he should have realized that by that time our relationship had been long gone, dead, buried, and pushing up daisies.

God is omniscient and I'm grateful that I have the wisdom to understand that and am able to roll with it. I've always wanted children and prayed for them; however, it never upset me to a point that I would entertain the thought of fertility, knowing that if God would have a child born through my womb, all of the demons in hell couldn't stop it. I immediately understood that God knew more than I did and He obviously saw a reason for children not to be born in that union. I was always happy with God's choice and it didn't bother me. Reverend Defenbar knew that I wanted children, so he thought he could hurt me in an argument by telling me that he didn't want a baby by me, and that I wasn't woman enough to get pregnant. He didn't realize that at that point I wouldn't have a child by him anyway besides the fact that there was no activity to produce a child, but it was still and all an ugly thing to say to someone.

He found a way to fix his lips one day and call me yet another whore just because I had a headache and stomach pains two days prior to my cycle and he wanted to sleep with me. The only reason I gave him an explanation during that time was because I hadn't yet cut him off completely, although I was already cringing, shedding tears, and motionless while he did his thing before going back downstairs.

Although men don't possess the same intuition that women do, Hank clearly knew that the attraction, affection, and all feelings were gone but he wanted to make me suffer because of the piece of paper that said I was his wife. Hank has selective memory and acted as if he didn't remember turning me down every day in the first few years. Once he realized he had no control and that I was no longer interested, he suddenly wanted to be with me in that way. He also had the balls to laugh and humorously say at times, "Do you want a baby?" He thought I didn't know that he really meant that, thinking he would be able to hold on to me, but it was way too late and the very thought of it was disgusting to me at that point. I always responded in the same way he presented it, laughing and saying "hail naw! Eeeeew." Every day he would find a way to indicate sex and ask for it but I ignored him, then he would get angry and say, "I don't want nothing from you, and I won't bother you anymore about it." The very next day that vicious cycle repeated itself, and he would ask again. I knew I needed more than ever to get out of there. My being harassed everyday about sex from someone that makes me barf was stressful.

A month or so after my surgery, the one with the infamous "Third day home" story, and prior to my opening a business, Hank said, "Can I ask a question?"

I knew he was starting controversial crap so I just looked at him and didn't say "Yes," or "What."

He then said, "What do you call someone that buys you dinner and then nothing happens?"

I was so disgusted with his ignorant cantankerous questions and I hated being in his presence so I abruptly replied, "A friend."

"Oh, so I'm a friend. Well when I return from out of town I need to call your doctor to see if the surgery affects sex drive."

I looked at him like he was out of his mind, *he* affects sex drive. I guess he forgot about chasing me out of the house just three days after being home from surgery when I had to sleep in the park.

As always, he left for an out-of-town trip and I took advantage of that time to clean the house to a pristine condition which was a two day project if I worked diligently, almost around the clock. Taking a break between the two days wasn't an option because Hank was always rushing back home as if he couldn't be away from me, or perhaps with his introvert condition mixed with depression he just felt the need to be in that room downstairs. Since he only expressed despise toward me, he should have wanted to stay away; I know *I* didn't want him back so soon. Hank would leave on Monday morning and be back at six o'clock am Wednesday morning. I couldn't stand it, what was he always rushing back to? Did he need to watch me, or did he have to fight in order to breathe? In any case I had to work fast, long, and hard.

From washing walls; bleaching curtains and mini-blinds; cleaning mirrors; mopping floors; vacuuming; moving furniture; dusting; running up and down the stairs, in and out of the garage to do laundry; and putting away clothes etcetera, with no help, made my entire body ache. The accumulation of tar in the cigarette smoke that came off of the blinds, curtains, and walls was unimaginable, turning the water in the bathtub to a dense black mud. Although I was exhausted upon completion, the next day I conducted my weekly bible study at my house for the first time instead of at the church, and I cooked a hearty meal for my students. I prepared collard greens, turkey wings, fried fish, corn on the cob, and rice, and they loved it. I also had to tutor a high school Junior that day prior to having my class; I was like a super woman.

Upon Hank's arrival the next day he became aware of all that I've done and for some strange reason I thought maybe, just maybe he'd be nice to me knowing how hard I've labored in cleaning, and was still able to fulfill my obligations to tutor as well as conduct my class. Later that night around two o'clock in the morning, I was sitting at the kitchen table quietly snacking on something and Butterscotch was eating something out of his bowl. As fate would have it, Hank came upstairs to harass me, having no regard as to how tired I was and how my body ached. He didn't care about my well being whatsoever.

As soon as I heard him walking up the stairs I thought, "Oh God, here he comes."

Sure enough he said, "You don't ever want to spend time with me and as much as I talk about it, it doesn't do any good. I've been gone since Sunday and just got back, that's why I sleep downstairs, I can't even touch you."

That was like an Amityville Horror moment "He's baaaack!" All I could think was, "Wow! He really thinks a person would want to be around him." I was so exasperated that I didn't even respond, and so began his monologue.

"Is this the type of relationship you had with your boyfriends? They come home and you tell them what you did during the day, or did you spend time with them? I go months and months at a time and all I do is write out checks."

Even for Hank I found it odd that he thought it was abnormal to discuss your day with your spouse. I thought it was a part of life and that's what married people do. Incidents like that was the reason I had to play dead as long as I could, because it didn't matter where we were on the twenty-four hour clock, if I was awake and Hank knew it, then we were going to fight. What a way to live. I was mentally and physically tired and Hank wanted to argue about my ex's at two in the morning. I got up and walked away in total disbelief because it was so unreal how it never ended with him.

The simplest things were mountains to Hank; even when it was a good thing, he turned it into a bad thing, which to me is more detrimental than having an argument for a just cause.

As I was cooking fish for him one day he said, "If you use the white car, you'll have to put oil in it."

"Ok, I just put some in the black car yesterday," I said.

I was also the mechanic in our house, and I thought putting oil in the car *he* drove most was a good gesture. The black car was a 2009 CTS, and the white car was a 2000 DTS, both made by Cadillac which appears to be stereotypical of a preacher, but we actually liked them. Hank drove the black one the majority of the time unless I needed Onstar for directions, then I'd take the black car which I named "Kit."

He became so angry and yelled, "That's not what it needs, it needs an oil change!"

"I understand that, but I checked it and it needed oil for now, it was very low."

"You're gonna have your way, so you can rule," he shouted.

I wanted to be sure that he understood me so that he could see that his response didn't go with what I said. I was lost. I wanted to rule because I put oil in a car that needed it? I thought, how did that make sense?

So again, I explained the oil situation and homeboy went in yet another direction and said, "I've been asking you for a day, my time, and I'm not playing second fiddle to anything, not your business, nobody, nothing, I never have, and I'm not second fiddle. You're gonna leave anyway when you make enough money to."

At that point I realized he was confused and I just looked at him.

He then asked, "Are you interested in someone else?"

I repeated his very question and asked him, "Are *you* interested in someone else?"

"No, I'm interested in you, but you're not interested in me, I turn you off?"

Wait a minute; did he possibly think that he turned me on and that I was still interested in him? Oh my yuk! He actually had the chutzpah to ask me that. The relationship had become one clown short of a three ring circus.

Chapter Forty Three

The Great Escape had arrived and it was unequivocally kismet the way it all lined up and played out without my help or interference. When I realized it was time to pack my bags and go, ambiguity set in and I became sad, happy, excited, and nervous, all rolled up into one. It was extremely difficult suppressing my feelings of feeling sorry for Hank because he was at the brink of manifesting his very words of being alone, but I needed to do what my mind knew was the right thing to do.

Constantly complaining to Lamont and Mary Ellen had become complacent due to the lack of funds I thought I needed in order to move, and not knowing what else to do or how to do it. I hadn't realized the harm that stress would have ultimately created to my physical body; however, they continued to warn me by saying, "This isn't healthy for either of you." Bending their ears went on for years and years, and finally the questions started to come.

It was around the same time back in the earlier years when Mary Ellen suggested the tape recorder that she threatened to call my parents and tell them all that I was going through if I didn't go home that very day and pack my bags. Knowing how protective my parents are of me she was going to encourage them to go over and demand that I leave but I was ashamed, so I literally begged her not to. I also hoped things would change for the better in the marriage.

Lamont just boldly asked me one day nearing the end of the marriage, "What is it going to take for you to get outta there? You have to get outta there." I always thought long and hard about that because Hank had done so much for me financially and I wanted desperately to pay him back for everything he'd done plus some, just in good faith. I'm well aware that was a warped way of thinking for most because he was my husband and he was obligated to do those things. As much crap as I've been through over sixteen long years, he still owes me, I have change due to me. The thought of it reminds me of a movie that shows a woman with a calculator at the kitchen table tabulating all of the work, effort, and sufferings of a bad marriage in order to come up with its monetary equivalent.

It's amazing what words can do once released into the universe, and how verbal abuse never goes away. Because of the insults and names he'd hurl at me constantly over the years, i.e. thief, whore, bitch, user, poor, son-of-a-bitch, nigga woman, you ain't nothing, you only want my money, you only care about what you can get, etc., I had this thing inside of me that wanted to see him suffer the consequences of every bad thing he's ever said and done to me. Thank God that feeling has vanished long ago as I forgive him and release him to his higher good. I wonder if he ever realized that everything he's done for me meant nothing because he threw it back in my face and accused me of what I'm not. I want him to see that I am somebody; I am a child of the King.

What I have divulged thus far is only scratching the surface of the deplorable way I lived, and what I had to endure daily.

I came up with an answer and told Lamont, "If I had three hundred thousand dollars, I could give Hank two hundred thousand and I would leave with one hundred thousand."

I needed to be sure that he would be ok and I wanted to give him back every dime he ever spent on me. I felt obligated to stay there through the financial low which was mainly due to my business folding, and his retirement didn't help. My ideal was to leave once everything was built back up. That was the incorrect way to think but unfortunately that was my standpoint for years. I have no doubt that Hank is telling people that "She stayed while the money was here and good, and now that it's gone, she left." That couldn't be further from the truth, it was a life or death situation that I had to leave; sink or swim, and that boat was capsizing and I can't swim.

Furthermore it was inevitable, we didn't stand a chance, not as much as a snowball's chance in Hades. Hank spoke it into existence for sixteen years. He was ridiculously redundant in saying, "I want a divorce, I'm leaving you, I'm going to make sure I leave you broke, and I'm getting out of here when I retire," etc., etc.

I always knew in my heart that I would leave as soon as I could but by my standards; it was just a matter of time and money. On the contrary, I didn't know that Lamont never believed me all of those years. He didn't think I'd ever leave, and he never revealed that to me until nearing the end. He explained to me that when very bad things would happen he was sure I'd leave because the average person would have ran, but I still remained, so his faith in me dissipated. Lamont has a gift of foreseeing

things that would always come to pass. One day, just a few months prior to my leaving he said to me, "You're leaving, I know you're leaving, I believe you now. It's a feeling that I have, and it's different this time, I believe you."
I was shocked and I said to him, "What do you mean you believe me now? You didn't believe me before? How could you think anyone would stay there?"
That's when he revealed how he never believed me because it seemed to be all talk. Just the very thought of Lamont not knowing me as well as I thought he did was daunting.

It's always a sure "Win" when you follow the Word of God, being a doer of the Word and not just a hearer of the Word. I on the other hand having been engulfed in my then current situation did just the opposite of what the Word says. Being a learned person of the Word, fortunately I was able to bounce back, just give me less than ten minutes. The Word says in the book of Romans 4:17 "Call things that be not, as though they were," but I was calling things as they were and kept complaining.

At times I believed Lamont felt that he wanted me gone from there more than I did, but no one could have wanted it more than me. He was so fed up with hearing "Hank" episodes and my remaining there not making a move that he became cynical with me and said things like, "Good, that's what you like," and "The next time I hear Hank's name, I'm hanging up on you." I can't say I blamed him although I got angry and didn't call him for a couple of days. Before long I was right back to complaining about what I was suffering, and he was right back to listening.

I was finally able to overcome and ignore reality. I began thanking God for beautiful relationships, and for peace although it wasn't there. I understood and began to call things that were not as though they were.

God in His infinite wisdom set me up to be able to network with the right people and rub shoulders with those holding household names in the world. I was able to make acquaintances and friends with people that have already been where I want to go. He was putting things in place necessary for my departure; He is always working in the background.

Things had gotten so bad that I ended up in fight or flight mode, and I decided to take a flight, I was tired of fighting. That's when the pain of remaining the same became greater than the pain of change, and I got sick and tired of being sick and tired. God works in mysterious ways, and miraculously during such a low point in my life and three months before I moved out I made contact with Chase Rydell on Facebook, someone that I've known twenty five years prior but had lost contact. Chase is one that I hold in high regard as he always made perfect sense to me and is now a motivational speaker and an entrepreneur also. I immediately confided in him and explained what I was currently and had been going through. He responded only once saying, "You have to get out of there. You have no children, no love, no peace or anything, so tell me again *why* are you there?" Chase is extremely clever and he posed that question in such a way that made it seem as if I previously gave him a reason that justified my remaining in torment. Chase laid all of the cards on the table and gave me the opportunity to think for myself and answer that question. It made me feel inadequate, which was his intention because there was no reason that I had to stay there and suffer, and I couldn't answer the question which he already knew. Straightway I made a decision to leave with zero dollars let alone three hundred thousand, and that is when my real journey began. Chase had three words of wisdom for me "Keep moving forward."

After that decision, the very next Sunday I received a Rhema through a sermon I heard at the church we attended after Hank's retirement, and I was convicted. God could not have been anymore clearer to me in revealing that He didn't intend for my life as His child to be that way. The chains that bound me were broken and I knew I had to leave on faith and no money. It no longer mattered what Hank thought. Actually, in light of my never sharing the idea with Hank of my hopes of leaving him with two hundred thousand dollars, he obviously didn't expect anything when he would always say, "I want a divorce when I retire." He would have assumed it was impossible anyway due to my financial status at that time mixed with his little faith.

I had to escape for my life. Genesis 19:22 states, "Hurry escape there for I cannot do anything until you arrive there." I began to understand first hand that God can't do anything until you get to where you need to be. I had to get into position and I didn't want to miss my blessing. It's clear that I couldn't work there in the house with Hank, nothing but confusion was there, I couldn't think productively, and I couldn't write this book, I was stagnant. Had I stayed I would have remained stagnant because all I was doing was running out of the house frustrated, and complaining.

God was speaking to me and I had to move. Our blessings are waiting for us in a place called obedience. I had to get over the fear that was holding me in the place where I was; fear of leaving him alone, fear of no money, and fear of going into the unknown. I couldn't go on cursing and carrying on, I decided that I needed to be a person of character and in right standing with God across the board. I asked for forgiveness daily of any wrongdoing by thought, word, or deed, but I needed repentance. In all honesty I wasn't there yet so I refused to repent when I knew that in retaliation I would be cursing Hank out the next day, it was what it was.

Having heard that Word preached mixed with my already divine inspiration that came through Chase Rydell to leave with zero dollars on faith and trusting God, was the icing on the cake and it was a wrap, that's all she wrote, the fat lady had already delivered her rendition, and Lydia had left the building.

I knew that I was walking into the unknown having no idea where I was going, how I was getting there, with what money, or what my next move was, so I had to strategize. My business that I operated out of my rented office space wasn't booming so there wasn't any income, but at that point it wasn't a factor, whereas for most it would have been the main factor. I had to encourage myself by speaking over my life and circumstances in spite of reality which I had to ignore or I'd still be there, but the devil is a lie! I love the Lord wholeheartedly and in the book of 1 Corinthians 2:9 it states, "Eyes have not seen, ears have not heard, nor has it entered into the hearts of man what God has prepared for those who love Him," so I knew something was already prepared because the God I serve can't lie.

My mind was made up, it was a cut and dry situation, I was leaving on sheer faith because I didn't have enough money to buy a mosquito a wrestling jacket. Although my mind was apprehensive, my hands and feet were in action. I made it to my office as fast as I could to get on the computer, as my first order of business was to see what kind of prices were out there for my particular living standards, being that I was accustomed to a certain way of existing. I can't live with bugs in my dwelling place, I mean I won't even go to sleep if a fly is in my house, not until he is dead. I can't live around hoodlums, I can't live in an inner city setting or torn down neighborhoods, etcetera. I'm a suburban girl born and reared.

I found a website that requested all of my criteria, i.e. how many bedrooms, baths, square footage, price range, and whether the search is for an apartment or a house. Once the information is logged into the computer, locations suiting your needs are generated and listed. The very first place I chose and visited was the place I ended up with. That is actually the same thing that happened when Reverend Defenbar and I bought our house. The first house I circled in the paper and visited became our house. When you ask God first, trusting and believing Him, He gives you the desires of your heart; and both of those places were perfect in all aspects including being centrally located.

Everything was so sudden, and I didn't quite know how to include the good reverend. I needed to digest it and come to terms with it first which was extremely difficult, but I knew I had to give a fair notice. I was putting dude on notice. I didn't hesitate with my plan. As soon as I received the revelation from God, I acted without skepticism. I made an appointment for a site visit and when I put the address into my global positioning system, the distance in time was close to two hours. I frequently did site visits for my business so that was just another one which was what I told Hank. I was glad to take the ride, it was peaceful and the scenery was God's country as was my destination. Talk about head for the hills!

Never having heard of the place or any neighboring town is proof that God was the Planner because I could not have possibly picked a better place. Upon arrival, as I pulled up to the visitor's center/rental office I noticed that the grounds were kept beautifully with tennis and basketball courts, a gym, and a swimming pool. I also learned that section of town was the more accomplished section within five minutes of the indoor mall. Every major and minor store, restaurant, auto shop, grocery store, cineplex, the railroad, office supply, dollar stores, churches, fabric store, craft stores, beauty supply, home stores, home building stores, super stores, and wholesale club stores that you could possibly name or imagine was in bike riding distance. I could not have done that if I tried, and I had no clue geographically speaking as to where to begin my search.

As I was touring the place, reality and melancholy set in and I found it hard to accept that I was at a point like that in my life. As I began to weep, I apologized and the salesperson gave me a Kleenex.

"It's ok, I know it has to be hard," she said sympathetically, understanding the brief synopsis of my situation.

I didn't have to worry about the schools, so there was no need to check them. I liked everything that I saw and went back to the rental office to fill out the necessary paperwork, and then I had to wait the longest few days for an approval.

My cell phone rang and I noticed the phone number to be that of Julia, the saleswoman from my future residence that I was already claiming.

I picked up, "Hello?"

"Hi, this is Julia, everything went through ok, and you were approved! When can you come back to leave a deposit and select a move-in date? It has to correspond with our availability."

As she was talking my heart hit the floor, I became afraid, it was about to go down. This was really happening and Hank didn't know.

I told her, "I can be there next week."

"Ok, thanks, I'll see you then," she said.

"Ok, and thank you."

At that point I was nervous thinking now what? I thought to myself, "What is my next move?" I had to call on El Shaddai, God Almighty. Reverend Defenbar always taught us to consult God first before making any decision, especially a major one.

The week passed by with speed and before I knew it I was on the road driving to God's country again. I left very early in the morning so that my arrival time would be around nine o'clock. I told Hank that I was going to another site visit which was a little under a couple of hours away. It was true, it just wasn't the whole truth at that time. I wanted to have my facts in order with the move-in date when I told Hank, and I had to wait on God to give me the words to say and how to say them. Everything was all so new to me, and I was clueless in America. After all, I was departing from a sixteen year marriage and by no means was that an easy task.

Hank would always give me the CTS when I was driving a long distance alone because it had Onstar, and oddly enough he did care about my wellbeing on the road. I listened to my gospel compact disks as usual and thanked God. As I drove I felt freedom, I felt disbelief, I felt nervousness, I felt numb, I felt sad, I felt my inner strength of who the real Lydia was, I felt happy, and I felt the love of God. I cried and cried, I shouted Hallelujah, I shouted thank you Jesus, and I praised God.

When I thought of Hank, I became annoyed as to why he would allow that to happen, why did he speak it into existence for the entire sixteen years, why couldn't he love me enough or was that the only way he knew how to love?

I had to get myself together, cry it out before I reached my destination because that lady didn't need to see me crying again. I had to get myself on some rah!rah! stuff before walking through those doors so that I only exhibited my inner happiness, and all of those other feelings I needed to leave in the car.

I pulled into one of the six parking spaces which was dedicated to potential residents. A pole was in front of it with a classy green wooden engraved plaque with gold lettering, that read: "Future Resident Parking." Those words at that point had meaning as I read them, more than they did the first time, it was so surreal. This was going to be my new home, so far away from home as I once knew it. I no longer had to live vicariously through visualization of one day living in peace.

With money order in hand, I walked into the rental office as my stomach fluttered, it was really happening. Julia and I greeted each other with smiles on our faces as if seeing a long lost friend. We sat in our respective chairs, and the signing of the paperwork began. It was like being at a closing there were so many papers. I had to show my driver's license; I had to sign and pay for the gym; and I had to sign for my cat, as well as give her his up-to-date immunization records etcetera; it seemed unending. The move-in date was established and was two months in the future due to their availability. I was given a copy of everything, we shook hands, and I left.

I drove back to my office that day and filed my papers away there, intact in the envelope. I said a heartfelt and sincere breath prayer, "God, please tell me when and how to tell Hank." I thought the sooner the better would be ideal so that he'd have time to get used to the idea, but I had to wait for God to help me with wording and timing. I don't think Hank knew me well enough to know or to even contemplate the thought that I'd ever actually leave or had the strength to do so. Although my hitting the road was like karma because of the way he treated me, one would think he should have been happy to see me go, but for some strange reason I felt that Hank would be unpleasantly surprised.

Other than Hank and my two sounding boards, Lamont and Mary Ellen, I didn't tell anyone else, not even my parents until a week before I was to move in because I needed everything to be drama-free. Lamont said, "It's been a long time coming, and your change has finally come. Now you'll have peace, and you can work." I cried over the phone because I was worried about Hank being ok, and Lamont kept assuring me that

God will make sure that Hank would be ok, which later on was confirmed by two others.

I didn't want to tell my mother because the location was so far away, I had no family or friends there, and she wouldn't be able to get to me in five minutes if she needed to like she has my entire life. I'm the youngest of my parents children and I didn't know if mommy would have had separation anxiety or what, but I knew my daddy would be fine because he knows I'm a surviving conqueror and a trooper.

After signing the lease, for the next few days I immediately went about my daily routine without meditating on telling Hank because I knew that God's timing was the best. I did wonder however, how long I'd have to wait on God and whether or not He was planning to give Hank ample time to get used to the idea. It is nothing short of amazing to watch God's Word manifest in your life right before your eyes, thereby allowing you to become a more powerful witness to His works. The book of Mark 13:11 states, and I quote: "But when they arrest you and deliver you up, do not worry beforehand, or premeditate what you will speak. But whatever is given you in that hour, speak that; for it is not you who speak, but the Holy Spirit." Those same instructions that Jesus gave to His disciples; Peter, James, John, and Andrew, works for me also.

Just as sure as the world, Reverend Defenbar redeemed me on his own. Subconsciously I knew he would because all it would take is one argument, and he'd be screaming one of his all time favorite sayings, "Why don't you leave," and that would be my cue.

I was driving alone in the car on my way to a craft store to purchase items that would aid me in producing a prototype of an invention I came up with when Hank's fateful call came in. The weather was beautiful that day, and I'll never forget it. My cell phone rang and the name popped up on the screen, "Hank Cell," and my neck got tight.

I pressed the button on my earpiece and said, "Hello?"

"Ah, yeah Lydia, are you coming home anytime soon because I'd like to get something to eat around here."

His sound came across as if he was on the warpath, and I knew there was more to it.

I tried to remain cool, hoping to keep him cool, and I said, "Are you telling me you didn't eat all day?"

"No I haven't."

"Ok, why would you do that?"

I couldn't believe that he didn't eat everyday because I went to the office and wasn't there to feed him. Hank would get crazy if I dared ask him a question, simple or not, and so he went off. He started to say how I wasn't a wife, and that I was no good to him.

He blurted out, "I'll be glad when you leave, why don't you leave, I don't want you!"

Bells and whistles went off in my head like I hit the jackpot on a slot machine, but I wanted to see his face when I respond to that remark so I hung up on him. I made the fastest U-turn known to man and I hurried home to be sure he remained right there in that mental state, I didn't want him to cool down because he'll flip in a minute.

I walked through the door of my house and I quickly said, "What did you say to me while I was driving?"

He took it hook, line, and sinker, and repeated himself saying, "I said, why don't you leave?"

I thought to myself, "Yesssss!"

"As a matter of fact I am, I found a place online and my move-in date is in two months. I signed the lease and gave my deposit."

"Good," he said abruptly, and went downstairs.

I believe he was shocked or didn't believe me because he didn't ask any questions at that moment. I was so happy, the hard part was over, and Hank had been put on notice. I rejoiced quietly in my closet, "Thank you God, thank you God." I wanted to jump up in the air and click my heels to the side.

For certain that was a barricade night just in case he thought a little harder. It's always the ones that spectators speak of saying, "They were so nice, so quiet, you wouldn't think they'd ever do something like that." I was not interested in becoming a statistic, not that I thought I would, but one can never be too safe.

As the morning dawned, I was curious to see how Hank was from the new found information that probably haunted him the night before. I didn't play dead that morning because I was too anxious to see his reaction and whether or not he had my coffee sitting on the kitchen table, which I refused to think he'd spike. To my surprise the coffee was there, and I drank it. From past experience, I knew that it was more likely than not that I could have been headed for a tornado and I needed my caffeine before I was attacked. Had I been an alcoholic, I would have had a cocktail for breakfast *that* day.

It had become customary that once I was up and my footsteps were heard, the good reverend made his way upstairs to the kitchen to see what was going on. Although I never knew what to expect with Hank, seeing that it depended on which way the wind was blowing, that day I *really* didn't know what to expect, so I made a conscious effort to keep a composed behavior. He walked into the kitchen and I was astonished that he was in a great mood.

"Good morning," he said.

I responded, "Hey, thanks for the coffee."

I didn't mention anything further about moving, and I continued in my routine, fixing Butterscotch's morning food and drinking my coffee.
Hank broke the silence, "What date did you say you were leaving?"
"The fifteenth, September fifteenth, I just have two months to go."
"Oh alright, I spoke to Jessica, and she wants me to move closer to her and the family, so I have to decide if I'm going to go, or stay here."
"Hank I don't think you should stay here alone, you should move to that area."
"Well I have to make up my mind, because I like where I am, and I've gotten used to this area. It's good that you found a place, because we weren't happy here, and that is best."
He then chuckles and continues to say, "Now I don't have to spend so much money."
"I have to go and get boxes. Oh, and I don't want any of the furniture, and what I would like to take I'll only take it if you don't want it."
I was sure to take my L-shaped executive office desk set with the matching credenza and hutch which I actually never used; it was purchased for my office at the spa but ended up being used for the office I made out of the smaller bedroom in my new apartment. I wanted to be as accommodating as possible in hopes of him remaining agreeable and argument free because at the end of the day it wasn't an argument, I was out.

      While getting myself ready to leave for the office I was in awe, that God in His power made this so easy for me. God confirmed that I've served my purpose in that marriage and have been through enough. I had gotten myself all worked up for nothing, thinking I would have the fight of my life about this, and I was prepared for World War III. When I got in the car I called Mary Ellen and Lamont to report how it all played out, and to witness how God's yoke is easy and His burden is light.

She was happy and laughing at me saying, "You thought he was going to be upset, and he was so happy. He was thinking the same thing as you were, wondering when you were going to leave. Well that's good, now all you have to do is pack and go!" She and I continued talking in happiness and disbelief about the situation.

When I called Lamont, he said, "See there, Hank wanted you gone, out of there this whole time, and you thought he'd be mad. Well I'm happy for you." We laughed and rejoiced, then hung up.

Chapter Forty Four

Looking back and rehashing what I went through, sometimes having church members at odds with me over something that I'm not aware of, and most times at odds with Reverend, it feels great to say, "I'm still standing." What the church members didn't realize was that I had to fight Pastor Defenbar every day, so fighting them either silently through body language or verbally, was nothing, a piece of cake. There were many times I wanted to tell some of them, "You ain't nobaaady, trying to be somebaaaady."

One thing I do know is that the way I was forced to live was no way to live, life is meant to be abundant in all areas. In the Amplified version of the bible, John 10:10 states: "The thief comes only in order to steal and kill and destroy. I came that they may have *and* enjoy life, and have it in abundance (to the full, till it overflows.)" I want everything God has for me, I refuse to let anyone hinder me from getting it, and I was being robbed of an abundant life. Stepping out and looking in, it almost seems humanly impossible to have survived through hell with my head always up and in my right mind, rather than being in an insane asylum or taking some form of barbiturates.

I mentally have a recollection of all the drama that took place, but supernaturally my heart didn't feel the pain that it appeared it should have. As I went through the fire, I know it was because God made me fireproof that the effects weren't crippling. God is immutable, therefore, He's the same yesterday, today, and forever more, and He has done the same thing for me that He did for the three Hebrew boys; Shadrach, Meshach, and Abednego. When they were thrown into the fiery furnace Jesus was with them, and they didn't feel a thing, nor did they get as much as a singe on their bodies. The bible says when the guards looked into the furnace they assured King Nebuchadnezzar that they threw only three in, but said they now see four. El Shaddai didn't necessarily want me to just simply *go* through the fire, I see now that He wanted me to *grow* through the fire so that I can lift others up and encourage them through my experiences. God chose me for that job of being the first lady, and He equipped me, and ordained me to do it, all according to His plan.

Although I tried, I couldn't destroy the sin and evil that was there in my house and I couldn't let it destroy me. People will only change when they are ready to, and Hank didn't want to change, or didn't know how to change.

I was avoiding the next step of getting boxes and bringing them in the house in front of Hank, it was just too hard and I didn't want it in his face like that. It didn't bother me for him to see the boxes already placed in the closet, I just didn't want to be carting them pass him as a constant indicator of my leaving. On the other hand, Mary Ellen kept reminding me that I was a procrastinator and that I shouldn't wait until the last minute to try and start packing sixteen years worth of accumulated stuff, and she was right. I decided to stop at one of the home improvement stores to purchase boxes and tape. I didn't remove them from the car until Hank left the house, and then I'd sneak them in and put them in my closet the same way I used to sneak new hats into the house.

My movements were robotic with every corrugated box that I taped together and packed. I was only doing what I knew needed to be done as my stomach shivered the entire time until I was actually gone. Hank never came upstairs when I was packing, and I was grateful that he finally went out of town during the process in which I got as much done at that time as possible. I refused to cry in front of Hank, so I would close my closet door when I wasn't able to fight the feeling. While he was gone, I found myself walking around the house taking a good look at what was home for the past umpteen years, and I stopped in the living room and broke down, clinching my shirt at my stomach and yelling, "Oh God, Oh God." The tears were flooding my face and it hurt in my gut, it was the closest I've ever come to my brother's passing a year prior to meeting Rev. Defenbar, which is the worst pain I've experienced thus far. During the packing phase these breakdowns would occur almost daily. However, once I calmed down I heard the voice of Chase Rydell in my head saying, "Keep moving forward," and it gave me strength to do so and right back to packing I was.

After a couple of weeks had passed nearing my move-out, Hank returned to his true self. He approached me one day as I was in the bedroom packing and said, "You never told me you were moving, and I know you've been planning this all along, you're nothing but a sneak." I thought, "Here we go, I knew it was too good to be true." The calmness of it all and agreement to this just didn't match up to who Hank was, something wasn't right about it; I knew there had to be a dead cat on the line somewhere!

"I did tell you, it was a few days after I found out that I was approved, you knew two months in advance."

He stuck to his story, and I'm certain that's the lie he spread to his family because that's what he was telling *me*, and I'm the one who told him two months in advance!

From that point forward, anytime Hank wanted to start a fight, I'd quickly interject "We don't have to fight about this anymore, I'm leaving, we have nothing to fight about," and that's when he'd start that "I never told him I was leaving" thing. Hank's disparaging words went from being previously demoralizing to being totally prolific in that they had become like little power pills to me causing me to pack even faster and get out of there. His evil words also let me know that I was indeed doing the right thing and on the right track. Again, Chase Rydell's voice in my head repeating, "Keep moving forward," is what I heard.

The changes encountered by both of us with Hank complaining that I never told him that I was leaving, to being happy that I was leaving; and my going from not being able to pack fast enough, to crying, no bawling due to the sadness of it all, were nerve wrecking. The breakdown moments were a tremendous strain when everything would hit me all at once. Sitting on the edge of the bed one night I started to tear up and become overwhelmed with emotions, not being able to pinpoint any one in particular, everything just hurt. I wasn't crying because I'd miss the plethora of verbal abuse, because just a simple flashback of it had me packing so fast I would perspire. I was bombarded with grief, wondering if Reverend Defenbar would be ok, and I didn't want to leave him there alone, I only wanted to leave the abuse, but there was no way to separate the two.

All of the strength that I needed and obtained to make such a pertinent decision mostly came from Reverend Defenbar's teachings of the Word, and he taught the "Truth," which is synonymous to the "Word." I took advantage of being directly under his leadership, always getting firsthand information about studying the bible and its interpretation, as Pastor Defenbar is extremely intelligent when it comes to that. During that dark time in my life, I understood that I could do all things, that I was God's child and more than a conqueror, that no weapon formed against me shall prosper, that I deserved the best and an abundant life, that death and life is in the power of the tongue, that satan has no power over my destiny or life, that I had to walk by faith and not by sight, and that God would never leave me or forsake me. One thing for sure is that the season of your life will determine the interpretation of the scripture.

Through teaching the Truth, it was Pastor Defenbar that actually helped me to get away from Pastor Defenbar because it's the truth that brings the conviction necessary for change. Talk about God making your enemy your footstool, metaphorically speaking, ha! I had to come to terms with the fact that you will never change what you're willing to tolerate, and you will never change what you're unwilling to confront. I wasn't willing to tolerate that treatment any longer, I was taking it head on, and I moved from victim to victor! Chase Rydell was the match that ignited the fire that was already inside of me. My decision has determined my conduct, my character, and my destiny.

The day was fast approaching, I've never seen a month pass by so fast. Everything was finally packed and boxes were everywhere; in the living room, dining room, bedroom, and closet. It may sound absurd, but I didn't barricade myself any of those nights because I knew that God didn't bring me that far to leave me.

I rented a large truck and was fortunate enough to have Lloyd and Christopher, my adopted brother and cousin respectively, load the truck for me and drive me nearly one hundred miles away. The only time that was convenient for the three of us to load was during the evening when it was dark out. When we were done it was well after one o'clock in the morning, and we were exhausted. Hank didn't leave his downstairs room that night, he never saw a box leave the house, and it took hours to load that truck with taking five here and there. Hank not coming out of that room to address my family members was the norm. However, none of us wanted Hank to feel bad so we were moving as quietly and quickly as possible, in a manner as if he didn't know we were there. All we were able to do was to keep our voices low, and try our best not to bump into walls with the bulky items. The house began to look empty as we removed the boxes, plants, treadmill, the loveseat sofa, pictures, portable massage table, clothes, shoes, hats, hats, and more hats, and handbags.

All of my suits and dry cleaned items hung all around the railing inside the truck just about fashioning a closet, and everything else filled in. The hardest part was over. The truck was packed with the main items for the most part that were too large or too heavy for me to handle singlehandedly. The wait to drive out of there the next day, along with looking at the packed truck in the driveway, was worse than waiting to tell Hank that I was taking his advice and leaving. My rest wasn't easy that night; the anticipation was overpowering.

That imminent hour had come, and I yelled downstairs through his closed bedroom door, "Hank, we're leaving."
He answered somberly, "Ok."
I don't know how I felt at that moment. I didn't bring Butterscotch that day because it wasn't yet official, there were at least five more car loads

that had to be taken, and I also had to return the truck. Lloyd brought along his friend Peggy to help and for company in the truck; Chris rode shotgun in the car with me. As we pulled out of the driveway loaded down, both car and truck, I looked back at my house and felt numb.

The drive was indubitably liberating, and the countryside was magnificent with breathtaking views of the mountains. We stopped for coffee at a rest stop where I purchased a sweatshirt with the State's name across the front and put it on. I felt my old self returning, I felt new, and my smile was genuine again. We pulled up to my new home and we all got out and went inside to first assess the premises. Everything looked great, I felt proud of myself, and I could see the proud look on their faces also. That was a miracle. I delegated which room each box was to go in, and we worked like ants in getting everything situated. The truck was a one-way rental and we worked into the evening, then having to find the drop-off location in the dark in unfamiliar territory. Thank God for navigation. After returning the truck, Lloyd drove my car back with Peggy in the front, and Chris and I were in the back.

Entering that empty house felt weird, and I'm sure Hank felt uneasiness also so he went out of town to visit his family the next day. By the time I tied up loose ends and packed my car again, it was around ten o'clock at night. With Hank not being there it didn't feel as sad, and a small weight was lifted. I put Butterscotch into his carrier, grabbed my purse, and we were on our way. Butterscotch usually cried in the car, but that night he was silent for the entire time, nearly two hours; he knew we had to leave and was on our way to safety, as he used to run and hide when Hank and I were screaming.

I left everything in the car and walked into my sanctuary with only Butterscotch and my purse. I let him out, and he sniffed around walking into every room, and I exhaled with joy. I'm in the catbird seat now! Jubilee, Jubilee!

Chapter Forty Five

HELPING OTHERS TO OVERCOME OBSTACLES AND ABUSE OF ANY KIND

It was by no means easy to get out of an abusive relationship being married to someone that was an authoritative figure. I felt trapped at times, not knowing how this would end, but I never gave up hope or dreams in spite of my physical circumstances. It takes great effort on the victim's part to exercise faith, belief in the Word, and to remain focused. If there is anything that you feel you are incapable of doing, I implore you to change your way of thinking now. You must walk with the Word, knowing that you can do all things through Christ that strengthens you.

There are twelve keys to my success, but sometimes I was so inundated with grief that I fell off by the wayside, although with me it was only for a good minute because I've been practicing this phenomenon of the Word and the laws of the universe for some time. I would put one or more of the following keys to work and get right back on track. The good thing however, is that it works for everyone that puts it to use, it's yours for the taking.

It's my opinion that the first and most important thing for a victim to realize is that the ordeal they're going through isn't of God, and that there are only two forces in operation in this universe, and that's good and evil. Taking that bit of information into account, I beseech you to understand what the scripture is saying in 1 John 4:4, which states, "Ye are of God, little children, and have overcome them: because greater is He that is in you than he that is in the world." One translation puts it this way, "My dear children, you belong to God and have defeated them; because God's Spirit, who is in you, is greater than the devil, who is in the world." Once you recognize the power that already rests within you, then the ordeal becomes powerless and you become powerful.

The second of my keys is that you must have an attitude of gratitude, which can be hard at times due to current situations that are blatantly in your face. The fact of the matter is, if you're not thanking God for what you already have, what exactly would make Him think you would be grateful for more, and at what point does more become more to you? God's gifts are unlimited, so when do you start to say "Thank you," and do you ever stop saying thank you? "Thou hast been faithful over a few things, I will make thee ruler over many things," says the Lord in the book of Matthew. I was thanking God for the car that I had already received by faith, although it hadn't yet manifested. Likewise, I was thanking God for the peace that wasn't there, but I believed would come in calling things that be not as though they were.

The third key would be to meditate every day, or as often as you can. Relax for about twenty minutes in an uninterrupted and quiet space and recite a positive mantra, one that will help you in becoming the person God intended you to be. This was difficult for me because I had a hard time finding twenty free minutes for myself, but nevertheless, I forced it. I practiced using the method of transcendental meditation, but all the same you can sit with your eyes closed and repetitiously thank God in advance for what you want in your life, what you'd like to see in your life, and what you'd like to happen in your life. When you meditate on the Word, and God's promises, you will be a success because He says that His Words will not return to Him void. The scripture states in the book of Joshua, "Be strong and very courageous. Be careful to obey all the law my servant Moses gave you; do not turn from it to the right or to the left, that you may be successful wherever you go. 8 Keep this Book of the Law always on your lips; meditate on it day and night, so that you may be careful to do everything written in it. Then you will be prosperous and successful." Thank God for Jesus fulfilling the law, and that we're under a new covenant living in the dispensation of Grace.

The next key being the fourth, is in knowing that you are an unlimited being. In the third chapter of the book of Ephesians it states, "Now unto him that is able to do exceeding abundantly above all that we ask or think, according to the power that worketh in us." The key here is that the power is already in us to do great things, but we have to work the power and the power is unlimited, thereby making us unlimited.

The fifth key, is that I know God supplies all of my needs according to His riches in glory, not *my* riches but His, therefore, I have abundance and no lack. I would repeat in my prayers, "Thank you Father that I have abundance and no lack." Understanding that faith comes by hearing, and hearing by the Word of God, I always speak the promises out loud so that I can *hear* myself saying the words. Eventually, the promises become second nature to you after hearing them so much and you reach the point of, you know that you know that you know, that you already have received by faith what God's Word has promised, and then that's when the manifestation takes place. Remember that without faith, it's impossible to please God; you *must* believe before you receive. The scripture references are Hebrews 11:6, and Mark 11:24, respectively. Also keep in mind Hebrews 11:1 which states, "Faith is the substance of things hoped for and the evidence of things NOT SEEN."

In giving my opinion regarding which key I feel is very important, has no bearing on the way I used them. There is no order or routine that I carried out to put these keys of mine to work making them effective. I actually gave thought as to how I made it through and escaped from a harmful situation, and the things mentioned here are major players in what I've done over the years in order to reach the point where I am now.

The most prominent factor that I have in my favor is that I sincerely believe every word in the bible, which is the inspired Word of God. However, I also understand that everything in the bible is truly stated, but isn't a statement of truth. When you follow God's way using the methods that He put in place for you, His children, you can't fail. Peace and happiness, wealth and health, abundance and redemption, belongs and has been given to the children of God. The downside of this is that if you don't know these things then you can't work these things, and they remain dormant in your life!

The sixth key is to know that wealth is a mindset! It is impossible to obtain wealth if it never enters your mind. Thoughts become things and that's a fact. Where the mind goes the man follows. For example, have you ever brushed your teeth without the thought "I have to brush my teeth" first entering your mind? Likewise with everything else, you think about it before you do it, like going to the store, going to work, taking in a movie, calling a friend, etc. If you don't see yourself wealthy, you will never be wealthy. I would always keep it in my mind that I'm powerful enough with the power vested in me by God to have what I want, and to live a certain lifestyle without having to depend on anyone else, especially my abuser.

This seventh key should probably be at the top of everyone's list, and that is to go for peace and happiness because without that it's very hard to accomplish any goal while living in the midst of turmoil. I am fortunate enough to have been born with intestinal fortitude, and I fought my way through to reach certain small goals which was very hard to do, but I did it. Having that experience was evident enough to let me know that in order to reach higher goals or my ultimate goal, I would unmistakably need peace and happiness first so that I can concentrate on what's really important.

Focusing only on *what* you want rather than on what it is you *don't* want, is "The great eight" key. This is one of the hardest of my keys to adopt and I had tremendous problems with it, but it is as equally essential as any other, if not more. We as humans tend to vent to those closest to us about our current issues, not realizing that what you think about, you bring about, and that you will have what you say, as stated in Mark 11:23-24. The more we talk about something, the more we are creating it to happen or to continue happening. I had to learn to stop saying Hank did or said this or that, or I need to get out of this marriage and this house. I realized what I needed to say was "Thank you God for my beautiful husband that cherishes me, adores me, and respects me," and so on, listing all that I would like in a husband, and let *those* words bring that type of husband into my life. In talking to Lamont or Mary Ellen, it was so hard not to tell them why I was upset if I was at that moment, as I didn't see the harm in telling them what had just happened. This key is actually powerful enough to change situations that haven't yet reached the point of no return, where there's still a spark left. Unfortunately for me, all of the love, trust, and respect, had been stripped away long ago but it was still crucial for me not to talk about the woes because I would have been an aide in keeping it going, so I had to focus, and talk about what I wanted.

Prosperity to me isn't having money alone, it's also having great relationships, the best of health, and successful businesses; however, this should be tailored to each individual as necessary. I can only mention what it means to me, and the methods I used on the road to freedom. I focused on health, prosperity, I studied the bible, listened to Reverend Defenbar, and watched televangelists, realizing all of the promises of God as I received them by faith. I've read many motivational books, watched DVDs on faith and positivity, studied the law of attraction, and these things I meditated on over and over and over. I can't say that it didn't take years and years, but I believed it all and refused to give up. I say to you in this ninth key, to focus on prosperity.

Key ten is visualization, which is very powerful and easy to do. When you visualize you materialize. I played soothing instrumental music and closed my eyes for as long as I chose to and saw myself having the life I wanted. I also purchased a large art board and put photos on it of the house I want, the car, and so on, and I would just stare at it as a reminder, making it easier to visualize having it because I now had a picture in my mind. I even put a piece of jewelry on it that I saw in a magazine. This step is powerful and simple, so do it.

Key eleven is to just "Feel it." If you need to get in that house to see what it feels like being inside, then find a way to get in there, and how about test driving that car that you want; this makes the power behind visualizing stronger. I will share an experience of mine as an example of how literal I take and believe the Word of God. What I did was based on the scripture in Deuteronomy 11:24-25, which states: "Every place on which the sole of your foot treads shall be yours: from the wilderness and Lebanon, from the river, the River Euphrates, even to the Western Sea, shall be your territory. ²⁵ No man shall be able to stand against you; the L ORD your God will put the dread of you and the fear of you upon all the land where you tread, just as He has said to you." I phoned a realtor to see the home I wanted and upon entering, I took off my boots and let the soles of my feet, the Word didn't say the soles of your boots, tread all over that house. I jumped in the shower when the realtor was down the hall, walked in all the closets, walked through the grass, and I also put my feet in the swimming pool, therefore, I believed the house was mine.

Key twelve is my favorite, and I purposely saved the best for last. You must sow seeds for what it is you desire. Seedtime and harvest will never pass away. I sowed seeds for health, peace, and wisdom, things that are intangible, as well as for things tangible. I personally didn't just sow them to my local church, but to other worthy ministries as well, specifying to God what that particular seed was for. Many of my manifestations has already taken place. The scripture tells us in 2 Corinthians 9:10, "Now he that ministereth seed to the sower both minister bread for your food, and multiply your seed sown, and increase the fruits of your righteousness."

I've given you the keys that helped me on this journey that I'm on. It's not all about just running away from your problems or getting out of a bad situation or marriage, it's bigger than that. It's about not repeating the same agony with someone else, it's about how your life should be in all areas, and embracing how God intended for you to live while on this earth.

For me, mastering these keys weren't easy by any means; it took time and understanding, faith, belief, patience, and a whole lot of praying. Don't forget to pray the prayer of faith. "The effectual fervent prayer of a righteous man avails much!" James 5:16.

"Hurry escape there for I cannot do anything until you arrive there." Genesis 19:22.

Where is your place that God can bless you?

THERE IS HELP!
ASOPIPA – (Abused Spouses of People in Power Anonymous)

Having lived this life, I understand the importance of remaining discreet for the sake of the ministry and I'd like to offer ways to help those in similar positions.

Ministry comes from a place that you've been, because you can't preach, teach, or enlighten anyone about something you haven't experienced.

I will do what I can to go around the country in an effort to form ASOPIPA meetings, empowering those in need. These meetings will be for those that are looking for ways to cope with being married to a public figure, and for those that are in need of leaving an abusive situation. In an effort to ensure that there isn't any trepidation on your part of being exposed, there will be a screening, confirming you are who you say you are for these meetings. Going online to register is also in the forefront.

MOTIVATIONAL CREED FOR BELIEVERS

I BELIEVE THAT FOR ME TO SUCCEED IMMEDIATELY IN A WORLD WHERE SPIRITUAL FORCES ARE AT BATTLE TO GAIN MY DESTINY, I MUST REMAIN FOCUSED, STEADFAST, DILIGENT AND UNDERSTAND THAT PROCRASTINATION IS NOT AN OPTION. I HAVE FAITH AND BELIEVE IN GOD'S HOLY WORD. I WILL USE THE WORD, NAME AND BLOOD OF JESUS AS MY WEAPON AGAINST ANY EVIL FORCE. DEATH AND LIFE ARE IN THE POWER OF THE TONGUE, AND THEY THAT LOVE IT SHALL EAT THE FRUIT THEREOF. THE POWER IS WITHIN ME TO BRING FORTH HAPPINESS, WEALTH, AND HEALTH, AND TO DO AWAY WITH DISCONTENT. I BELIEVE THAT FAITH WITHOUT WORKS IS DEAD!

© 2006 Theresa Ann Clark

www.ingramcontent.com/pod-product-compliance
Lightning Source LLC
Chambersburg PA
CBHW021119300426
44113CB00006B/210